ROBERT W. HARPER

OLD GLOUCESTER COUNTY AND THE AMERICAN REVOLUTION
1763-1778
Including Atlantic, Burlington, Cape May,
Cumberland and Salem Counties

GLOUCESTER COUNTY CULTURAL AND HERITAGE COMMISSION
Woodbury, New Jersey

DEDICATION

Dedicated to:

Professor Marius Livingston, late Chairman of the Department of History at Glassboro State College, who gave me the opportunity to teach The History of New Jersey; to Thomas Bowen, Editor and Publisher, Emeritus, of "Today's Sunbeam," Salem, New Jersey, who gave me the opportunity to publish thousands of words on the History of South Jersey; and to Dr. Thomas Rozanski, who gave me two "new" eyes after successful cataract surgery.

ILLUSTRATIONS

Key: AC (Author's Collection); HSP (Historical Society of Pennsylvania); NJHS (New Jersey Historical Society); NYPL (New York Public Library); RUL (Rutgers University Library); PHMC (Pennsylvania Historical Museum Commission); PCHC (Philadelphia City Hall Collection); NPC (Naval Photographic Center); LC (Library of Congress).

OLD GLOUCESTER COUNTY AND THE AMERICAN REVOLUTION
1763-1778
Including Atlantic, Burlington, Cape May,
Cumberland and Salem Counties

This publication is part of the Tercentenary Celebration of "Old Gloucester County," (1686-1986), and is made possible through the encouragement and support of the Gloucester County Board of Chosen Freeholders:

John R. Maier - Director
James G. Atkinson - Deputy Director
Stephen B. Atkinson
Paul A. Oland
Steven R. Salvatore
Jay Sharp
Gary W. Stuhltrager

Publication is also made possible by the encouragement and support of the Gloucester County Cultural and Heritage Commission:

Charles Crabbe Thomas - Chairperson
Eugene Eipper - Deputy Chairperson
Alice Corsey
Lois Green - Secretary
Dr. Robert W. Harper
Marie Kennedy
Jerome Solomon
Kathy Spinosi
John B. Squillace
Paul A. Oland - Freeholder Liason
Eleanor Rogers - Recording Secretary
Dr. Robert Haynes, Director, Gloucester County
Tercenterary Committee, 1686–1986

BOOKS BY THE AUTHOR

John Fenwick and Salem County in the Province of West New Jersey, 1609-1700, including Burlington, Cape May, Cumberland and Gloucester Counties.

Friends and Indians in South Jersey

The Jefferson Printing Company, Glassboro, New Jersey

PREFACE

While Larry Gerlach has stated that "we surely know more about the American Revolution than any other national rebellion in history," it needs to be noted that his comment does not apply to "Old Gloucester County" and South Jersey, for consensus historians have accepted only what is known and have not sought out the wealth of untouched primary source materials available at the county and state levels, as well as those to be found in contiguous states and at the National Archives in Washington, D.C. Had such research been done, it would not be necessary for this work to be brought into being.

The rationale for what follows is rather simple. We do not know as much as we ought to about the role of "Old Gloucester County" in the American Revolution; and, as George Buttrick noted in his "Christ and History," "A Preface usually offers 'Reasons' why the author has written the book," I submit that my reasons for this effort are two: The need for the work and because I felt compelled to write it!

By the way of an introductory clarification for non-South Jersey readers of "Old Gloucester County and the American Revolution, 1763-1778, including Atlantic, Burlington, Cape May, Cumberland and Salem Counties," it seems appropriate to point out that Atlantic County was detached from "Old Gloucester" in 1837 and Camden County was severed in 1844, thus much of the Revolutionary War history of the two 19th century creations is to be found in great part with that of "Old Gloucester."

Several important military events took place in "Old Gloucester County" from the Delaware River to the Atlantic Ocean portions of the old county; however, New Jersey, dwarfed by New York to the north and Philadelphia to the west, has had much of its important Revolutionary War history ignored or overlooked by both New Jersey and out-of-state historians. This has left the historical canvas quite bare in spots.

What follows here is an attempt, albeit a provincial one, to present a revisionist view of the contributions of "Old Gloucester County," its citizens and soldiers to the winning of national independence. It needs to be mentioned that some of the material in this publication appeared in two long series of historical articles which were printed in the Gloucester County Times in 1976 and again in 1978 and 1979. In addition, many articles pertinent to South Jersey also appeared in Today's Sunbeam of Salem, New Jersey, during the same time period.

Since those years, as a result of on-going research, much additional material has come to light which makes it possible to further enrich an important segment of our local, national and state history. Still, there remains much more work to be done to complete our "Old Gloucester County" history.

The work on the following pages was made possible by the encouragement of both the Gloucester County Board of Chosen Freeholders and the Gloucester County Cultural and Heritage Commission. In addition, without the support of my wife, Kathryn, and my daughters, Bevin and April, it would not have been possible to devote the energy and time necessary to complete even a modest effort such as this.

I have appreciated the assistance of Ms. Clara Kirner and Mrs. Ethel Traub of the "Special Collections" (The Stewart Room) section of the Glassboro State College Library. Mrs. Edith Holle, librarian (and historian herself) of the Gloucester County Historical Society in Woodbury, New Jersey, has been her usual helpful self. Mr. Frank L. Suplee, Jr., of Glassboro and a former student of mine, has called my attention to important primary source documents, some of which have been used in this book. I would also like to thank Mr. Scott Leslie of Pitman, another former student of mine, for several of the photographs used herein. Ms. "Jackie" Fisher, a student at Glassboro State College, is thanked for typing much of the manuscript. Finally, I am indebted to Mr. Charles Crabbe Thomas of Woodbury for helping to proof-read the manuscript and for giving many words of encouragement.

Robert W. Harper, Ph.D
Professor of History
Glassboro State College

Spring 1986

INTRODUCTION

"George Washington is God!" "Benedict Arnold is the devil!" "The American Revolution began with the signing of the Declaration of Independence!" "Trenton, Yorktown, and Valley Forge — these were the American Revolution!" Such patriotic utterances have echoed through the pages of our history books for almost two centuries. Indeed, as Gary B. Nash commented in his "Red, White and Black - The Peoples of Early America, we have "as school children, as college students, and as presumably informed adults . . . been nurtured on what has passed for the greatest story of human history," albeit, there is much myth, distortion and often serious ommission in the epic.

Until the turn of this century, many writers of history, who were not necessarily trained historians, were often lacking in ambition and repeated the standard heroics. By this is meant that they too infrequently sought out new primary source documents and were willing to repeat in their works what had been written by historians of the 18th and 19th centuries.

This was to change when the scientific historians, under the influence of the great German historian, Leopold von Ranke, sought to revise history of earlier periods by the use of primary source materials, many of which had not been known by the "copier" historians. Valuable documents in the "ash-can" of history were to be brought to historical light, thus providing new visions and truths.

It follows that, as some historians do change, many of them in the post-World War II period have tried to revise the history of the American Revolution, not just for the exercise, but in order to show that the use of previously unknown or unused primary source documents reveals serious deficiencies in the generally accepted consensus presentation of what happened during the period 1763-1781. Such revisionism need not be used just to defrock or tarnish the images of our great heroes; it is to enrich the drama of the American Revolution by adding those persons, places and happenings of consequence, which have been ommitted by the consensus historians.

It is the ommissions connected with the New Jersey contributions that will concern us in the following pages, especially events in "Old Gloucester County," in particular, and in South Jersey, in general. The premise will be made that the military events at Forts Billings and Mercer were of significance; that the "Great Cattle Drive" from Salem, New Jersey to Valley Forge, Pennsylvania, through "Old Gloucester County," saved General George Washington's starving army; that the stunning defeat of the Hessians at Red Bank on October 22, 1777, convinced the French of the worth of the American cause, as much as did the defeat of General John Burgoyne at Saratoga, New York, on

October 17th; that the failure of British foraging attempts in South Jersey during February and March of 1778 brought the British to the conclusion that Philadelphia had to be evacuated, thus leading to American success at the Battle of Monmouth, on June 28, 1778.

In addition to the above exciting events, an attempt will be made to bring to further light and focus, the contributions of Brigadier General Silas Newcomb of the South Jersey Militia. Newcomb and his men fought bravely with General George Washington at the Battle of Long Island on August 28, 1776 and were with him during the dreary days of retreat over the Hudson River and through the state of New Jersey until Washington's troops approached the outskirts of Trenton.

It must be confessed that I have long wanted to restore the dignity of General Newcomb and the South Jersey Militia from "Old Gloucester," Atlantic, Burlington, Cape May, Cumberland and Salem Counties, for the Militia has been castigated by many writers of history, past and present, for its role in the defense of Forts Billings and Mercer. As will be seen, a revisionist approach has revealed that Newcomb's South Jersey Militia Brigade and the West Jersey Artillery under Captain Samuel Hugg from Gloucester Town distinguished themselves in the Delaware Valley, at Morristown, in North Jersey, at Princeton and elsewhere.

Chapter I

Towards Revolution

1763-1769

At the conclusion of the French and Indian War, 1756-1763, Great Britain was in control of the Atlantic seaboard from Georgia to Canada. It was a great victory for the British and the colonists in New Jersey, and elsewhere in Great Britian's North American colonies. Even South Jersey Lenni Lenape Indians had been recruited for service in the British army. The Reverend John Brainard, superintendent of the Bretherton Reservation in Burlington County, attested to this:

> "Indians have every year since the commencement of this War, inlisted in the King's service, far beyond their proportions, and generally, more or less, every Campaign have died in the Army."

Few future Americans in 1763 thought of themselves as other than loyal Englishmen and women; albeit, there were examples of non-support of British war policies by the pacifist Quakers of "Old Gloucester" and Salem counties. Even so, George Mason of Virginia stated the colonial attitude in a typical manner: " . . . in crossing the Atlantic Ocean, we have only changed our climate, not our minds; our natures and dispositions remain unaltered." Mason was English, to the core!

In view of the extreme cooperation between Great Britain and her 13 mainland colonies during the French and Indian War, it is more than remarkable that in the short thirteen year period, 1763-1776, relationships soured on both sides of the Atlantic to the extent that the colonies were to declare their independence on July 4, 1776.

A change in British attitudes after the successful French and Indian War was to cast an increasing gloom over New Jersey and the other colonies. From the beginning of colonization until 1763, the colonies had experienced a large degree of "Beneign neglect" due to the distance between Britain and America. In addition, the British had their own inner political, economic and religious turmoils, compounded by external conflicts with France and other European powers.

The French and Indian War was a costly one which increased England's self-indebtedness and it was a severe drain on the English treasury. Indeed, "the national debt was, in eighteenth century terms, astronomical, and taxes, particularly on the English landed gentlemen who dominated Parliament, commensurately burdensome . . . Parliament insisted on relief."

Soon to be gone were the days of British expenditures on the colonies without colonial contributions. The policy of "no taxes" was to be followed by one of rigid controls of the colonies' wealth and the institution of "taxation without representation" by the British Parliament."

The Lords of the Treasury noted on October 4, 1763 that they observed "with concern that through neglect, connivance, and fraud, not only the revenue is impaired, but the commerce of the colonies is diverted from its natural course and the salutary provisions of many wise laws to secure it to the mother country are in great measure defeated." In addition, it was said that "smuggling in the New England colonies alone had cost the British government some 100 thousand pounds in lost revenue."

Such a sorry situation from the British point of view had to be rectified and it could only be done so by forcing the colonies to pay a share of colonial expenditures, including the 350 thousand pounds required to maintain an anticipated ten thousand British troops to be stationed in the 13 colonies. Parliament responded to this fiscal dilemma by passing the American Revenue Act of 1764. Known more generally as the Sugar Act, it was intended to raise much of the money needed to operate the colonial governments. Funds were to be generated by placing duties on such as sugar, molasses, wine, coffee and foreign rum.

Suffice it to say that there was a severe depression following the French and Indian War. It was felt in all the colonies and was compounded by the fact that the colonies were no longer allowed to trade with the West Indies. In addition in 1764, Parliament forbid the colonies to print new paper money to aid their faltering economies. As John Cunningham tells us: "New Jersey, whose provincial debt of 300,000 pounds topped that of all the colonies, teetered on the brink of financial ruin. Without new paper money . . . New Jersey faced deflation and wide spread depression."

The Colonial Currency Act of 1764 alarmed all the colonies and the New York Assembly pointed out that " . . . If the said Plan be carried into Execution, it will not only highly reflect on the Credit, Honour, and Punctuality of this Colony, but also reduce it to a State of Bankruptcy" At issue was the colonial practice of converting bills of credit into currency and King George III was advised on February 9,1764 that it was not known " . . . from what causes this absurd and destructive notion of converting paper Bills of Credit into legal Currency first took it's rise . . . "

Daniel Coxe, a descendant of one of the oldest and wealthiest families in South Jersey, noted, on April 12, 1764, in a letter to his friend Joseph Reed:

> "What in the name of Sense has possess'd the English Nation or rather its Parliament, for I find a paragraph in the last papers that a Scheme is on foot for Obliging Us to furnish 500,000 (Proclamation pounds) among the Colonies. My God! What Madness this is; think they that We are in any Ways able to raise that Sum or half of it? How are we to do it? Our Trade is confined and limitted . . . Money we have not in Specie . . . America is but in its Infant State, unable of itself to bear any heaven Burdens . . . "

During late August 1764, Robert Ogden, speaker of the New Jersey Assembly, notified Courtlandt Skinner, a delegate to the Assembly, that in Boston it was felt that the colonies ought to unite and "Exert themselves to the utmost to Keep of (f) the Threatening blow, of Imposing Taxes, Duties, &c., so Distructive of the Libertys the Colonies hitherton enjoyed."

By September of 1764, there was increased concern in New Jersey that the British Parliament might inflict additional hardships on the colonists, thus it is found that The New Jersey Committee of Correspondents, consisting of Charles Read, Samuel Smith and Jacob Spicer, wrote their lobbyists in London as follows:

2

"If any thing comes on the slate next Session of Parliament either
for repealing the Duties laid on the Trade of the Northern Colonies
and prohibiting a paper Currency as last Session, or for adding any
thing new by way of Tax on this Colony, the Committee of Correspondents direct that you will humbly & Dutifully Set for in the
name and on behalf of this Colony that we look upon all Taxes laid
upon us without our Consent as a fundamental infringement of the
Rights and priveleges Secured to us as English Subjects . . . "

The recently arrived governor, William Franklin, fell heir to the hissing caul-
dron of discontent that began shortly after his arrival in 1763. Citizens of New
Jersey were optimistic because they had heard good things about the 33 year
old son of Benjamin Franklin. He was a well educated and travelled young man
who looked forward to a long career; however, the events which transpired during his 13 year tenure were to be his undoing because of his loyalty to the
crown of England. There isn't any doubt that he believed a detente could be
reached between King George III and the colonies, once the taxation problems
were resolved. Many times, he took issue with British actions which he felt were
unfair towards New Jersey.

As for "Old Gloucester County," it was said in 1765 to be fortunate in "its
situation opposite and contiguous to Philadelphia," for that fact afforded "great
opportunities to make the most of the productions of the county . . . They raise
beef, pork, mutton, butter, cheese, etc. They have three villages, Gloucester,
Haddonfield and Woodbury; at the first the courts for the county are held. Of
houses of worship, the people called Quakers have seven, the presbyterians five,
episcopalians one, Sweeds Luthern one, baptists one, moravians one." The
"Sweeds luthern"church was at Raccoon (Swedesboro) and the "moravians"
church was located just north of Oldman's Creek where it forms the boundry
line between Gloucester and Salem Counties.

Despite the seeming general tranquility, the crowning insult to New Jersey
and its sister colonies was the Stamp Act of 1765. Governor Franklin made plans
to comply and appointed William Coxe as Stamp Officer for the Province of
New Jersey. Mr Coxe came from Philadelphia to survey the situation and on September 3, he notified Governor Franklin as follows:

"I think it incumbent upon me to aquaint your Excellency, that on
my return from New-Jersey, on Sunday last, I came to a Resolution
to Surrender the Office of Distributor of Stamps for that
Province . . . "

Apparently it was not widely known that Coxe had resigned because the
"Sons of Liberty" of New Jersey notified Mr. Coxe on December 28 that:

"Whereas you have been appointed to the most odious and detesta-
ble office of Distributor of Stamps for the government of New-
Jersey . . . We the Sons of Liberty in said Government, hereby desire
your resignation . . . Now, Sir, we desire and insist, that you . . . acquaint us of all . . . deputies (if any there be) that they may be dealt
with in a proper manner . . . "

The "Sons of Liberty" then told Coxe in very strong terms that "If , Sir, you
refuse our very reasonable request, it will put us to the trouble of waiting upon
you, in such a way and manner, as perhaps will be disagreeable both to yourself
and us . . . " Obviously, Governor Franklin was both disturbed and worried, for

Gov. William Franklin, 1763—1776

he reported to London that" . . . the principal Matter which agitates the Minds of the People, & indeed seems to ingross All Attention, is the Act of Parliament for establishing a Stamp Duty in America."
Franklin further stated:

> "The Person who was appointed Distributor of Stamps for New—jersey has . . . taken fright at the outrageous Proceedings which have happened in other Colonies, & resigned his Office . . . He was assured from me, that he should have all the Protection which the Powers of Government could afford . . . but he could not be prevail'd to act."

Between the Coxe resignation and November 1765, the sketchy records tend to indicate that John Hatton, an "Old Gloucester" and Salem man, apparently agreed to become the Distributor of Stamps under the despised Stamp Act, at least for Salem County. From the *Pennsylvania Gazette* of November 26, it is learned:

> "A number of the Inhabitants of this County being informed that Mr. John Hatton, of Salem, wanted to be employed as a Distributor of Stamps, they assembled here, being the Day of Quarter Sessions, and, after some consideration about the Affair, four of them were deputed to go and wait on that Gentleman, in order to know the Truth of the Report."

It would appear that the Salem County men wasted no words with John Hatton, for he signed the following declaration:

> "I do solemnly declare, that I, nor any Person for me, shall not act as Stamp Master, or Distributor of Stamps, nor attempt to carry that Law into Execution in this Province, until it shall be, or appear to be, the Desire of the People Generally, by their and your calling upon me publickly to execute the said Act. This Declaration, Gentlemen, I do freely and voluntarily make, and will strictly abide by."

John Hatton, who later played an active role as a Tory supporter of King George III during the American Revolution, came to South Jersey when he was approximately sixteen years old, and with his inheritance bought land in Cape May, Gloucester and perhaps Salem counties. His main home is still standing on King's Highway near present day Swedesboro.

Governor Franklin assessed the situation in New Jersey and reported to London that he had heard "in the neighbouring Colonies, the People intend to force the Officers of the Government to carry on Business as formerly, without any regard to the Stamp Act, and, if they succeed in the Attempt, I doubt not but the people of New Jersey will follow their example." Even the lawyers of New Jersey "entered into an Agreement not to act under the Stamp Law," thus gaining credit for being the first colonial lawyers "'to make an effective opposition to the Stamp Act."

A Stamp Act Congress was called into being in New York City during October 1765, initially on the incentive of Massachusettes. Here were to be planted the seeds of the Declaration of Independence only 11 years away. Severe disturbances broke out in many of the colonies and Governor Franklin noted that "the Infection has spread and a great part of the Inhabitants of this Colony are not become actuated with the same kind of spirit which before raged so furiously in the neighbouring Provinces. They have not as yet, indeed, proceeded to the

5

same Length in Acts of Riot and Violence, but the most prudent Management has been . . . necessary to prevent them."

Resistance continued and was so strong that the Stamp Act was repealed by King George III and Parliament on March 4, 1766. Governor Franklin said to the Assembly that "It gives me great satisfaction that I have it now in my power to Communicate to you an Act for the repeal of that Statue, and to present you with my sincere Congratulations on the happy Termination of this most Important Affair. Happily the Storm which for some time past raged so Violently as to threaten the future welfare of Great Britain & her Colonies is at length Subsided . . . "

Northcoat pinx   Leney fct

King George III

Unfortunately, the British Parliament followed the repeal of the Stamp Act with the Declaratory Act of 1766 which atttempted to tighten England's control over the internal affairs of the colonies. It was stated that "the said colonies . . . have been, are, and of right ought to be, subordinate unto, and dependent upon the imperial crown and parliament of Great Britain . . . All resolutions . . . and proceedings in any of the said colonies . . . are . . . deleated to be utterly null and void" if they denied the authority of the British Parliament.

There followed tensions over the Quartering Act of 1765, which had been overlooked during the Stamp Act controversy. This act called for the housing of British soldiers, when necessary, in taverns, inns, un-inhabited houses and barns. In New Jersey, Governor Franklin was ultimately able to get the Assembly to pass an act supporting the Quartering Act, provided that five military barracks were built at Burlington, Elizabeth-Town, New Brunswick, Perth Amboy and Trenton. The soldiers, then, would not be a bother to the citizens of New Jersey.

The New Jersey Assembly had also resisted that part of the Quartering Act which required that the colonials provide the British troops with food, "and small beer or cyder, not exceeding five pints, or a half a pint of rum mixed with water to each man . . . " Governor Franklin finally got Assembly approval to supply the British troops with food and drink.

Unfortunately, it is not known how the members of the Assembly from "Old Gloucester County" voted on the Quartering Act, but one of them, Robert Friend Price, had been an Assemblyman since 1761. The Pennsylvania Gazette of June 23, 1768 noted that "On Thursday last **Robert Friend Price** and **John Hinchman,** Esquires, were elected Representatives for Gloucester County, in New-Jersey."

The British Parliament continued to inflict new taxes via the Duty or Revenue Act of 1767. New duties were to be placed on such items as glass, lead, painter's colors, paper and tea. As for glass, Governor Franklin reported to London on June 14, 1768 that "A Glass House was erected about Twenty Years ago in Salem County, which makes bottles, and a very coarse Green Glass for windows, used only in some of the Houses of the poorer sort of People. Fine glass can still be imported into America cheaper than it could be made there." Franklin was making reference to the glass factory at Alloways, known earlier as Wistarburg. The Stanger brothers, who started the glass industry at Glassboro in the 1770's, arrived from Germany in 1768 and worked at Wistarburg until it became evident that the factory's future was nil.

In "Old Gloucester County," its citizens were becoming increasingly concerned about taxes and equality of treatment for all of the people. On October 1, 1768, twenty-two men of the county sent a petition to "The Honorable House of Representatives of the Colony of New Jersey in General Assembly Convened." In part, the petition noted:

" . . . We humbly Conceive Taxes Ought to be regulated, and not on the Income, which is making a Man pay for his labour, is in fact a Penalty for being Industrious."
" . . . To this is added an Estimate of the real Value of Estates, and tho certainty in a matter of this nature cannot be expected, it nevertheless Sufficiently shows the Extreem Disproportion the Taxes bear of the Estates taxed..."

The signatories to this petition were: "Sam. Harrison, Alexr Randall, James Cooper, Samuel Webster, John Jessup, David Cooper for Eft. Hopkins, Abrm Chatting, William Snowden, Samuel Ladd, Isaac Dallinger, Mark Miller, Caleb

Bickham, George Flannigan, William Griscom, Samuel Kenard, Thomas Redman, Benjamin Rambo, Joshua Lord, David Branson, Jacob Spicer, Benjn Lodge and Peter Cheesman."

Reaction to increased British taxes was mixed in the colonies, from radical opposition, to means of getting around the inflicted duties. In 1769, the Massachusetts Gazette reported:

"The whole continent from New England to Georgia seems firmly fixed; like a strong, well-constructed arch, the more weight there is laid upon it, the firmer it stands; and thus with Americans, the more we are loaded, the more we are united."

Even though the Religious Society of Friends (Quakers) were still dominant in "Old Gloucester County" in 1769, many of its members were people of means, thus smarting under the increasing yoke of British taxation and tyranny. The following petition of October 3, 1769, was sent to Robert Friend Price and John Hinchman, the county's elected delegated to the New Jersey General Assembly:

"Gentlemen
As We have Chosen you to ye most important of Trusts, Even that of Guardians & Defenders of our Liberties, Privileges & Property, We think it expedient at this time to intimate what we shall expect from You at this Alarming Crisis; When ye others Colonys are Struggleing with ye utmost Ardour to preserve American Freedom, it is our desire that ye Representatives of New Jersey may Zealously unite with them & not appear as unconcern'd Spectators. Therefor That You Endeavor to have Resolves entered on ye Journals of ye House similar to those of ye Assemblys of divers other Colonys, with respect to raising a Revenue on America by Act of Parliament, Suspending Legislation, Sending for Persons from Hence to England for their Tryals, Our Sole right of Taxing our Selves and ye necessity of Uniteing with ye other Colonys in defence of our Rights &c. This is a Debt due to posterity, that should our Constitutional Privileges be Torn from us, it may appear not to have been with ye Approbations of our Representatives.
That you Countenance every Measure that will tend to Encourage & promote Industry, Frugality & American Manufactures & wean from ye Extravigant fondness people too generally have for foreign Comoditys, this appearing ye most probible means in our power of Transmitting Freedom to our Posterity."

The above remarkable "Old Gloucester County" document is located in "The Stewart Room" at Glassboro State College and from it, the following signatories have been identified:

"Joshua Stokes, John Gill, Jacob Clement, Sam. Clement, Joseph Clement, Joshua Cozens, S. Blackwood, Jo. Hugg, William Hugg, John Brown, William Snowden, Mark Miller, Tho. Clark, Arch Maffett, Jonathan Chew, John Hopkins, Ja. Wilkins, David Brown, John Jessup, Thomas Rambo, James Whitall, Restore Lippincott, Thomas Redman, Samuel Borrough, Joseph Borrough, Ebenezer Hopkins, John Redman, William Griffeth, Benj. Vanleer, Joseph Collins, Ed. Gibbs, Wm. Hinchman, Josiah Albortson, Nehemiah Andrews, William Griscom, Simeon Ellis, John Matlack, David Hurley, Simeon Breach, Joseph Champion,

Peter Breach, John Kay, Benjamin Hartley, Sam. Harrison, Josiah Shivers, Isaac Burrough, Dan. Cooper, John Eastlack, Jacob Stokes and Benj. Thackray."

As 1769 began to approach its end, all of the original colonies, save New Hamshire, had officially boycotted British imports. In New Jersey, the Assembly upon a motion by John Hinchman of "Old Gloucester County," put forth on October 18, 1769, the following resolution:

" . . . That the Thanks of this House be given to the Merchants and Traders of this Colony, and of the colonies of New-York and Pennsylvania, for their disinterested and public spirited Conduct, in withholding their Importations of British Merchandize, until certain Acts of Parliament laying restrictions on American Commerce, for the express Purpose of raising a Revenue in America, be repealed; and that Mr. Speaker be directed to write to the respective Committees of Merchants in said Colonies transmitting to them a Copy of this Resolve.

1770-1774

The boycotting of British imports was to take its toll on the mother country and by March 3, 1770, both King George III and the Parliment announced that the hated Townsend Acts were repealed. It was not, however, until April 14th that the governors in the colonies learned that " . . . so much of an Act made in the 7th year of His present Majesty for granting certain duties . . . as relates to the Duties upon Glass, Red-Lead, White-Lead, Paints, Colours, Papers &c . . . was at and end. Tea was the only item to be taxed by Great Britain.

The stationing of 10,000 British troops in the 13 colonies was to bring about many unfortunate incidents, the most serious of which was the "Boston Massacre" of March 5, 1770. During the disturbance in the Boston Common, Crispus Attucks, a Black American, and four others were killed by British gunfire.

John Adams, who defended successfully the commanding officer of the British soldiers, wrote that "on that night the foundation of American Independence was laid." The "Boston Massacre" was commemorated in 1771 and James Lowell, a rebel from Massachusetts, noted that the colonials "wanted more than to be spared oppression." Free people he said were "those who have a constitutional check upon the power to oppress."

Massachusetts continued to be in turmoil and to keep the flames of liberty alive. Samuel Adams, sometimes referred to as the "Father of the Revelution" said in 1770 "that your young Men begin to be ambitious of making themselves perfect Masters of the Art military." Of Adams, Massachusetts Governor Hutchinson said: "I doubt whether there is a greater incendiary in the King's dominion."

As Larry Gerlack pointed out in his "New Jersey in the American Revelution," New Jersey "was spared the acts of violence that racked other colonies." Even so, in January 1770, "New York became the scene if a serious riot. British troops cut down a liberty pole put up by the radicals and piled up the pieces in front of the Sons of Liberty headquarter."

Governor William Franklin was an astute prophet, for he wrote:

"Mens minds are sour'd, a sullen Discontent prevails, and, in my opinion, no Force on Earth is sufficient to make the (colonial) Assemblies acknowledge that the Parliament has the right to impose taxes on America . . . I apprehend that, as long as this

Temper continues, they will do all . . . to prevent the consumption of British Manufactures in the Colonies, that the Mother Country may thereby lose more in her Commerce than she can possibly gain by way of Revenue."

During the spring of 1770, all was not tranquil and James Madison, the future fourth president of the United States under the Constitution, wrote to his father on July 23, 1770 that the students at the College of New Jersey at Princeton were in turmoil because certain New York City merchants were no longer boycotting British woven goods. Madison noted that the 22 graduates of the class of 1770 "had agreed to attend commencement exercises in September dressed 'in American Cloth'"

The decision of the students was highly applauded in an item in a New York newspaper of July 24, 1770:

> "We are credibly informed from Princeton, 'That the Senior Class at Nassau-Hall, have unanimously agreed to appear at their ensuing Commencement, dressed in American Manufactures,' How happy ought we to esteem ourselves, when we see some of our Youth, who will probably fill some of the highest stations in their Country, when their fathers have fallen asleep, so early declaring their love to their country . . . "

Despite continued New Jersey protest against those who had weakened their resolve to enforce economic sactions against Great Britain, Governor William Franklin continued on fairly cordial terms with the Assembly. He wrote to London on January 14,1771 that John Ladd of "Old Gloucester County" had died and that he wanted to replace him in the Governor's Council with either Daniel Coxe of Trenton or John Lawrence of Burlington. Of Lawrence, Franklin noted that he "was lately a Member of Assembly, has a good Estate & is a lawyer by profession. Both of them are members of the Church of England." Ultimately, both men became members of Franklin's Council.

As 1771 unfolded, tensions began to increase between Franklin and the Assembly. He reported to London on April 30th that he had called a meeting at Burlington but that the Assembly "absolutely refused granting any Money for the Purpose of providing the King's troops. The Assembly declared that funds were not available. Franklin insisted that there were funds and he stated that the Assembly "returned an angry and somewhat abusive Answer, denying the Facts to be as I stated them."

Speaker Stephen Crane of the Assembly pointed out to Franklin that "This House informed your Excellency that they could not grant further supplies for His Majesty's Troops without laying Taxes on the good People of this Colony, who are already burdened with a heavy Debt contracted for His Majesty's Service during the last War (The French and Indian War, 1756-1763)."

Assembly Robert Friend Price of "Old Gloucester County" and Theunis Dye of Bergen County presented a strong rebuttal of Franklin's insinuation that New Jersey could afford to support the King's troops. Part of their message pointed out that:

> "Whereas the great Distress in which this Colony for several Years passed has been involved in for Want of a sufficient Currency, both as a Medium of Commerce and to pay Debts, hath compelled very many af the inhabitants to sell their Estates . . . You see nothing but Affluence; we see the distress of the People. Therefore we have the

best Right to Credit, as we have the best means for Information."

One of the most outspoken opponents of the stationing of British troops in New Jersey was Aaron Leaming of Cape May County. In some comments to the citizens of his county, Leaming stated that the British had " . . . quartered Troops in Pennsylvania and all the Eastern colonies" and that "the professed design of the troops are, to keep us in Subjection to the Crown & parliament of Great Britain. We acknowledge Subjection to the Crown of Great Britain, but none to the Parliament. They are our fellow Subjects. And this is the contest between us," as of May 26, 1771.

Leaming pointed out that "at first there were about 240 troops quartered in this Colony . . . but in hopes they would soon be drawn out if this province, we annually provided for them, by Acts of our own. And they keep increasing the troops apon us, 'till now they amount to 431 . . . the province was & is in profound peace."

By December 27, 1771, Governor William Franklin was able to notify London that "his endeavors have been attended with Success, and that the Assembly have at length granted a Sum of Money to discharge the Arrears due for the support of the Troops." Franklin has agreed to present the Assembly's opinions of the heavily inflicted taxes even though he did not "concur with them in Sentiments either with Respect to the Weight of the Taxes, or the Burthen of supporting Troops."

On February 21. 1772, Governor Franklin was in Burlington and met with his Council members for West New Jersey. The six members present were Charles Read, Samuel Smith, Richard Stockton, Steven Skinner. Daniel Coxe and John Lawrence. The first order of business was the nomination of Samuel Blackwood of Deptford Township and Thomas Clark of Greenwich Township to be Justices of the Peace in "Old Gloucester County."

It might be said that during the period 1771-1774, each of the colonies had its own particular problems with Great Britain and that a certain spark was needed ti unite all 13 colonies against King George III and the Parliament. One possible incident that might have produced a severe rupture was the destruction of a British revenue vessel, "The Gaspee," by angry Rhode Islanders on June 9, 1772. Of interest for New Jersey is the fact that the Chief Justice of New Jersey, Frederick Smyth, was instructed from London to proceed to Rhode Island serve on a special investigating commission seeking causes and culprits for the burning of the "Gaspee".

On July 2, 1772. the Lords of Trade in London were notified that the previous sessions of the New Jersey Assembly had approved twenty five acts, two of which pertained to "Old Gloucester County":

"An Act to impower the Inhabitants of the township of Deptford in the County of Gloucester, to repair their Public Highways by Hire and raise Money for that purpose."

"An Act to enable the Owners and Possessors of the Meadows lying on the Southerly Branch of Newton Creek in the County of Gloucester to repair and maintain a Bank, Dam and Water Works."

During late 1772, Committes of Correspondence were revived in Massachusetts by Samuel Adams and his friends. As Lawrence Gipson has stated: "With the appointment by the various colonies of committees of correspondence for the purpose of promoting intercolonial solidarity, a revolutionary American political union was in the making." The slow communications, by modern standards, between the colonies on matters of

11

mutual concern was most effective.

During May 1773, Parliament saw fit to pass the Regulating and Tea Acts. Both were to benefit the East India Company which would be able to sell its tea directly to the Colonies in a monopolistic fashion. While the price to American consumers would be lower under the new plan, colonial merchants stood to be driven out of the market and it was feared that tea would only be the first step towards the crippling of other colonial commercial ventures.

On December 16, 1773, three British merchant-vessels were boarded in the Boston Harbor by "Indians" and approximately ninety thousand pounds of tea were dumped into the water. Known romantically to school children today as "The Boston Tea Party", the dumping of the tea was an act of wanton destruction of the property of the East India Company and open defiance of an act of Parliament.

The "Tea Fever" spread to many other colonies, including New Jersey where in December 1774, a group of disguised citizens of Greenwich (Cumberland County) burned a cargo of tea that had been landed from the brig "Greyhound" The tea-burners were disguised as "Indians" who were never convicted for their vandalism. In addition, a group of students at the College of New Jersey in Princeton burned tea in protest against the British.

As might be expected, when the news of the "Boston Tea Party"reached Great Britain, Parliament responded with the Boston Port Bill which closed the harbor until the East India Company was given restitution for the tea, estimated to be worth fifteen thousand pounds. In addition, there followed a series of stringent "Intolerable" or "Coercive" acts aimed at bringing the colonies back into line. One of the most objectionable was the Quartering Act of 1774, which allowed colonial authorities to find quarters for British troops near to any area where the colonials needed to be observed.

Another act of 1774, the so-called "Quebec Act", enlarged "the Province of Quebec to include the territory north of the Ohio River and east of the Mississippi, where Massachusetts, Connecticut and Virginia all had claims which the Quebec Act ignored. The three colonies claiming Western territory felt that Great Britain was restricting their expansionist aspirations and that they were being punished; however, the Treaty of Paris which ended the French and Indian War in 1763 had not been fully implemented. French Catholics were now given the right of freedom of worship.

Within a few months, the issue of religion was to enter the Anglo-American turmoil and the Suffolk County, Massachusetts, Resolves of September 6, 1774, stated:

> That the late Act of Parliament for establishing the Roman Catholic religion and the French laws in that extensive country now called Canada, is dangerous to an extreme degree to the protestant religion and to the civil rights and liberties of all America."

Approximately two months earlier, it is learned from the Pennsylvania Journal of July 20, 1774:

> "At a general meeting of the magistrates, lawyers, freeholders, and other respectable inhabitants of the county of Gloucester, in New Jersey, held at the court-house in the said county, July 18,1774, the following resolutions were read, maturely considered, and unanimously agreed to:"

The first of the fourteen resolutions pointed out "that Boston is now suffering

12

the common cause of all British America; and therefore merits the most speedy and effectual aid in the in the power of the whole to give." Resolution two stated "that if the other colonies withhold their assistance, until Massachusetts is crushed and deprived of her liberty by the high and dangerous arm of Parliamentary power, now stretched forth over her for that purpose, they may, with good reason, expect soon to share the same fate."

Resolution four is of great interest:

> " . . . If we suffer the Parliament of Great Britain to tax us without our consent, they may then establish over us, at our expense . . . a military force, sufficient completely to subject us to the arbitrary will of the Minister, or, on his own words: 'to lay us at his feet.' "

"Old Gloucester County's" eleventh resolution indicates that attitudes "Towards Revolution" were becoming well defined:

> "That as a general Congress of Delegates from each respective Colony is prepared to be held at Philadelphia, in order to deliberate upon some general legal p;an of opposition to the arbitrary measures of the British Parliament . . . we do appoint Robert Friend Price, John Hinchman, Samuel Harrison, John Cooper, John Sparks, James Hinchman, Joseph Ellis, Samuel Clement, Joseph Hugg, Isaac Mickle, Joseph Morgan, Thomas Clark, and Isaac Tomlinson to act as a Committee of Correspondence with the other colonies, and who shall also have the power to appoint a committee of three of their own Members, to meet the committees of the other counties of this Province, to choose delegates to represent them . . . "

On July 21, 1774, a convention was called of the New Jersey Committees of Correspondence at New Brunswick and 72 members attended. It was stated that "The Committees taking into serious consideration the dangerous and destructive nature of sundry Acts of the British Parliament, with respect to the fundamental liberties of the American colonies, conceive it their indispensable duty to bear open testimony against them."

In addition, New Jersey's sympathies for Boston are evident in this statement rendered by members of the New Brunswick Convention:

> "We think the several late Acts of Parliament for shutting up the port of Boston, invading the Charter rights of the Province of Massachusetts Bay, and subjecting supposed offenders to be sent for trial to other Colonies, or to Great Britain . . . are not only subversive of the undoubted rights of his Majesty's American subjects, but also repugnant to the common principles of humanity and justice . . . "

The members of the New Brunswick Convention felt it "to be a duty, incumbent on the good people of this Province, to afford some immediate relief to the many suffering inhabitants of the town of Boston." Subscriptions were urged and the money collected was to be sent either directly to Boston or to a special committee for the aid of Boston. This committee consisted of James Neilson, John Dennis, William Ouke, Abraham Hunt, Samuel Tucker, Dr. Isaac Smith, Grant Gibbons, Thomas Sinnickson and John Carey.

In "Old Gloucester County," the following citizens were appointed a Relief Committee on August 19, 1774 to "receive donations from those who are charitably disposed" to help their suffering fellow Americans in Boston:

Waterford - Samuel Spicer, Abraham Inskeep, David Davis, Joseph Borrough and Kendall Cole;

Newton -	Marmaduke Cooper, Joseph Cooper, Ebenezer Hopkins and Thomas Redman;
Gloucester Town -	Joseph Hugg;
Gloucester Township -	Peter Cheesman, Robert Mattocks, Josiah Hillman and Benjamin Pitfield;
Deptford -	The Rev. Benjamin Chesnut, John Hopkins, Charles Fisher, John Wilkins, Jr., and Jonathan Chew;
Greenwich -	Docr. Bodo Otto, Daniel Cozens, Solomon Lippencott and Jonathan Fisher;
Woolwich -	Jacob Spicer, George Vanleer, James Tallman, William Guest and Robert Brown;
Great Egg Harbor and Galloway -	Richard Somers, Richard Wescott, Elijah Clark, Samuel Risley, Robert Smith, James Somers, Lemuel Sayre and Thomas Stites.

It is learned from The Pennsylvania Gazette of November 8, 1774 that the citizens of "Old Gloucester County" responded well to the call for aid to the people of Boston:

> "We hear that Mr Joseph Ellis, of Gloucester County, lately paid into the hands of Thomas Cushing, Esq., five hundred and thirty four dollars, being generously subscribed by the inhabitants of that county, for the relief of the poor of Boston."

It is apparent then that the events at Boston during 1774 created a deep feeling of sympathy in all of the 13 British Colonies. In New Jersey, the situation was viewed seriously and the July 21-24 New Brunswick Convention united the counties in the common cause against Great Britain. In addition, it was significantly resolved that "James Kinsey, William Livingston, John DeHart, Stephen Crane and Richard Smith Esquires . . . be delegates to represent this Province in the General Constitutional Congress, to be held at the city of Philadelphia, on or about the first of September next . . . to determine upon all such prudent and lawful measures as may be judged most expedient for the Colonies . . . in order to obtain relief for an oppressed people, and the redress of our general grievances."

Larry Gerlach has located a previously "undated, unpublished essay by the Reverend John Witherspoon, president of the College of New Jersey. It is Gerlach's opinion that the essay may safely be dated circa August 1774, for it speaks to the problems to be faced by the First Continental Congress, which was to convene on September 5th. Witherspoon, one of the 5 New Jersey signatories to the future Declaration of Independence, stated " . . . that the great object of the approaching Congress should be to unite the colonies, and make them as one body, in any measure of self-defense, to assure the people of Great Britain that we will not submit voluntarily, and convince them that it would be either impossible or unprofitable for them to compel us by open violence."

It is important to note that Benjamin Franklin was in London during the summer of 1774 and was serving as an Agent for the Province of New Jersey. The Standing Committee of Correspondence and Equiry, consisting of Robert Friend Price of "Old Gloucester County," Samuel Tucker and John Mehelm of Hunterdon County, and Henry Paxson of Burlington County, wrote to Franklin. They informed him that they had been "appointed a committee, to obtain amongst other things the most early and authentic intelligence of all acts and resolutions of the Parliament of Great Britain . . . We know of no person so proper to make application to, on this occasion, as to you, our Agent."

Chapter II
The First Continental Congress, 1774

In late August 1774, the delegates to the First Continental Congress were arriving in Philadelphia. Most of then had experienced long, hard journeys by horse and coach; however, as they arrived on the outskirts of the city, "they were . . . greeted by a company of riflemen and infantry with a band of musicians and conducted proudly into Philadelphia."

Massachusetts delegate John Adams commented that "by a computation made this evening . . . , there will be at the Congress about 56 members, 22 of them lawyers." The New Jersey delegation consisted of James Kinsey, John DeHart, Stephen Crane, William Livingston and Richard Smith. One of these New Jersey delegates noted in a secret and confidential letter of September 3, 1774:

"I am just returned from Philadelphia where I have been to wait on, and endeavor to found out the Temper of the Delegates. Near two Thirds of them are arrived, and I conclude all will be ready to proceed on Business on Monday. I have not had any great Opportunity of sounding them . . . "

On September 5, 1774, at 10 o'clock in the morning, citizens of the city of Philadelphia observed some 500 well-dressed gentlemen walking in determined fashion from the comfortable Smith's City Tavern to Carpenter's Hall. This group of American leaders, delegates from 12 of the disturbed British Colonies (Georgia was unable to send its delegates), were to bring into being the First Continental Congress, that "nursery of American Statesmen," as John Adams remarked. Indeed, as history bears out, it was a successful, first attempt at creating a national government in the Americas and Philadelphia still remains the American "cradle of liberty."

From the pen of one New Jersey delegate, it is learned that:

"The Congress this Day met at Carpenter's Hall, not-withstanding the offer of the Assembly Room a much more proper Place. They next proceeded to choose a Secretary, and, to my surprise Charles Thomson was unanimously elected—The New Yorkers and myself and a few others, finding a great Majority, did not think it prudent to oppose it . . . "

In addition to the choosing the radical Son of Liberty, Charles Thompson, of Philadelphia as Secretary of Congress, it was necessary to select a leader to preside over Congress. This might have been a divisive experience, for regional differences existed and there were many outstanding provincial leaders present from the Carolinas to New Hampshire. Who would the leader be? Present were such as Patrick Henry, George Washington and Peyton Randolph from Virginia; John and Samuel Adams from Massachusetts; Silas Deane from Connecticut; Joseph Galloway and John Dickinson from Pennsylvania; William Livingston and Stephen Crane from New Jersey; and Thomas Lynch and John Rutledge from South Carolina, among others.

Instead of regional jockeying for power, there was no disharmony. The delegates rallied behind the recommendation of Thomas Lynch from South Carolina. John Adams tells us that "Mr. Lynch arose, and said there was a gentleman present, who had presided with great dignity over a very respectable Society, greatly to the advantage of America, and he therefore prosposed that the Honorable

FROM THE ORIGINAL DRAWING BY H. A. OGDEN

DELEGATES LEAVING CARPENTER'S HALL AFTER A SESSION

Peyton Randolph, Esquire, one of the delegates from Virginia and the late Speaker of their House of Burgess, should be appointed chairman and he doubted not it would be unanimous--the question was put and he was unanimously chosen" The first President of the United States under the Continental Congress.

Calling their body a Congress and their leader a President, the delegates ultimately drew up a declaration of grievances which they insisted was indictative of British tyranny. Catalogued by the delegates were such felt injustices as the Stamp Act, Sugar Act, Coercive Acts, Quartering Act, Boston Port Bill, Quebec Act, and others of an oppresive nature.

On September 6, 1774, one day after the convening of the First Continental Congress in Philadelphia, Governor William Franklin wrote to the Earl of Dartmouth, stating that "Since my last, nothing of a public Nature worth communicating has occured in this province, except that there has been a general Meeting of the Several Counties at New Brunswick, when they came to Resolutions Similar to those of the other colonies . . . "

It is worth conjecturing whether Governor Franklin was deceiving himself or the Earl of Dartmouth, for the First Continental Congress was to sharpen focus on all of the issues between Great Britain and her 13 American Colonies. The solution of these issues might have prevented the promulgation of the Declaration of Independence less than two years after the Convention at New Brunswick and the convening of the First Continental Congress on September 5, 1774.

Under President Randolph, the First Continental Congress thoroughly examined all of the ramifications of a conciliation with Great Britain. After lengthy discussions for more than a month, the Congress, with no legislative powers per se , approved what has become known as "The Continental Association" on October 20, 1774. Article 2 stated:

"THAT WE WILL NEITHER IMPORT NOR PURCHASE ANY SLAVE imported after the first day of December next; after which time we will wholly discontinue the SLAVE TRADE . . . "

In addition to a non-trade article against Great Britain, Article 14 stated:

"And we do further agree and resolve that we will have no trade, commerce, dealings, or intercourse whatsoever, with any colony or province in North America, which shall not accede to, or which shall hereafter violate this Association, but will hold them as UNWORTHY OF THE RIGHTS OF FREEMEN, AND AS INIMICAL TO THE LIBERITES OF THIS COUNTRY."

Governor William Franklin of New Jersey, in commenting on the proceedings of the Continental Congress, realistically told the Earl of Dartmouth that:

"Altho' the Proceedings of the Congress are not altogether satisfactory to many of the Inhabitants of the Colonies, yet there seems at present little Reason to doubt but that the Terms of the Association will be generally carried into execution, even by those who dislike Parts of it."

Franklin also noted that "few have the Courage to declare their Disapprobation publicly, as they well know, if they do not conform, they are in Danger of becoming Objects of popular Resentment, from which it is not in the Power of Government here to protect them. Indeed the Officers of Government in all the Colonies (except at Boston) have but little or no Protection themselves."

The First Continental Congress was only in session a brief fifty-one days, from September 5 to October 26, 1774; however, in addition to the "Continental Association," the Congress encouraged the colonies to raise their own troops for the threatened struggle with Great Britain. Even so, the delegates drew up a petition to King George III in which they begged "Leave to lay our grievances before your Majesty, that your royal authority and interposition may be used for our relief; and that a gracious answer may be given to this petition." It is interesting to note that William Livingston, John DeHart, Stephen Crane and Richard Smith signed the petition. The name of the other New Jersey delegate, James Kinsey, does not appear.

The members of the First Continental Congress left for home optimistically, hoping that the petition would move King George III in their direction. It was not to be so and the Earl of Dartmouth notified all colonial governors on January 14, 1775 that the king was disturbed that the delegates had scheduled a Second Continental Congress during May 1775. In particular, Dartmouth stated:

"Certain persons styling themselves Delegates of several of His Majesties Colonies in America, having presumed, without his Majesties authority or consent, to assemble together at Philadelphia, in the months of September and October last; and having thought fit, amongst other unwarrantable proceedings, to resolve that it will be necessary, that another Congress should be held, at the same place, on the 10th of May next, unless redress for certain pretended grievances be obtained...I am commanded by the King to signify to you his Majestys pleasure, that you so use your utmost endeavors to present any such appointment..."

Meanwhile in "Old Gloucester County," the events of Philadelphia were being keenly followed, for "At a General Meeting of the inhabitants of the county of Gloucester, in New Jersey, held at the Court-house, on the 12th of December, 1774; the association formed and entered into by the General American Congress...in behalf of themselves and these Colonies in general, being read and approved, it was

I. Resolved unanimously, That the said Association be adopted and carried into execution throughout this county."

One of the articles of the "Continental Association" stated "that a committee be chosen in every county, city, and town...to observe the conduct of all persons touching this Association." In essence, no citizens in the 13 Colonies were to conduct business with any agent of Great Britain. If persons did trade with an Englishman, their names were to be published and they would be considered as foes "to the rights of British America...and universally condemned as the ENEMIES OF AMERICAN LIBERTY..."

In "Old Gloucester County," on December 12, 1774 it was "resolved unanimously, That a Committee of Observation, consisting of 77 members, be chose by a majority of electors 'qualified to vote for representatives in the legislature..." Fortunately, Frank Stewart, the eminent Gloucester County historian, acquired the original documents of this immediate period and they are in the archives of the Gloucester County Historical Society, thus it is possible to identify the 77 members by political division:

Waterford
Samuel Spicer
Joseph Morgan
Joshua Stokes
Kendal Coles
Abraham Inskeep

Newton
Isaac Mickle
Samuel Clements
John Gill
William Cooper
Samuel Cooper
Doctor (Benj.) Vanleer
Marmaduke Cooper
Ben. Cathrall
Joseph Cooper
Ben. Cathrall
Joseph Cooper
(John Mickle)

Gloucester Town
Sam'l Harrison
Robt. Fr'd. Price
John Hinchman
Joseph Ellis
Wm. Hugg Jun'r
James Dundas
Joseph Hugg

Gloucester Township
Mich'l Fisher
Isaac Tomlinson
Peter Cheesman
John Hider Jr.
Josiah Hillman
Robert Mattocks
Jacob Roberts
Benj. Pittfield
John Hedger

Deptford
John Cooper
John Sparks
James Whitall Sr.
John Hopkins
Joseph Low
James Wilkins
John Wilkins Jr.
Doctor Thos. Hendry
Israel Shreve
Charles Fisher

Thomas Denny

Woolwich
James Hinchman
George Vanleer
John Steelman
Matthew Gill
Robert Brown
James Talman
Constantine Wilkins
John Kelly
John Cozens
Wm. Zane
Samuel Hewes
Wm. Guest
Jno. Rambo

Greenwich
Alexander Randall
Thos. Clark
Restore Lippincott
Doctor Bodo Otto
Dan'l Cozens
Arch. Maffet
Thomas Taber
John Barns

Egg Harbour
Elijah Clark
Rich'd Wescott
Rich'd Somers
John Somers
Ben Brush
Jos. Johnson
Thos. Stites
Thos. Clark
Jno. Somers Jr.
Lemuel Sayre
Robert Morse
Robert Smith
Richard Price
David Clark

19

It was further resolved at the Court House Meeting that the young women of 'Old Gloucester County" instead "of trifling their time away do prudently employ it in learning the use of the spinning wheel...The time calls for diligence, and no hand ought to be idle, that is capable of contributing, in the least degree, to the support of the public cause."

The last resolution called for the 77 member Committee to remain active until December 12, 1775, "unless our grievances are before that time redressed, or such new resolutions entered into by the General Congress, as shall render a fresh choice necessary; and that, should the latter of these cases happen, they do then immediately convene the county, in order that such fresh choice may accordingly take place."

On December 19, 1774, "The Committee of Observation for the County of Gloucester" appointed "Robert Friend Price, John Hinchman, John Cooper, John Sparks, Joseph Ellis and Joseph Hugg, as a committee to meet the committees of the other counties...and that three or more of said Committee shall attend for choosing Delegates to serve in the Continental Congress at Philadelphia, on the 10th of May next." The committee of all the county committees returned James Kinsey, John DeHart, Stephen Crane, William Livingston and Richard Smith as the New Jersey delegates to the coming May 1775 meeting of the Second Continental Congress.

Unfortunately, the colonial grievances went generally unheeded in England. Lord Chatham, however, made a formal plea on January 20, 1775 for reconciliation between Great Britain and her 13 colonies. Chatham believed the British troops should be removed from Boston and if this were done, it would begin to "open the ways towards a happy settlement of the dangerous troubles in America by beginning to allay ferments and soften animosities there." Regretfully, the "House of Lords refused...to accede to Chatham's request by a vote of sixty-eight to eighteen."

On February 15, 1775, Parliament responded by enacting the first of two "Restraining Acts" which were intended "to subdue the rebellious spirit in America." These acts placed further restrictions in colonial trading and fishing rights, hence they were to further infuriate the colonists. In addition, Massachusetts was declared to be in a state of rebellion, which was to be crushed by the ten thousand British troops in the Boston area.

It is not to be implied that other plans for reconciliation were not being proposed in England. Lord North submitted a plan on February 20, 1775 which he said "plainly defines the line to be held in America; and as it puts an end to Congress, it certainly will have a good effect in this Country, and I hope in at least some of the colonies." It was not to be so in any of the colonies, for liberty once gained is not meekly surrendered.

Royal government in America was ineffective; however, on March 7, 1775, Governor William Franklin of New Jersey transmitted to the Earl of Dartmouth in London a list of the names of the members of the King's Council for New Jersey. They were Peter Kembel, David Ogden, William Alexander (Earl of Stirling), John Stevens, Samuel Smith, James Parker, Frederick Smyth, Richard Stockton, Stephen Skinner, Daniel Coxe, John Lawrence and Francis Hopkinson.

In England, Edmund Burke made his famous conciliation speech in the House of Commons on March 22, 1775. He suggested that it would be wise "to establish the equity and justice of taxation of America by grant and not by imposition." He suggested many of the obnoxious acts should be repealed;

however, Burke's proposals were soundly defeated in the House of Commons.

Within a few weeks, General Gage, commander of the British Troops in America, decided to destroy colonial military supplies located near Concord, Massachusetts. The American Revolution was to have its military beginning on the morning of April 19, 1775 when British troops and Massachusetts minutemen exchanged gun-fire in what has been romantically called "the shot heard around the world." No matter, blood was to be shed and there would be no turning back on the "road to revolution."

Chapter III

The Second Continental Congress, 1775-1778

Three weeks before the Second Continental Congress was to convene at Philadelphia on May 10, 1775, 800 British troops marched to Lexington, Massachusetts, where they were confronted by approximately 70 minutemen. The main battle between the "Red-Coats" and the provincial troops occurred at Concord, where 1800 British soldiers did battle with 3700 Americans. British losses were 273 and those of the minutemen, approximately 95. Dramatically the events at Lexington and Concord electrified the other colonies and a "new spirit of resistance was mounting. Many a hesitant American was swung over to the patriot cause of armed opposition."

Express riders were dispatched from Lexington and Concord on April 19, the day of battle. From the records of the "Gloucester County Historical Society," it is learned that "on Sunday afternoon the 23rd of April the Committee of Correspondence of New York dispatched an express rider to New Brunswick ... Expresses were undoubtedly sent to the different Committees of Correspondence of the various counties of South Jersey."

It would appear "that the news of the first spilling of blood between the armed forces of England and its American Colonies reached Old Gloucester County either late in the afternoon of April 24 or early in the morning of April 25, 1775," 15 days before the Second Continental Congress was to assemble at Philadelphia.

In early May, Governor William Franklin of New Jersey wrote the Earl of Dartmouth that "the Accounts we have from Massachusetts Bay respecting the Proceedings of the King's Troops, and the late Engagement between them and the Inhabitants of that Province, have occasioned such an Alarm and excited so much Uneasiness among the People throughout this and other Colonies, that there is Danger of their committing some outrageous Violences before the present Heats subside."

Franklin realistically noted that "it is greatly to be regretted that the late Skirmish happened at the Time it did, as it has, in its Consequences, proved one of the most unlucky Incidents that could have occurred in the present Situation of Affairs. It will not only be a Means of retarding, if not entirely defeating the Wishes and Measures of His Majesty for a happy Reconciliation; but will endanger the Lives & properties of every Officer of Government in the King's Colonies to the Southward of New England ..."

On May 5, 1775, there was convened "A Meeting of a majority of the Committee of Correspondence for the County of Gloucester ... Present Samuel Harrison, Esq., Chairman, John Hinchman, John Cooper, John Sparks, Joseph Ellis, Joseph Low, Isaac Mickle, Joseph Hugg." The Committee ordered that:

> "In consequence of the intelligence received from the Committee of Correspondence from New Brunswick and at their request the above named have taken into consideration and do unanimously agree and think it our indispensable duty in this alarming crisis forthwith to request a meeting of the inhabitants of this county for the purpose of choosing of members to meet at the Provincial Congress at Trenton ..."

Over in Philadelphia on Wednesday morning, May 10, 1775, with the streets

22

blazing with banners proclaiming "Liberty or Death," solemn members of the Second Continental Congress convened and unanimously re-elected Peyton Randolph of Virginia as President and Charles Thomson of Philadelphia as Secretary. It was Mr. Thomson who had indicated in a letter to Benjamin Franklin that tensions were mounting and that Britain and her 13 colonies were on "the brink of precipice."

On the same day that the Congress first met, Captain Ethan Allen and his 83 "Green Mountain Boys" of Vermont captured Fort Ticonderoga on Lake Champlain. Asked by the British commander on whose authority he acted, Allen replied: "In the name of the great Jehovah and the Continental Congress." The victory was not only a boost to colonial morale, but it also produced significant amounts of military hardware and ammunition which were sorely needed.

In "Old Gloucester County," it was ordered that the Committee of Correspondence meet at William Hugg's house on May 18, 1775. At this meeting, "the inhabitants taking into consideration the intelligence communicated from the Committee of Correspondence of New Brunswick do unanimously Resolve: That it is highly necessary that there should be a Provincial Congress held ... and agree that seven persons be chosen for said purpose to represent this County. And accordingly, Robert Friend Price, John Hinchman, Elijah Clark, Esquires, and Messrs. John Cooper, Joseph Ellis, John Sparks and Joseph Hugg were unanimously chosen ..."

Also on May 18, it came to light that John Cox of Woolwich Township had conducted himself in an anti-American manner, for he "was charged with being inimical to the liberties of America ..." Cox confessed as follows:

"I, John Cox of the Township of Woolwich and County of Gloucester do hereby acknowledge that I have inadvertently violated the resolves of Congress for which I am sincerely sorry and do hereby promise that in future, I will strictly observe and keep every association and resolve recommended by either Continental or Provincial Congress."

On May 27, 1775, Governor Franklin wrote to the Earl of Dartmouth that "Ever since that unfortunate Affair at Lexington, the Colonies have been in the utmost Commotion. The People are not contented to wait for the Determination of the Continental Congress, but are continually holding County Committees and Provincial Conventions in every Colony."

In New Jersey, Franklin noted, the Provincial Congress came to "a Resolution of raising Ten Thousand pounds in order to support a Body of Militia in this Province, which they propose to have well disciplined and ready for immediate service ... I have already received a Number of Resignations from the Militia Officers who held Commissions under me ... Their Ambition is now, it seems, to have Commissions from the Congress or Conventions."

On June 2, 1775, the Second Continental Congress received a statement from Dr. Joseph Warren of Massachusetts. It read: "We are now compelled to raise an army, which with the assistance of the other colonies, we hope under the smiles of Heaven, we will be able to defend us and all America from further butcheries and devastation by our implacable enemies." Within 2 weeks, Warren died in the action around Bunker Hill. Benjamin Franklin was so disturbed that he wrote to his English friend, Mr. Strahan of the Parliament: "You are now my enemy."

The Congress resolved on June 3 that "A Committee be appointed for the purpose of borrowing six thousand pounds for the use of America" and that the Committee "apply the sum of money to the purchase of gun-powder for the use of the Continental Army." Obviously, the American Revolution had already begun but still awaited a formal declaration of independence.

On June 12, it was said in Congress that "This Congress ... considering the critical, alarming and calamitious state of these colonies, do earnestly recommend that Thursday, the 20th of July next, be observed by the inhabitants of all the English Colonies on this continent, as a day of public humiliation, fasting and prayer."

Shortly, Peyton Randolph of Virginia, now a delegate to the Congress, while John Hancock of Massachusetts served as president, urged his fellow delegates to appoint George Washington as commander of the colonial armies. On June 16, 1775, President Hancock "from the Chair informed George Washington, Esquire, that he had the order of Congress to acquaint him, that the Congress had by a unanimous vote made choice of him to be general and commander in chief of the forces raised, and to be raised, in defense of American Liberty."

Leaving Philadelphia on June 23, General Washington arrived at Cambridge, Massachusetts, in early July to view his army of approximately 15,000, most of whom were poorly trained and armed. The new commanding officer, after some early difficulty and hostility, was able to bring discipline and organization into being. Fortunately, the Congress was also able to supply funds for some military expenditures out of the 2 million dollars authorized in late June.

Not many eye-brows were raised on June 21 when "Mr. Thomas Jefferson appeared as a delegate for the Colony of Virginia and produced his Credentials which were read and approved." Jefferson's intellignece and militant attitudes were soon recognized and he joined the camp of such militants as Benjamin Franklin, Samuel Adams, John Hancock and John Adams, among others. This was the "independence or bust" faction which stood opposed to those who held out for conciliation with the British. The third and largest of the colonial factions felt that an impressive show of military force would bring the British to their senses, making independence un-necessary.

On June 27, 1775, there was convened "a Meeting of the Justice & Free-holders of the County of Gloucester at the Court House in the Town of Glou-cester." The justices were (Gloucester Township) Michael Fisher, (Gloucester Town) John Hinchman, (Greenwich) Thomas Clark, (Woolwich) James Hinchman, (Egg Harbor) James Somers, Samuel Risley, Robert Morse and (Dept-ford) Israel Shreve. The freeholders present were Nathanial Lippincott (Water-ford), John Gill and David Branson (Newton), Joseph Hugg (Gloucester Town), Peter Cheesman and Josiah Hillman (Gloucester Township), David Cooper and James Whittall (Deptford), Joshua Cozens and Thomas West (Greenwich), Jacob Spicer and Constantine Wilkins (Woolwich) and Frederick Steelman (Egg Harbour/Galloway).

In Philadelphia, despite the different factions in Congress, that body on June 30, 1775 "approved The Articles of War" which contained 69 individual articles. Governor Franklin immediately wrote the Earl of Dartmouth that "A Formal Declaration has been published by the Congress & every preparation made for carrying on a War which is in their power ... There is indeed, a Dread in the Minds of many here, that some of the Leaders of the people are aiming to estab-lish a Republic ..."

On July 4, 1775, a year before the adoption of the Declaration of Independ-ence, Governor Franklin wrote to London that it was "reported that a Thousand of the New Jersey Militia are ordered to march to the City of New York, to join the Connecticut People now there under the Command of one Wooster ... I am just informed that 400 Rifle-Men are to march this Day from Philadelphia to join the New England Army at Cambridge," now under the command of George Washington.

Benjamin Franklin

A day later on July 5, the Earl of Dartmouth wrote to Governor Franklin that

"In this Situation ... it is the King's firm Resolution that the most vigorous Efforts should be made both by Sea and Land, to reduce His rebellious Subjects to Obedience ... & the proper measures are now pursuing not only for augmenting the Army under General Gage, but also for making such Addition to our Naval Strength in No. America as may enable Admiral Graves to make ... a disposition of his Fleet ..."

On July 8, 1775, in hopes of averting open war with Great Britain, Congress approved the "Olive Branch Petition" of Pennsylvania's John Dickinson. The colonial leaders confirmed their loyalty to King George III but asked that their grievances be alleviated. To prove their sincerity, the "Petition" was taken to London by an arch-loyalist Richard Penn, a descendent of William Penn.

Unfortunately, King George III did not receive Penn and he refused to even look at the "Olive Branch Petition" and those Americans who had hoped for some conciliation with the King and Parliament were disappointed, for on August 23, the King declared the colonies to be in a state of rebellion.

Governor Franklin notified the Earl of Dartmouth in early September that he was informed that "General Gage has received Information of its being Determined by the General and principal Officers of the Continental Army (as it is called) to make an Attack on the town of Boston ... and endeavour to destroy the King's Forces ... before any Re-inforcement can arrive." Washington's troops were able to conduct a rather successful seige of Boston during the fall of 1775, but it was not until the spring of 1776 that the British were forced to evacuate Boston, never to return.

On November 1, 1775, Franklin reported to London that "The Provincial Convention of this Province, I hear, have at the Instigation of the Continental Congress, agreed to raise two Battallions consisting of eight Companies each, and 68 Privates to a Company. The Officers, I am told, are now recruiting and 30,000 (pounds) of Paper Bills of Credit, is ordered to be immediately struck ... Unless the Army under Schuyler or that under Washington should happen to be defeated or repulsed, there seems little probability but that the Inhabitants in general will implicitly follow the Continental Congress in all their Extravagancies. It seems to be generally agreed that many of that Body are for an entire separation from the Mother Country, and some of them publicly avow Sentiments of Independence."

While spirits were high during the fall of 1775, realists were aware that the enlistments of most of Washington's troops would expire at the end of the year, and "most of the common soldiers felt that they had done their stint." Recruitment was not to be an easy task for those who were leading the 13 colonies down the road to revolution.

In addition, the Continental Congress authorized an attack on Canada by two American armies. It was hoped that the Canadians would sympathize and would desire to join the other 13 colonies in an effort to obtain independence from Great Britain.

By December of 1775, General Richard Montgomery had led his troops up from New York to Montreal. Meanwhile Colonel Benedict Arnold had successfully led his forces through the wilderness of Maine and joined forces with Montgomery. The two commanders, with Montreal secured, then decided to attack Quebec and thereby obtain vitally needed military supplies

General George Washington

Unfortunately this "Northern Campaign" of the Americans ended in a severe defeat. The loss included the death of General Montgomery and his aide-de-camp, Captain John MacPherson, Jr., of Philadelphia, plus dozens of other Americans. In addition, Colonel Benedict Arnold was wounded and "had the misfortune to have his leg splintered by a shot, and was obliged to be carried to the hospital."

Benedict Arnold is usually portrayed as the great traitor; however, a contemporary account of his march to Quebec tells us much of the man:

> "Seldom was there an expedition attempted during the American war, in which more hardship was endured ... than in this of Arnold's ... They had swamps and woods, mountains and precipices alternately to surpass. Added to their other trials, their provisions failed,

27

and, to support life, they were obliged to eat their dogs, cartouch boxes, clothes and shoes ... After thirty one days of incessant toil through a hideous wilderness, they reached the habitations of men."

As 1776 began, American troops were still camped close to Quebec and they still were in possession of Montreal. During the ensuing months, small pox and a shortage of military supplies were to take their toll and by June 1776, the ragged Americans were at Fort Ticonderoga. "The Northern Campaign" had been a bitter and costly failure.

At this low ebb, the great American trupmhet was sounded throughout the Delaware Valley on January 10, 1776 by Thomas Paine, an English immigrant to Philadelphia two years earlier. Paine's "Common Sense" was a very polemical document, for it boldly advocated a "Declaration of Independence" for the 13 American Colonies six months before the actual declaration.

Thomas Jefferson

Little other than an act of treason against King George III from a British point of view, Paine's "Common Sense" could well have cost him his head. Even so, he went ahead and "in three months it sold probably a hundred thousand copies," no doubt circulating from hand to hand to more than triple that number in the Delaware Valley alone.

By the stroke of his quill, Paine became "the most articulate spokesman of the American Revolution," as well as "the epitome of a world in revolution." He was echoing the teachings of John Locke and the Enlightenment Frenchmen, such as Voltaire and Rousseau, who followed Locke.

Paine said "the period of debate is closed" and that "arms as the last resource decide the contest; the appeal was the choice of the king, and the continent has accepted the challenge." It was his strong conviction that:

> "The sun never shined on a cause of greater worth. 'Tis not the affair of a city, a county, a province, or a kingdom; but of a continent -- of at least one-eighth part of the habitable globe. 'Tis not the concern of a day, a year, or an age ... Now is the seedtime of continental union, faith, and honor ... Even the distance at which the Almighty hath placed England and America is a strong and natural proof that the authority of the one over the other, was never the design of heaven ..."

Thomas Paine raised this question: "But where, say some, is the king of America." He answered: "I'll tell you, friend, he reigns above, and doth not make havoc of mankind like the Royal Brute of Great Britain ... in America THE LAW IS KING. For as in absolute governments the king is law, so in free countries the law OUGHT to be king, and there ought to be no other ... O ye that love mankind! Ye that dare oppose not only the tyranny but the tyrant, stand forth!"

It was Thomas Paine then, the poor immigrant Quaker, who told Americans during the bleak days of early 1776 that it was "the business of little minds to shrink" from the business at hand, that of freeing 13 British Colonies from the tyranny of the British throne and the Mercantile System. Paine's mind was never to shrink, during a life time of pursuing democratic causes, from the business of attacking injustices and to man's inhumanity to man.

While Larry Gerlach states in his "The Road to Revolution" in New Jersey that Paine's "Common Sense" did not prompt "any open debate" in this province, it is to be noted that the Constitutional Gazette of February 24, 1776 commented that:

> "This animated piece dispels, with irresistible energy, the prejudice of the mind against the doctrine of independence, and pours in upon it such an innunciation of light and truth, as will produce an instantaneous and marvellous change in the temper -- in the views and feelings of an American. The ineffable delight with which it is pursued and its doctrines imbibed is a demonstration that the seeds of independence ... will grow surprisingly well with proper cultivation in the fields of America ...

Chapter IV

The Declaration of Independence

During the summer of 1775, "Old Gloucester County" did not possess a large military establishment; however, it did have three battalions of militia-type "minute men." The first battalion was commanded by Colonel Israel Shreve and his two top officers were Colonel Bodo Otto and Robert Taylor. Battalion two was commanded by Colonel Joseph Ellis, with Lt. Colonel Elijah Clark and Major William Ellis as his supporting officers. The third "Gloucester" battalion was commanded by Colonel Richard Somers, with Major Richard Westcott, George Payne and Jermiah Smith as his main staff officers. All of these commanders and their troops were to see a great deal of action when the theatre of war shifted to Central and South Jersey during the campaigns of 1776 and 1777.

On December 12, 1775, the Committee of Observation and Correspondence of "Old Gloucester County" met and the following patriots were chosen from these townships:

Waterford: Kendall Coles, Joshua Stokes, Abraham Inskeep:
Newton: Isaac Mickle, Samuel Clements, Joseph Cooper, William Cooper, Samuel Cooper, Doctor Vanleer;
Gloucester Town: Samuel Harrison, Robert Frd. Price, John Hinchman, Joseph Ellis, William Hugg, Jr., Joseph Hugg:
Gloucester Township: Peter Cheeseman, Josiah Hillman, Benj. Pitfield, John Hider, Robert Matlack, John Hedger, Isaac Tomlinson;
Deptford: John Sparks, John Cooper, Israel Shreve, Doctor Hendry, James Wilkins, Joseph Low, John Wilkins, Jr., James Whitall;
Greenwich: Thomas Clark, Doctor Otto, Daniel Cozens, John Barns, Archibald Moffett, Robert Correy, John Cozens :
Woolwich: James Hinchman, George Vanleer, Robert Brown, William Zane, James Talman, Matthew Gill, John Rambo, WIlliam Guest, John Kelley;
Great Egg Harbor and: Elijah Clark, Richard Westcott, Richard Somers, Galloway   Samuel Sayre, Thomas Stites. Samuel Risley, John Somers.

During the first week of January 1776, Governor William Franklin of New Jersey wrote a "secret and confidential" report to the Earl of Dartmouth in which he noted that the New Jersey Assembly was in a mood to petition King George III again "on the Subject of the present uhappy Disputes." Before the Assembly could act, "a Committee of the general Congress at Philadelphia came in great haste to Burlington . . . and pursuaded them to drop their Design." The three man committee from Philadelphia consisted of John Dickinson of Pennsylvania, John Jay of New York and George Wythe of Virginia.

Having for all intents and purposes seized the power of government away from Franklin, he reported to London that "the Provincial Congress here have given Leave to some Persons to export Country Produce, on the Condition of importing the value in Powder, and other military stores." In particular, Richard

Westcott of "old Gloucester County" was authorized "to freight a Vessel to some foreign Port with the produce of this Colony to purchase Gunpowder & other military Stored for the use of their Province."

On January 8, 1776, Governor Franklin's home was surrounded by provincial troops and Lt. Colonel Winds sent a brief letter inside the house:

"I have Hints that you intended to leave the Province if the Letters that were intercepted should be sent to the Continental Congress . . . I desire that you will give me your Word and Honour that you will not depart this Province till I know the Will & Pleasure of the Continental Congress concerning that Matter."

Franklin replied: " I have not the least Intention to quit the Province, nor shall unless compelled by Violence." Even so, Franklin felt that the "Congress will order me to be seized and sent to the Interior Part of the Country, that I may not have the Opportunity of transmitting any more Intelligence to your Lordship," the Earl of Dartmouth.

On February 20,1776, it was noted in the Journals of the Continental Congress that "Old Gloucester County" had been greatly honored:

"IN PROVINCIAL CONGRESS, NEW JERSEY, BRUNSWICK, 14th Feb. 1776 On motion, Resolved, unanimously, That William Livingston, John D'Hart, Richard Smith, John Cooper and Jonathan Dickinson Sergeant, Esqrs. be Delegates to represent this Province in the Continental Congress, for the Space of one Year, or until others shall be legally appointed in their Stead; and that they, or any three or more of them, have full and ample Power to consent and agree to all Measures which such Congress shall deem necessary; and this Province bind themselves to execute, to the utmost of their Power, all Resolutions which the said Congress may adopt. And further, if the said Congress shall think necessary to adjourn, we do authorize our said Delegates to represent and act for this Province, in any one Congress to be held by Virtue if such adjournments, during their Delegation. A true Copy from the Minutes,

William Paterson, Secretary"

For the record, John Cooper of Woodbury was a member of the Second Continental Congress from February 14th to June 22nd, 1776, missing by 12 days the great honor of signing the Declaration of Independence. Unfortunately, it does not appear in the records of the Congressional Journals that John Cooper participated in any of the deliberations taking place at Philadephia. It also seems conclusive that he did not attend any meetings of the Congress. Instead, John Cooper, as a delegate to the Continental Congress, continued to function very actively as one of "Old Gloucester County's" delegates to the Provincial Congress of New Jersey.

By March 1776, Governor Franklin was on serious difficulty with the revolutionary authorities. He had commanded Lt. Colonel Winds to remove the guard around his home "as he would answer the contrary at his Peril." Winds' superior officer, Lord Sterling, ordered the Royal Governor arrested and he was to be sent under heavy guard to Elizabeth town. Franklin tell us that "Accordingly I was made Prisoner by a Party of about 100 Soldiers . . . it not being in my Power in the present Situation of Affairs to make the least Resistance."

As March 1776 was coming to a close, citizens of "Old Gloucester County" were to realize that the threat of war was a real possibility, for on March 25th, two British men-of-war were to appear off the Delaware capes. Henry Fisher of Lewes, Delaware, who was charged with the responsibility of promptly notifying the Committee of Safety at Philadelphia sent the following message up the river:

"This serves to inform you that there is a Sloop of War now coming into our Road with a small tender. And as it is now night, I cannot inform you whether they are bound up the Bay or not; the Wind is now at the South, therefore have Reason to believe that they will proceed up the Bay . . . "

The next day, Henry Fisher was able to be more specific in his dispatch to the Committee of Safety:

"This comes Express to all whom it may concern, giving notice that last Evening came into Whorekiln Road, a Man of War, not less than forty Guns; this morning they took a sloop at the mouth of Lewes Creek and my Pilot Boat . . . all persons along the Bay are here by warn'd to be on their guard . . . "

At Philadelphia during the early days of April 1776, the Committee of Safety became increasingly concerned that British interference in Delaware River shipping was taking its toll. Accordingly, the Committee

"RESOLVED, That the Letter receiv'd from Henry Fisher of Lewes be immediately sent to the Delegates of this Province, to be laid before the Congress, and the said Delegates be requested to represent it as the sense of the Committee, that if two or more fast sailing vessels of small draft of Water were properly equipt they might protect the Trade of this & Neighboring colonies in the Bay of Delaware, now infested with Tenders and small armed Vessels of the Enemy . . . "

The Roebuck of forty-four guns, commanded by Captain Andrew Snape Hammond of the Royal British Navy, was an imposing and frightening sight for the citizens of the Delaware Valley, Captain Hammond had wished to attack the city of Philadelphia but his superiors ordered him to continued to play havoc with American shipping in the Delaware Bay

By the end of April, Captain Hammond began to move up the Delaware River, for in his narrative, he noted:

"As I now began to grow short of water, and had lighten'd the Ship to as easy a draught of water as I could . . . I took the Liverpool with me & sailed up the River in order to fill my empty Casks, and reconnoitre the enemys force of the River . . . "

When the Roebuck and Liverpool hoisted anchors at 6 A.M. on May 5, 1776, the reality of war became evident to the citizens of Cumberland, Salem and "Old Gloucester" counties. In addition to the ultimate "Great Battle in our Rever," as phrased by James Wood of Philadelphia, the farmers if South Jersey could expect increased British foraging raids in order to supply feed for the British sailors.

Indeed as we learn from Peter Force's "American Archives," Thomas Harris, Chairman of the Cumberland County Committee of Correspondence, reported the following during May 1776 to the New Jersey delegates to the Continental Congress:

"As our situation on the Delaware exposes us to frequent depredations of our enemies—we having already two alarms, and this day a number of our cattle killed and taken away, and we not having sufficient quantity of powder and ball in store to protect our shore, and hourly expecting more visits from the ships that lie in the bay— I am directed to apply to you to solicit the Congress for a further supply of two hundred pounds of lead . . . "

As the Roebuck and the Liverpool continued up the Delaware River, Frank Stewart tells us in his "Battle of Red Bank" that Job Whitall at Red Bank noted in his diary: "alarm guns were fired betwixt twelve and one of the clock which occasioned great commotion amongst the people of Old Gloucester County.

It was on May 8th, 1776 that the first naval engagement between American and British forces took place in the Delaware Valley. From Captain Hammond's "Narrative," it is learned that the Pennsylvania Navy "consisted of 13 Row Galleys, each carrying one gun from 32 Pounders to 18pdrs, a Floating Battery of 10 Eighteen pdrs and a Sloop fitted as a fire ship." Hammond spoke of the naval battle as follows:

"We met them under sail (as the Tide ran too rapid to ride with a

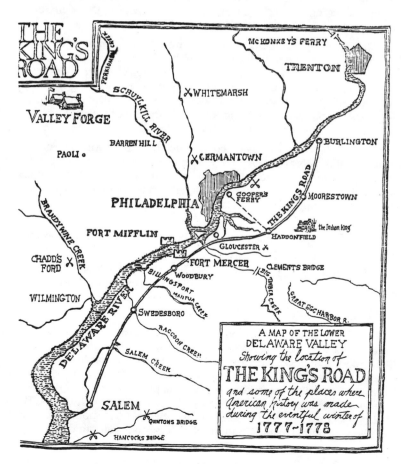

A MAP OF THE LOWER
DELAWARE VALLEY
Showing the location of
THE KING'S ROAD
and some of the places where
American history was made
during the eventful winter of
1777-1778

Spring upon the Cable) and lay under the disadvantage of being obliged to engage them at the distance they chose to fix, which was scarcely within point blank Shot . . . We fired upon them near two hours before they thought proper to retire and row off . . . "

In "Old Gloucester County," at Red Bank, Job Whitall recorded that he had "heard a cannonading with the row gallies and a man-of-war or two which lasted three hours or more. The people getting arms as fast as possible."

The battle between the American and British vessels continued a second day and many rumors were current. In his "Diary," Christopher Marshall of Philadelphia noted that " . . . after dinner went to coffee house, where various reports were Circulated, how the "Roebuck" ran aground &c but upon the whole it appeared that little Damage has been sustained on our Side, but as no express has arrived this day was are in Suspence."

James Wood's "Account Book" affords a vivid account of the action:

"the Next day they began to fire at four a Clock and it lasted till after dark: one (h)our or two in which time they made three holes in the "Roebuck" man of war and seven in 'Liverpool' man of war . . . the Roe Gales lost 12 men . . . "

The Roebuck went aground in the shallow water off the coast of Penn's Neck. A contemporary letter of the day noted that "In the course of the engagement the 'Roebuck' ran ashore, and is now fast on the Jersey shore. at Kearney' Point, a little above Deep Water Point." By 4 o'clock the next morning, at high tide, the Roebuck was pulled out of the mud by the Liverpool. The British vessels moved back down the Delaware River to Reedy Island, where it took several days to repair the rather extensive damage inflicted by the Americans.

The "Battle in our Rever" discouraged any further British attempts to move on the city of Philadelphia, the Capitol of the United Colonies. It would not be until early fall of 1777 that further naval action would occur in the Delaware Valley.

With the British naval threat at rest, there remained the problem of what to do with Royal Governor William Franklin. Frederick Smyth, the Chief Justice of New Jersey, convinced Lord Stirling to allow Franklin to remain at his home. As Franklin wrote: "The Result was, that the Chief-Justice went to Lord Stirling— the guards were soon after his Return removed from my house, and I have continued unmolested ever since." Actually, Franklin remained under "house arrest" for another 2 months, shorn of all power by the Provincial Congress of New Jersey.

On May 30, 1776, Governor Franklin made the fatal error of notifying the General Assembly that he wished to meet with them on June 20th "in order that I might communicate to you matters of great importance to the public welfare." The Provincial Congress met at Burlington on June 14 and resolved:

"That, in the opinion of this Congress, the Proclamation of William Franklin, Esq; late Governor of New Jersey, bearing the date thirtieth day of May last, in the name of the King of Great Britain, appointing a meeting of the General Assembly to be held on the twentieth day of this instant (June) ought not to be obeyed."

It was further resolved that "in the opinion of this Congress, the said William Franklin, Esq: by such his Proclamation, has acted in direct contempt;and violation of the Resolve of the Continental Congress of the fifteenth day of May last." In addition, Franklin's salary was to cease, to which he replied that "Their last

Resolve which respects the stoppage of my salary is, I must say, an instance of meanness, which I never expected to have experienced from any body of men in New Jersey."

On the morning of June 17th, Colonel Nathaniel Heard of New Jersey Militia came to Governor Franklin's residence and presented a paper which Franklin was to sign. Actually, he was presented with a parole by which he would guarantee to remain either at Princeton, Bordentown or at his farm at Rancocus for the duration of the "war between Great Britain and the said United Colonies, or do, or say any thing in opposition to, or in prejudice of the measures and proceedings of any Congress for the said colonies, during the present troubles, or until .. duly discharged."

Still the legal governor, Franklin asked for Heard's authority and he was given two directives from Samuel Tucker, President of the Provincial Congress of New Jersey. Tucker advised Heard that it was "the desire of the Congress that this necessary business be conducted with all the delicacy and tenderness which the nature of the service can possibly admit of."

Loyalist to the end, Franklin noted: "suffice it to say, that I rejected the written parole (as they term it) with that contempt such an insult deserved from one who has the honour to represent his Majesty." He concluded "That no office or Honour in the Power of the Crown to bestow, will ever influence me to forget or neglect the Duty I owe my Country, nor the most furious Rage of the most intemperate Zealots induce me to swerve from the Duty I owe his Majesty."

When President Tucker was advised that Franklin refused to sign the parole, he notified Colonel Heard that it was the "desire of Congress, that you immediately bring William Franklin, Esquire, to this Place." Franklin was brought to Burlington under heavy guard and confined; however, it was felt by many that the prisoner ought to be sent either to Pennsylvania or Connecticut, for it would be improper to hold the former governor as prisoner in New Jersey.

The Continental Congress at Philadelphia resolved "That William Franklin, Esquire, be sent under guard to Governor Trumbull of Connecticut, who is desired to take his parole; and if Mr Franklin refuse to give his parole, that Governor Trumbull be desired to treat him agreeable to the resolutions of Congress respecting prisoners."

It was reported in the Pennsylvania Evening Post on July 11, 1776 that "Last Wednesday passed through this place (Hartford, Connecticut), Governor Franklin of New Jersey, on his way to Governor Trumbull at Lebanon." In a sarcastic manner, Lord Howe wrote that "Governor Franklin, who for a long time maintained his ground in Jersey (I suppose under the pretence of being a friend to America, but now discovered) has been lately taken into custody (by a most loyal people) . . . and is now a prisoner at Connecticut."

Franklin remained the "house prisoner" in Connecticut for two years. He was then brought to New York City for approximately six months, after which time he was exchanged for an American prisoner and allowed to return to England where he died in 1813, at the age of 83

During the hectic days of June 1776, New Jersey selected five new delegates to the Continental Congress at Philadelphia. They were Abraham Clark, Richard Stockton, John Hart, Francis Hopkinson and the Rev. Dr. John Witherspoon, who was the sixth president of the College of New Jersey (Princeton). All of the New Jersey delegates were to give vocal approval to the Declaration of Independence on July 4, 1776 and they were all to become signatories to that document.

And for the support of this declaration]
we mutually pledge to each other our
lives our fortunes, & our sacred honour.

John Hancock

Sam'l Adams *Phil Livingston*

The Declaration of Independence

It needs to be recalled that the war between Great Britain and her 13 Colonies was already in process before July 4, 1776 and that "Old Gloucester County" was being called upon to furnish troops for what was shaping up as the defense of New York City and Long Island. On March 17, the British evacuated Boston and a month later, General George Washington arrived in New York City to begin preparations for the defense of that city against an expected attack.

Even though the British forces did not appear, it was reasonable to assume that they would, hence New Jersey was asked by the Continental Congress to make approximately 3000 men available to General Washington from its militia. It follows that on June 15, 1776, President Samuel Tucker of the New Jersey Provincial Congress noted in remarks to his people that:

"This province has been requested by the Continental Congress to send without delay, from their militia, Three Thousand Three hundred men to New York, in consequence of the authentic information, that the grand attack of our common enemy this summer, which will prove the decisive campaign, is to be upon that city . . . We trust and hope, that while every province is making the most spirited efforts, New Jersey in its place and duty will be second to none."

"Old Gloucester County" was asked to furnish two companies of men, as were Burlington, Cumberland and Salem counties. The eight companies were to be formed into a battalion under the command of Colonel Silas Newcomb of Cumberland County. Within a month Colonel Newcomb's forces were stationed around New York City and they were later to participate in the disasterous battles for control of Long Island.

Inspite of the doubts in the minds of many at Philadelphia during the early days of July, an agreement was reached among the delegates, even though Thomas Jefferson was forced to delete the anti-slavery comments he had written, the Declaration of Independence was adopted on July 4, 1776. Washington did not receive his copy until July 6 and when it was read to the troops, great cheers filled the air around New York City.

It was not until July 8 that the Declaration of Independence was proclaimed at Trenton and it was reported by The Pennsylvania Packet that "the declaration and other proceedings were received with loud acclamations. The people are now convinced of what we ought long since to have known, that our enemies have left us no middle way between perfect freedom and abject slavery . . . The inhabitants of New-Jersey will be found ready to support the Freedom and Independence of America." At Princeton, it was reported by that same newspaper that " . . . Nassau Hall was grandly illuminated, and Independency proclaimed under a triple volley of musketry, and universal acclamation for the prosperity of the UNITED STATES. The ceremony was conducted with the greatest decorum."

With the 13 American Colonies now declared independent of Great Britain, a long and costly year was to ensue in order to gain the highly coveted independence. On July 15, 1776, Samuel Adams wrote to Richard Henry Lee of Virginia from Philadelphia that "the Militia of the Jerseys, Pennsylvania, and Maryland, are all in motion. General Mercer, (for whom Fort Mercer was named), commands the Flying-Camp in the Jerseys."

Adams went on to say that "Our Declararion of Independence has given vigour to the spirits of the people . . . New-Jersey has finished her form of government, a copy of which I enclose. They have sent five new Delegates, among whom are Dr. Witherspoon and Judge Stockton. All of them appear zealous to the American cause."

Ten days after the Declaration of Independence was proclaimed, South Jersey troops stationed at German Flats in the Mohawk River Valley of New York learned the news. Captain Joseph Bloomfield in command of the 7th Company, Third Battalion if the "New Jersey Line," had received a letter from his father "in which was enclosed a copy of the Declaration of Independence of the Continental Congress, passed the 4th day of July, declaring the Colonies free and independent States -which may God prosper and protect."

From the "Journal of Lt. Ebenezer Elmer from Bridgeton of Captain Bloomfield's 7th Company, we learn that on July 15, 1776: "About 12 o'clock an assembly was beat for the men to parade in order to receive a treat and drink to the States' health. When having made a barrel of grog, the Declaration of Independence was read, and the following toast given by Parson Caldwell - 'Harmony, virtue, honor and all propriety to the free and independent United States of America. Wise Legislatures, brave and victorious Armies, both by sea and land, to the American States.' When three hearty cheers were given . . . the grog flew around a main."

At Trenton on July 17th, the Provincial Congress of New Jersey resolved: "WHEREAS. the honorable Continental Congress have declared the United Colonies, Free and Independent States; We, the Deputies of New Jersey, in Provincial Congress assembled, do resolve and declare, That we will support the freedom and independence of the said States with our lives and fortunes, and This House from henceforth, instead of the style and title of the Provincial Congress of New Jersey, Do adopt and assume the style and title of the Convention of the State of New Jersey."

Meanwhile fortifications continued on the Delaware River and on July 19, 1776, Captain Robert White reported to the Philadelphia Committee of Safety that he had "sent a person to the Jerseys to know what number of Logs the Inhabitants (of "Old Gloucester County") would supply this Board with, who brought with him a list of the Following Gentlemen, who Generously gave the numbers of Logs mention'd opposite their names, vizt:

	Logs			Logs
Benjamin Whitall	55		Joseph Ward	10
John Wood	20		Joshua Hopper	15
Nathan Kinsey	10		Isaac Hopper	10
Richard Johns	50 (or more)		Levi Hopper	15
David Paul	20		James Wood	10
Joseph Low	30		Joseph Tatem	1
James Brown	10		Charles West	40
	195			101

The "Old Gloucester County" logs were to be used in the construction of the "chevaux-de-frize" designed to prevent British war vessels from proceeding up the Delaware River to attack Philadelphia. On July 21st, it was resolved by the Philadelphia Committe of Safety that it " . . . Furnish the Inhabitants of Gloucester County" with Two Teams to assist them in bringing logs down to the different Landing places."

The DEPUTIES of the *several Counties* of New–Jersey in
PROVINCIAL CONGRESS.

To *Doctor Ebenezer Elmer*

WE reposing especial Trust and Confidence in your Patriotism, Valour, Conduct and Fidelity, Do, by Virtue of the Power and Authority delegated to us by our Constituents, and in Pursuance of the Direction of the Honourable the Continental Congress, constitute and appoint you the said *Ebenezer Elmer Ensign First Lieutenant of the Company lately chosen by in the hundred and fourteenth of that Militia in the county of Cumberland whereof Jonathan Elmer Esqr is Captain and now under the will of the of the Provincial Congress* into your Charge and Care as *first Lieutenant* thereof, and duly to exercise both Officers and Soldiers of that *Company* in Arms. And as they are hereby directed to obey you as their *first Lieutenant* so you are likewise to observe and follow such Orders and Directions from Time to Time as you shall receive from your *Captain* or — superior Officer or Officers, *or* ☓☓☓☓☓☓☓☓☓☓ Provincial Congress or Committee of Safety: And for your so doing this shall be your Commission. Dated the *twenty fourth* Day of *October* — 177 *6*.

By Order of the Congress,

Wm Tucker President

Jm Facey Secy

Attested

While the fever of independence was running high among the American patriots, a quite different British attitude is noted in the "American Journal" of Ambrose Serle, Secretary to Lord Howe. Serle wrote on July 25, 1776 that the American "Leaders seem resolved to run all lengths, and to draw the poor miserable People after them. No Resource remains for Britain but her Sword, which she has often drawn in Defense and Protection of these ungrateful Regions. She stands justified to God and the World in having attempted every pacific means to bring them to a Sense of Duty & Allegiance . . . "

Serle commented further that the "New York Papers also contained Declarations of the Constitutions of New Jersey & Virginia, framed by their respective Congresses upon a System of absolute Democracy. They proclaim themselves several & separate States, and proceed so far as to treat Great Britain & the King as their natural 'cruel and unrelenting Enemies . . . ' The annals of no Country can produce an Instance of so virulent a Rebellion, of such implacable madness and Fury, originating from such trivial Causes, as those alledged by these unhappy People."

In South Jersey, at "Bridgetown," on August 7, 1776, "The Committee of Inspection for the county of Cumberland . . . the officers of the militia, and a great number of other Inhabitants, have met at Bridgetown, went in procession to the court-house, where the declaration of independency, the constitution of New Jersey, and the treason ordinance, were publicly read . . . " Jonathan Elmer delivered a "spirited address," after which "the peace officers' staves, on which were depicted the King's coat-of-arms, with other ensigns of royalty, were burnt in the street. The whole was conducted with the greatest decency and regularity." The Elmer address appears to be the only surviving "Declaration of Independence" statement from South Jersey.

Chapter V

The Battle of Long Island and Aftermath

As July 1776 began to unfold, it was indeed as Francis Lightfoot Lee phrased it, a time that found many Americans "In a most perilous state, from which nothing, but some extraordinary event" might extracate them. On July 1st itself, the New York Gazette and Weekly Mercury informed its readers that "the number of (British) Transports now at Sandy Hook, we hear amounts to 113 sails and we have not the least reason to doubt, that General (William) Howe is in this Fleet." An invasion of New York was now apparent even to the doubters, and New Jersey would surely find itself in the mainstream of war if Lee's "Extraordinary event" should be a definite break with the mother country.

As James T. Flexner noted in his "Washington: The Indispensable Man," the commander-in-chief of the American Army saw "gathering before him" prior to July 4, 1776, "what was in fact the largest expeditionary force of the eighteenth century. The total amounted to thirty thousand men, one third of them Hessians George III had rented from four German princes. The accompanying fleet included ten ships of the line and twenty frigates."

From "The American Journal of Ambrose Serle, who served under Lord Richard Howe during the period 1776-1778, it is learned that:

"...Besides Sloops, Bombs, Fire-ships, armed Vessels, &c., the whole fleet consists of about 350 sail. Such a fleet was never seen together in America before; which is allowed on all hands. Our Army now consists of 24,000 men, in a most remarkable State of Good Health & in high spirits. On the other hand, the Rebels are sickly & die very fast. 'Tis said by some People who came over this morning, that not less than 3000 are upon Sick List."

Obviously in the face of such British might, there were many Americans still unsure of what to do. General Washington in one of his infrequent political comments noted that many of the delegates to the Continental Congress were "still feeding themselves upon the dainty food of reconciliation."

In view of the British might facing the Americans, General Orders were issued from General Washington's headquarters on July 2nd, 1776, which fully reflected the seriousness of the situation:

"The time is now near at hand which must probably determine whether Americans are to be freemen or slaves; whether their houses and farms are to be pillaged and destroyed, and they consigned to a state of wretchedness, from which no human efforts will probably deliver them."

With a British landing expected at any moment, the General Orders further pointed out that:

"...the eyes of all our countymen are now upon us; and we shall have their blessings and praises if happy we are in being the instrument of saving them...Let us therefore animate and encourage each other, and show the whole world that freemen contending for liberty on their own ground are superior to any slavish mercenaries on earth."

From Philadelphia, an unknown American patriot was quoted in the Pennsylvania Evening Patriot as follows:

"Every moment that I reflect on our affairs, the more I am convinced of the necessity of a formal declaration of Independence. Reconciliation is thought of now by none but knaves, fools, and madmen...I shall rejoice to hear the title of the United States of America, in order that we may be on a proper footing to negotiate a peace."

Not all Americans, including some members of the Continental Congress convening at Philadelphia, were willing to take the drastic step of completely severiong relations with Great Britain Many still believed "it to be wrong to rise in opposition to the rule of the mother country." In addition, the pacifist Religious Society of Friends (Quakers),"...numerous in Pennsylvania, New Jersey, and Delaware, opposed war as wrong itself. The Moravians held similar views."

Steps had to be taken to deal with the doubters, non-associators and the dissenters, thus it was in early July 1776 that the Provincial Congress of New Jersey resolved that "Whereas by a regulation of the late Congress, the several Committees in this Colony, were authorized and directed to disarm the nonassociators and persons notoriously disaffected" and that the "several Colonels in this Colony do, without delay, proceed to disarm all such persons within their districts, whose religious principles will not permit them to bear arms; and likewise all such as have hitherto refused to bear arms..."

In "Old Gloucester County," where Quakerism was a significant force, pacifism, as taught by George Fox, was adhered to by most members; however, some Quakers were "read out of Meeting" for participating in revolutionary activities of whatever nature. For example, the political activities of John Cooper of Woodbury were severely frowned upon by the Religious Society of Friends.

As the pre-Revolutionary War tensions began to divide groups and communitites, July 4, 1776 came and went with only a handful of people at Philadelphia aware of the fact that The Second Continental Congress had signified its approval of the Declaration of Independence, albeit the signing was to be a slower process.

While July 4, 1776 has remained our most esteemed date, and rightfully so, it has been over-looked by historians that the next day, July 5, was of great importance to the American cause and to "Old Gloucester County," for while the Continental Congress had expressed great interest in fortifying the Delaware River, nothing had been done in terms of actual construction.

As early as October 1775, Josiah Quincy of Massachusetts, informs us via his letter to George Washington, that John Adams had told him that the citizens of "Old Gloucester County," had made "machines, to be sunk in the channel of Delaware River. Three rows of them are placed in the river, with large timbers, barbed with iron. They are frames of timber, sunk with stones; machines very proper for our channel in the narrows" of Boston Harbor.

The "machines," more properly known as "Chevaux-de-Frise," had been deposited on the floor of the Delaware River north of Billingsport; however, additional ones were to be constructed and sunk in conjunction with the building of Fort Billings, once land had been secured for that purpose.

In view of the sequence of events, it is apparent that negotiations for the purchase of land at Billingsport had been underway for sometime and does not appear to be dependent on the Declaration of Independence. No matter, the importance of Billingsport in "Old Gloucester County" is indicated by the purchase of 96 acres of land for military purpose by the Continental Congress, the first of such acquisitions by the Revolutionary government.

Negotiations between the agents of the Continental Congress and Mrs. Margarett Paul and her son Benjamin Weatherby resulted in the opening clause of the following deed deed of sale:

"THIS INDENTURE Made the fifth day of July in the Year of Our Lord One thousand seven Hundred seventy six between Margarett Paul of the Township of Greenwich in the County of Gloucester in the Western Division of the province of New Jersey, widow and relict of John Paul late of the said Township...& Benjamin Weatherby of the same place, Yeoman, One of the sons of the said Margarett...and George Clymer and Michael Hillegas...treasurers of the Thirteen United Colonies of America appointed by the Honorable the Continental Congress of the said Colonies..."

One day later on July 6, 1776, Judge Alexander Randal certified the sale as follows:

"Be it remembered that on the sixth day of July Anno Domini one thousand seven hundred and seventy six, personally came before me Alexander Randall one of the Judges of the County Courts for the holding of pleas for the County of GLoucester aforesaid Margarett Paul and Benjamin Weatherby...that they signed sealed and Delivered the above Instrument of Writing unto the above named George Clymer and Michael Hillegas..."

Margarett Paul and Benjamin Weatherby received "the sum of Six Hundred Pounds lawfull money of Pennsylvania" for the 96 acres of land which included "the message or Dwelling House and Kitchen with all the Buildings joining the said dwelling House now standing Erected on the within described Tract of a piece of Ninety six Acres of Land . . . " As will be seen, it was to be a year before construction started on the future Fort Billings.

On Friday, July 5, 1776, the Provinicial Congress of New Jersey orderd "that the artillery company, under the command of Captain Hugg (of "Old Gloucester County") be ordered to march immediately with their artillery to New Brunswick; and from thence to such places as General Livingston shall direct." Captain Samuel Hugg's Western New Jersey Artillery, which included many "Old Gloucester County" men, was first "raised under the Act of February 13, 1776 and was to consist of 4 officers and 60 men . . . "

President Samuel Tucker of the Provincial Congress of New Jersey wrote to President John Hancock of the Continental Congress on July 6th, expressing "hope that Congress will attend particularly to the Flying-Camp and establishing a magazine of powder, &c., in the eastern part of this place (Trenton), in order to more in the way of intelligence," etc.

On the same day, President Tucker notified John Hancock that "the western Counties...are still unprovided with ammunition; and as, in the present season, it is absolutely necessary that all the Militia should have some small supply; we request that Congress would grant us half a ton of powder, on account of the colony..."

On July 18, 1776, there was promulgated by the Convention of the State of New Jersey at Trenton what amounted to a "Treason Act." It read, in part, as follows:

"Whereas it is necessary in these times of danger, that crimes should receive their due punishment, and the safety of the people more especially requires, that all persons who shall be found so wicked as to devise the destruction of good government, or to aid or assist the avowed enemies of the state, be punished with death."

It was further stated by the Convention that any person or persons loyal to King George III or "to the enemies of the United States of America...shall be adjudged of High Treason, and suffer the pains and penalties thereof, in like manner as by the ancient laws of this state..." In addition, persons "found guilty of reviling the Government of this state...or of other seditious speeches or practices, shall be punished in like manner as by the former laws of this state..."

During the last weeks of July, South Jersey troops were among the American soldiers poised against the superior British Army stationed around New York harbor, especially on Staten Island, From the "Journal" of the Reverend Philip Vickers Fithian of Greenwich, Cumberland County, it is learned that on the afternoon of July 25th, "Col: Newcomb made us a visit...The Col: brings no letters for me; nor any Word other than that in common things go as usual in Conhansie." Colonel Silas Newcomb, it will be recalled, was stationed at New York City with six companies of his Brigade from South Jersey. They were to participate in the ensuing battles of Long Island, Washington Heights and White Plains.

On July 26th, the Rev. Fithian noted in his "Journal" that "after Evening Prayers I walked to the Hospitals of three Regiments; to ours; & the two New-England Battalions--a Sight the Forces Compassion——An unfeeling Heart here is Brutal--Youth of fine Constitutions, used to good & easy living...have stepped forth, when their country is bleeding, & are resolved to save it, or die."

Fithian found that "in every Apartment are many in the Dysentary. Many have putrid Fevers; Yet to such Places, must our Youth do, & mix with such Diseases; & here I must daily visit, among many in a contagious Disorder...But I am not discouraged, nor dispirited; I am willing to hazard & suffer equally with my Countrymen since I have a firm conviction that I am in my Duty." Within three months, Fithian was to die at Fort Washington, near the present-day George Washington Bridge.

In order to gain additional insight into what the harsh life was like for the outmanned American Army in the New York City area, the "Orderly Book" of Jedidiah Swan of New Jersey is a valuable primary source document. Indeed, Swan noted on July 27, 1776 that a John Bartley was "tried by a Genl Court Martial...for absenting himself from Guard without Leave, threatening to desert and take Man's life away & for abusive Language, found quilty and sentenced to receive 39 Lashes. James Steel of Capt. Pierce's Company...tried...for sleeping in his Post, is found Guilty and sentenced to receive 20 lashes."

On the next day, Jedidiah Swan indicated that "...the Number of sick increase" and that the "Barrack Master under the Directions of the Col. or Commanding Officer of each Regiment fix on some House convenient to the Regt. to be Improved as an Hospital for the Reception of Patients first taken down" with illness. Further, the Regimental Surgeons were to "Make a Weekly Return to the Director of the Comissary Gen... of the Sick in their Respective Regiments."

On July 29th, Swan makes reference to Colonel Silas Newcomb of Cumberland County who was in command of six companies of South Jersey Militia attached to the Continental Army around New York City: "The Two Companies of Coll Nucomb Regt on Long Island are to join their Regiment at New York Immediately." Fortunately, the "Journal" of Philaip Vickers Fithian allows us to positively identify the two companies of South Jersey troops on

Long Island as those of Captain William Kelsey of Cumberland County and Captain George Anderson of Burlington Coutny. In Fithian's own words, he recorded on July 31, 1776: 'Col. Newcomb came to see me & urged me to accept his Appointment, & I finally agreed. Capt: Kelsays, & Andersons Companies came from the Island this Day to the City & joined the Battalion."

The tension continued to build among the inexperienced American Troops in New York and on August 1, 1776, Fithian noted that "After Dinner we all passed over to Long Island, viewed the Works, Camps &c there. The Brigade met while we were there, & whipped an Offender for sleeping on his Post...After being whipped he was drummed out of the Brigade." In addition, "During the week from July 25 to August 1, eight soldiers were sentenced to be flogged, each received from 20 to 39 lashes." On August 3rd, Fithian notified his wife as follows: "Since I wrote to you last I have returned from Long Island to this City (New York) & joined Col. Newcomb's Battalion. I am myself in good Health; some are now sick, none dangerous." Even so, there was constant fear of British attack; however, Fithian stated that "We wait for the Time, & do not fear the Event."

A day earlier, August 2nd, at Philadelphia, "A warrant was issued for Apprending John Hatton, Sen'r., & John Hatton, jun'r." John Hatton, Senior, it will be recalled had been the controversial Collector of Customs at the Port of Salem and would be Distributor of Stamps. His continued Tory sympathies made him the subject of an extensive search by the Council of Safety. Mr. James Reed was instructed by the Council of Safety to proceed to Salem and perform the following:

> "You are hereby directed to go to the Committee of Inspection of Salem County, in the State of New Jersey, and to apply to them for proper powers of John Hatton, sen'r, & John Hatton, jun'r, and bring them before this Council, unless the Committee of Inspection should object to their being brought out of that State."

The Hattons were "charged with Treasonable Practices against the state of America," and Reed was told that he was to use his "best endeavor to seize Col. (Moses) Kirkland (whom this Board has reason to suspect is still in Jersey)." Kirkland was a notorius Tory and a friend of John Hatton, Senior, thus it was hoped that James Reed would find them all together.

Thomas Wharton, Junior, Chairman of the Philadelphia Council of Safety, addressed his remarks to the patriots at Salem by noting that "from your attachment to the cause of Liberty we expect exertions of a more extended kind and on more generous Principles, and firmly hope your endeavours will Meet with Success on securing two Men who are enemies to our Country & dangerous spies upon our Actions."

Wharton had also written to the Committee of Inspection of Cumberland County and on August 4, 1776, Jonathan Elmer notified the Council of Safety at Philadelphia that he had been told that "Old Hatton...is at his own home in Glou'ster County & with me it is matter of doubt whether either of the others are in this County...I judged it best for Lieut. Reed to return immediately to Glou'ster to secure Old Hatton" at his home on the King's Highway, south of Swedesboro, in "Old Gloucester County."

On August 5, 1776, Robert Smith, the Philadelphia architect responsible for sinking the chevaux-de-frise, wrote the Committee of Safety of Philadelphia from "Bellengsport" that he was "now ready to raise a Number of Frames, But the depth of the water opposite to where we have framed them, is not sufficient to bear them off, we must go lower down. The water there is deeper, but we have not room enough on the Beach to raise a number of Frames. I wo'd...propose that a Number of Labourers should be set to work...there is Lodging ready near the place for 312 men, there they may sleep. I beg, Gentlemen, that this may be attended to, otherways I shall be hindered much, and the public business (the defenses of the Delaware River) will lag behind."

WILLIAM LIVINGSTON.

William Livingston from the one hundredth Anniversary of the Promulgation of the Constitution of the United States. John A Kasson. From the original painting in the possession of the family.

Jedidiah Swan's "Orderly Book" entry of August 8th indicates that "Col'l Newcomb" was one of the "Field officers for the Piquet" and that the "movement of the Enemy and Intelligence by diserters give the utmost reason to believe that the great Struggle in which we are Contending for every thing dear to us and our Posterity is near at hand." Swan was reffering to the expected "Battle of Long Island," ultimately to prove a serious disaster for General Washington, one which led to a long series of retreats in New York and New Jersey.

On the next day, the Rev. Philip Vickers Fithian, now chaplain to the South Jersey troops commanded by Colonel Silas Newcomb, noted in his "Journal" that there were "no motions of our Enemy yet. All possible Care however is using to have our Guns in good repair. The continental, & other Gunsmiths are employed in all Hours...It was given out yesterday in general orders that the Army have all their Arms in certain Order: their Guns clean, & Locks if defective mended: Canteens filled with Water..."

Desertion was a continuing problems for the Revolutionary Army; however, with the Americans defeats in Canada and the presence a British Armada in New York, the rate of desertion began to greatly esculate. On August 10, 1776, the "Convention of the State of New-Jersey," meeting at New Brunswick, resolved:

> "That to prevent Desertion, no person or persons belonging to, or coming from, the army in the State of New-Jersey, be permitted to go over any of the ferries in, or travel through said State, without a pass, signed either by General Mercer, General Dickinson, General Livingston, Colonel Griffin, or Colonel Biddle..."

The three Generals referred to were General Hugh Mercer, for whom Fort Mercer was named at Red Bank, near Woodbury. He was the commanding officer of the "Flying Camp" and was to lose his life at the Battle of Princeton on January 3, 1777. General Philemon Dickinson was in command of the New Jersey Militia during the entire American Revolution. General Livingston was an early patriot from New Jersey and was the first governor elected under the July 2, 1776 Constitution. Actually, Governor William Livingston was elected to fourteen terms in office.

In order to prevent further desertions, General Hugh Mercer notified General George Washington on August 10th as follows:

> "I have written to the Congress to take some measures to stop this infamous desertion, and to the Convention of New Jersey to raise their Militia to take up the deserters and the supply proper guards for these posts. I have ordered one company of General Dickerson's brigade to be stationed at Trenton, one at Princeton, and one at Brunswick, to stop all deserters."

August 11, 1776 was a Sunday and the Rev. Fithian noted in his "Journal" that "The Lords Day is come once more. But the Sabbath is scarcely known in the Army. Profaned is all religious exercise. Dreadful is the thought that Men who expect an Engagement every Day with a obstinate, wise, & powerful Enemy, should dare be so ungodly. But the God of this World has blinded the Mind."

The British build-up in New York harbor continued and the Rev. Fithian noted on August 12th that "...Ship after Ship came floating up, til we counted forty one, & many of them large...An Express just now arrived from Gen: Green on Long Island, that the Fleet which enterd within Sandy Hook yesterday consists of fifty Sail. Be on our Side, O Lord, & we fear them not!"

On August 19th, Lt. Azariah Moore of Cumberland County wrote a letter to his brother from the American camp on Long Island. He noted that "notwithstanding the vast expense of the army on both Sides yet neither party have as yet thought proper to begin the Bloody work and indeed I believe according to the best judgment I can form it would be bad policy in either side to do it, however, it is thought by some that the enemy will try hard for this Island. It is something likely as they must be in great want of fresh provisions. Besides I am persuaded they can have no hopes of getting possession of the City..."

The rare letter of Lt. Azariah Moore of Cumberland County, which was recently discovered at the Gloucester County Historical Society in Woodbury, continued:

"Mr. Bennett tells me it was reported on the Road as he came along that our Army consisted of...more than 15 thousand men, that the General was seen to shed tears on that account. I am sure that nothing can be further from the truth."

Lt. Moore reported to his brother that "two weeks ago the Commissary General returned fifty thousand effective men. They have been coming in fast ever since some time. Three and four regiments a day so that the army can't be less than 70 thousand. What the necessity can be for drafting your Militia I can't conceive unless it is State-Policy as some have Conjectured. That it may be said hereafter that the American States in their Infancy raised an army of so many thousand men. However I shall not undertake to judge of these things. The enemy may be more formidable than we are aware of..."

On August 20th, 1776, Jedidiah Swan noted in his "Orderly Book" that the "Army may Expect an attack as soon as the Wind and tide may prove favourable." Swan wrote that General Sullivan hoped that "Every mans mind & Arms will be prepared for Action and when Called to it, Shew our Enemies and the Whole World that those Men Contending on their own Land are Superior to any Mercenarys on Earth."

As the tension continued to build for the expected British attack, Jeddiah Swan noted on August 21st that "Col'l Johnson's and Coll. Nucombs Regt. are to consider the Woods on the West Side of the Creek as their Alarm post till further Orders and to Repair there in case of an Alarm." Colonel Silas Newcomb's six companies from South Jersey appear then to have been posted in the woods along the Gowanus Creek area of modern day Brooklyn. The Rev. Philip Vickers Fithian from Greenwhich confirms this by noting: "We had prayers & the Battalion went to the wood destined for them to guard."

The August 22nd entry in the "American Journal" of Ambrose Serle reports that early that "...Morning the English Troops, the Highlanders, & Preston's Light Horse, landed on Long Island. The Disembarkation was effected upon the flat Shore, near Gravesend, without the least Resistance; the inhuman Rebels contenting themselves with burning as much of the People's Corn as they could...The Soldiers & Sailors seemed as merry as in a Holiday, and regaled themselvs with the fine apples (Newtown Pippins)."

Serle continued to say the "In a Word, the Disambarkation of about 15,000 Troops, upon a fine Beach, their forming upon the adjacent plain, a Fleet of above 300 Ships & Vessels with their Sails spread open to day...exhibited one of the finest & most picturesque Scenes that the Imagination can fancy or the eye behold."

Serle noted on August 23rd that "We could see the Rebels this Morning, retiring, carrying off, and burning; the Country seemed covered with Smoke...The rebels made more Conflagrations...of the poor Farmer's Stacks of Corn and other Property." For confirmation of Serle's "Conflagrations" by the Americans, the "New-York Diary" of Lt. Jabez Fitch of Connecticut tells us that the American "Riflemen also set Fire to several Houses Barns Stacks of Grain &c which was very near the Enemys Camp."

From Fitch, it is also learned that Colonel Ephraim Martin of the Fourth New Jersey Regiment was wounded on Saturday, August 24, 1776. Fitch wrote that "in the Evening Col: Marten was bro't into Camp, who had been Wounded with a Musqt: Shot in his Breast." From a military return of October 5th, it is noted that Martin was "wounded on Long-Island, went home, and is not got well yet."

The Rev. Fithian of Greenwhich reported in his "Journal" of August 25th that "Another holy Sabbath presents to our View. No social Worship to be performed this Day--Carts & Horses driving every Way among the Army--Men marching out & coming in to & from the front Camp--Small Arms & Field Pieces continually firing; all in Tumult."

The day before the "Battle of Long Island," the Rev. Fithian wrote a letter to his wife "Betsey" from the "Camp on Long Island, August 26th 1776." He said:

> "Last Thursday our Enemy landed down by the Narrows, to the Number it is yet said of Several thousand & began immediately...their Way toward New York...The Drums beat to Arms. And instantly this vast Body of men were at their respective Posts! For one single Hour, my dear Betsey, & not more than a single Hour, my Heart fluttered...Drums & Fires on all Quarters making the very Air echo "To Arms! To Arms!" All these made my thoughts flutter & divide for a few of the first Moments..."

Fithian lamented to his wife that "we could not hinder their Landing on Account of their Guns & the Country thro which they marched is wholly clear & level as a Meadow four miles Distance. But the remainder of their way here is for us most advantageous. It is very hilly...Nothing can better suit our Purpose."

In a more thankful vein, Fithian told his wife that "we have had none killed yet--several have been Wounded, some badly--Colonel Marten on Fryday was wounded in the Breast, it is however hoped he will recover--One of the Rifle-Men has his Thigh broke:--Another had his Leg shot away in the small by a Six-pounder, it was immediately cut off, & we hope he will not die--One poor Lad died yesterday of a Wound in his Belly; the first Victim here..."

According to Ambrose Serle, it was General Howe's plan to surprise the American forces on Long Island in the following manner: "General Howe, having under his Command, about 18,000 Men...began to move about 9 o'clock last Night (August 26th), in order to come up with the Rebels early in the Morning...The Rebels abandoned every Spot as fast, I should say faster, than the King' Troops advanced upon them."

It is from the August 27th 1776 entry in Fithian's "Journal" that we learn about the "Battle of Long Island" from a South Jersey point kof view. Wrote Fithian: "O doleful! doleful! doleful!--Blood! Carnage! Fire! Our People drove this Morning of excellent Men, went out into the Woods on the right & left Wing of the Enemy; Alas! numbers went never to return!--The Enemy surrounded them. Those who could, retreated within the lines! The Alarm Guns were fired a little before day. Many Battalions, of excellent Men, went out into

49

the Woods on the right & left Wing of the Enemy; Alas! numbers went never to return!--The Enemy surrounded them. Those who could, retreated within the Lines. Those who could not were obliged to fight their Way thro the Enemy at every Hazard--But many, many we fear are lost."

Lt. Jabez Fitch from Connecticut who was taken prisoner at the "Battle of Long Island" tell us of the heat of battle before his capture:

> "After this we met with several small attacks, in which we Generally Fought on Retreet, without much loss, untill we found ourselves Surrounded by the Enemy. We...took our March Eastward, with Intention to brake through the Enemy & Secure a Retreet that way...we soon found ourselves between two severe Fires from the Hessian Troops...a number of our officiers Assembled & concluded it best, as we were Intirely; Surrounded by the Enemy, to resign ourselves up to them in small Partys, & each one Take care for himself..."

On August 28th, 1776, the day after the "Battle of Long Island," the Rev. Philip Vickers Fithian from Cumberland County noted in his "Journal" that "our Enemies enlarge their Appearance; show us more Tents & begin a Breastwork...We cannot yet learn our Loss by our Retreat; the Generals Sullivan & Sterling are either killed or taken." Ambrose Serle in his "American Journal" confirms Fithian's belief by writing:

> "Ld. Stirling (so called) & Mr. (called Genl.) Sullivan, late one of the Members of the Congress, were taken among other Prisoners; the whole of which amounted to about 1200."

At this writing, it is not possible to ascertain How many "Old Gloucester County" troops were killed or wounded at the "Battle of Long Island." No matter, the following captains were in command of South Jersey troops on Long Island and in New York at the time of the battle: Abraham DuBois (Salem), William Kelsey (Cumberland), Samuel Ogden (Cumberland), George Anderson (Burlington), Allen Congleton (Salem) Benjamin Whitall (Gloucester) and Joseph Matlack (Gloucester).

Despite the defeat of the Americans at the "Battle of Long Island," the Rev. Fithian wrote on August 29th: "...yet we feat them not; even in Death we despise them. The weather is most unfavourable, very rainy...so much that the Trenches, Forts, Tents, & Camp are overflowed with water, & yet our Men must stand exposed & Firelocks to it all. Twenty four hours at least the Lines are manned by the same Persons, & some Regiments have been on Duty since Monday!"

On the first day of September 1776, the Rev. Philip Vickers Fithian wrote his wife that "the Day of the Battle was indeed terrible; Noise and Blood, & Flight before our Enemies! But we expected to fight when we left Home...The whole Army in now in Town (New York City)...We hear our Enemies are landing up the East River not far from Kings-Bridge, & are attempting once more to surround us. If they do we shall be compelled to fight them in the Field...I tell you again, my dear Betsey, that we are not afraid of this Army that belongs to Tory George...sacred indeed is their memory & fair & lasting will be their memory & fair & lasting will be their Fame, who fall fighting for America's Good..."

On September 2, 1776, General George Washington reported to the President of the Continental Congress about the state of military affairs at New York:

> "Our situation is truly distressing. The check our detachment

50

sustained in the 27th ultimo has dispirited too great a proportion of our troops, and filled their minds with apprehension and despair."

General Washington, bitter over the defeat on Long Island, held the basically untrained Militia greatly responsible and in his letter to President Hancock, he stated that:"the Militia, instead of calling forth their utmost efforts to a brave and manly opposition in order to repair our losses, &c. are dismayed, intractable, and impatient to return. Great numbers of then have gone off, in some instances almost by whole regiments, by half ones, and by companies at a time."

Washington continued to point out to Hancock that "our number of men at present fit for duty, are under twenty thousand. They were so by the last returns and best accounts I could get after the engagement on 'Long Island,' since which numbers have deserted. I have ordered General Mercer to send the men intended for the Flying Camp to this place (New York City), about one thousand in number, and to try with the Militia, if practicable, to make a diversion upon Staten Island."

The Rev. Philip Vickers Fithian wrote to his wife on September 3, 1776, stating:

"We are still in this City where Freedom is likely to suffer her sorest Persecution. Our proud & subtile Enemies envy us ye happy situation & are planning how they shall take it from us...we expect they will crown their Ships up the North River (Hudson), & by thus surrounding us, they expect to interrupt the coming of Provisions & thereby either make us Prisoners, or compel us to fight them in the field."

The next day found the Rev. Fithian aboard a ship and "lying a little below Mount Washington...We could not get ashore til between nine & ten, & then with much Difficulty...Our camp here is near the River, a little below Mount-Washington. The River is narrow, its Banks exceeding High..We hear a firing of Muskets this afternoon towards Hell—Gate--some say the Enemy are attempting to Land--Let them come we will fight them here."

Ambrose Serle reported in his "American Journal" on September 3rd that "the Woods near Brookland (Brooklyn) are so Noisome with the Stench of the dead Bodies of the Rebels, whom the Hessians and the Highlanders followed thither & destroyed, that they are quite inaccessible." Countering the patriotic attitude of the Rev. Fithian, Serle noted that "five men came off last Night in a Boat from New York, who confirm our former Intelligence, that the Rebels are in a State of Animosity, Feud, and Distrust, among themselves."

General George Washington was well aware that New York City "could afford only temporary refuge to the beleagured Americans," who were outnumbered by the superior British and Hessian forces. Faced with this reality, Washington was to ultimately withdraw his troops to White Plains, New York, leaving Colonel Robert Magaw of Pennsylvania in command of a substantial division at Fort Washington, where the Rev. Philip Vickers Fithian of Greenwhich was to die of disease at 10 A.M. on October 8, 1776.

It will be recalled that New York City fell to the British on September 14th, hence Washington's sagacity had prevented the wholesale capture of the American forces. General Nathaniel Greene wrote to Governor Nicholas Cooke of Rhode Island about the American Situation from the "Camp at Harlem Heights 17. Sept 1776:"

I suppose you have heard of the Retreat from Long Island and the Evacuation of New York. The Retreats were both Judicious and necessary; our numbers being very insufficient to hold such an extent of ground. His Excellency had proposed to Evacutate the City & Suburbs of New York sometime before the Enemy made their last landing..."

General Greene was to join a growing chorus of American officers who became increasingly critical of the Militia and he told Governor Cooke: "...we made a miserable disorderly Retreat from New York, owing to the disorderly conduct of the Milita who run at the Appearance of the Enemies Advance Guard...they struck a panick into the Troops in the Rear..."

At Perth Amboy, General Hugh Mercer, commander of the "Flying Camp," sent the following critique of the Militia to General George Washington.

"The Militia of Pennsylvania and New Jersey, stationed on Bergen and at Paulus-Hook (Jersey City) have behaved in a scandalous manner, running from their posts on the first cannonade from the ships of the enemy. At all the posts, we find it difficult to keep the Militia to their duty."

Such criticism was, of course, exaggerated, for while there were dissertions and many frightened young men, we find that the South Jersey troops of Colonel Silas Newcomb remained with General Washington and served at White Plains, Philipp's Manor, Newark, and elsewhere in New Jersey during the retreat over this state during November and December 1776.

The Jersey Prison-ship

52

The bravery and loyalty of the South Jersey troops is further attested to in a communication from Richard Stockton to Abraham, Clark, both signers of the Declaration of Independence. Writing from Saratoga, New York, on October 28, 1776, Stockton told Clark:

"The Colonel (Dayton) and Major Barber came here last evening, and the regiment is now within a few miles of this place, marching with cheerfulness, but great part of the men barefooted and barelegged. My heart melts with compassion for my brave countrymen who are thus venturing their lives in the publick service...There is not a single shoe or stocking to be had in this part of the world."

Richard Stockton was making reference to troops from South Jersey Counties who had been engaging the British and Indians in central and northern New York State since the Americans had been driven out of Canada during June 1776. According to Stockton, the requested shoes, stockings and clothing would be "distributed among our several regiments who will be all together at Tyconderoga in a few days. If any breeches and waistcoats be ready, send then along; but do not wait for them if the shoes and stockings are ready...Shall the brave troops from New Jersey stand in the lines in snow, without shoes or stockings? God forbid..." Among the suffering troops were the Salem County Companies of Captains William Shute and Anthony Sharp.

North of New York City, General George Washington, after a series of reverses, led his troops over the Hudson River on November 12, 1776 and marched to Fort Lee, New Jersey. With the fall of Fort Washington on Manhattan Island, large British forces were sent into northern New Jersey, forcing the Americans to retreat, bridge by bridge, mile by mile from "Fort Lee to Hackinsack, from Hackinsack to Acquaconack (Passaic)," from Aquaconack to Newark and from Newark to New Brunswick and Trenton. By early December, Washington brought the survivors of his army over the Delaware River to the hoped for safety of Pennsylvania.

A letter from "New-Ark," dated November 25th states that the author had "just time enough to inform you, that there is very good intelligence that the enemy intend to make a push for Philadelphia...We look to New-Jersey and Pennsylvania for their militia, and on their spirit depends the preservation of America. If in this hour of adversity they shrink from danger, they deserve to be slaves indeed!..."

From the priceless and little known "Military Journal of George Ewing" of Cumberland County, it is possible to view the trying period of November-December 1776 through the words of a South Jersey participant:

"...We remained and lay in our tents until the 15th of November when we marched for the Jerseys; our time of Service being expired..we came near Penny Town where I had the misfortunte to sprain my ancle...here I lay three days and then proceeded to Trenton. I reached this place the same day that the advanced guard of Gen'l Washington's army arrived there in their retreat through the Jerseys...I tarried a day or two and then Crossed the Delaware and went to Philad. Crosd again & in two days arrived at home to the no small joy of myslef and friends..."

George Ewing hoped "for a time to enjoy myself in peace in the land of my Nativity but herein I was mistaken; my rest was short for in two days after my arrival, the news arose that the Enemy had possesd themselves of Trenton." He tells us that the South Jersey Militia "of these parts were up in arms and I more regardless of my own ease than my Countrys safety joined them and marched to the unjust invaders of our rights; we marched first to Phila. where we lay near a week. Then crossed the River and Marched to Moorstown. Commanded by Capt. Daniel Maskell..."

Despite their steady forcing of the Americans over New Jersey, the British finally had to stop at Trenton for lack of water transportation over the Delaware River. Washington's wisdom is evident here, for on December 8, 1776, he had written to General William Maxwell, commanding officer of New Jersey's important "Maxwell's Brigade" that:

> "As it is a matter of the utmost importance to prevent the enemy from crossing the Delaware, and to effect it, that all the boats and water-craft whould be secured or destroyed, I do hereby earnestly request and desire that you will take upon you the care and superintendency of the matter."

A Minute Man

General Maxwell was informed that "at Tinicum a parcel of boats are to be collected for the transportation of the troops under the command of Major-General Lee...These boats should be kept under a strong guard. The boats at other places ought, in my opinion, to be destroyed or removed to Tinicum, lest they should be possessed by some stratagem of the enemy." Historians have said too little about the work and success of General Maxwell and his New Jersey troops, for had the boats not been collected, the British would have been able to cross the Delaware River and deal the final death blow to Washington's dwindling army and the hopes for American independence. As will be noted, the Maxwell mission made possible Washington's "Crossing of the Delaware" and the ultimate victories at Trenton and Princeton, both of which gave new life to the "American Dream" of 1776.

In addition to gathering up all the boats on the Delaware River, General George Washington was concerned that the British might try to cross the river near modern Camden, for it is learned from General John Cadwalader's letter to Captain Watkins of the Council of Safety for the State of Pennsylvania that:

"His Excely, General Washington, desire me to request that you will immediately dispatch a Party of men from Philad, to cut down & destroy the two Bridges on the Burlington Road, one on Pensawkin & the other on Cooper's Creek, as he is apprehensive the Enemy intend to pass to Philad. by that Rout..."

On December 19, 1776, the Pennsylvania Evening Post reported to its readers that "The Main body of the enemy's forces are yet at Trenton, from which place they send out parties of infantry and cavalry to harrass the country...Last week five hundred Hessians, and a party of light horse, took possession of the city of Burlington, but the rowgallies, belonging to this state, obliged them to abandon it in a few hours..."

Five days later, the same newspaper reported:

"We hear from good authority, that on Sunday last, betwixt Slab Town and the Black Horse, in the Jersies, a party of our army under the command of Col. Griffin had a skirmish with the Hessians, and that the enemy was forced to retreat with precipitation, having some killed..."

Colonel Griffin was Colonel Samuel Griffin and he reported from "Head Quarters Mount Holly, 21st Dec. 1776"that:

"We arrived at this place yesterday about 3 o'clock. The enemy abandoned it about 10 in the Morn'g, to all appearance in great confusion...They are now at the Black Horse, from this 7 miles, we are not 600 strong, they at least 700, with 3 field pieces, and from every acct. expect Reinforcement...this is a very dangerous Post, & can't be held without a large Reinforcement."

Men from the South Jersey Militia were involved in this skirmish with the Hessians and from the "Military Journal of George Ewing," it is learned that "an express arived and informed us that the enemy were marching from Mount Holly to surprise and take us; upon this Capt Maskell thout best to retire to Coopers Ferry...the Next day we marched to Haddonfield where we remained for some time when we marched to Mount Holly where at our approach the Enemy fled here."

On Christmas Day, December 25, 1776, Colonel Silas Newcomb's Brigade was at Haddonfield. Two of the six companies present were commanded by

Colonels Samuel Dick and John Holmes from Salem County. The other four companies under the command of Silas Newcomb were those of Colonels Joseph Ellis and Richard Somers from "Old Gloucester County" and those of Colonels David Potter and Enos Seeley from Cumberland County. It is readily seen then that officers and men from South Jersey played important roles in making it possible for General George Washington to cross the Delaware River "on the night of Christmas, and about three o'clock A.M. were on their march, by two routs, towards Trenton..."

The "great" victory at Trenton and the one that followed at Princeton involved troops from Salem and Cumberland Counties, as well as the West Jersey Artillery under the command of Captain Samuel Hugg of "Old Gloucester County." These victories during December 1776 and January 1777 caused a great deal of displeasure in Great Britain Indeed, King George III, the British Parliament and people wished to see an end to the Rebellion in the 13 colonies. Conversely, there was a hardening of the resistance among the Americans and it is learned from the "Military Journal of George Ewing" of Cumbeland County that on January 20, 1777:

> "This day the Enemy came out a foriging as far as Millstone Bridge; the party under the Command of Brigd Genl Dickerson marchd down and attack them and put them to the rout; took forty seven waggons and horses, a number of Cattle and twelve prisoners, killing about thirty...This Galland action was preformed by about four hundred Militia under the command of Genl Dickerson...opposed by near three thousand of the British troops."

As was the custom during 18th centruy wars, both the American and British troops went into winter quarters, Washington at Morristown and the British around New York City. During this lull in the fighting, except for "foriging" activites on both sides, the British devised plans for a "three-cornered-Campaign" by which they would capture Fort Ticonderoga, dominate the Hudson River Valley and split New England from the rest of the colonies.

If the British were successful, colonial leaders knew too well that the Delaware River Valley and Philadelphia would be next on the British agenda. William Richards, on January 12, 1777, wrote the Pennsylvania Council of Safety of his concern:

> "Should General Washington be so lucky as to drive the Enemy out of the Jersies, will they not make a bold push to attack us by water, and the much Earlier in the Spring than we are aware of? Is not Bilings Port by nature Capable of being made very Strong, so as to support the Cheveux de Frise that may be sunk in the Channel, that, with our other Force, may be a means of keeping then back, with the help of the Fire ships and Boats?..."

Chapter VI

New Jersey's Delaware River Forts

A - Fort Billings (1775-1777)

As we have seen, almost a full year before the Declaration of Independence on July 4, 1776, visionary American leaders had come to the conclusion that ultimately, the British would attempt to capture both New York and Philadelphia. As the Continental Congress conducted its business at Philadelphia, it was logical to deduce that the Delaware Valley would be a British objective, hence "Old Gloucester County" would be involved in at least naval operations if the Royal Navy attempted to gain control of the Delaware River.

As early as July 19, 1775, a committee was appointed in "Old Gloucester County" to investigate the feasibility of constructing "Chevaux de Frize" defenses on the Jersey side of the Delaware River. From the "Pennsylvania Archives," it is learned that "The Committee of Observation of the County of Gloucester, having Taken into Consideration a Plan Communicated to them by the Committee of Safety of the City of Philadelphia, for obstructing the Navigation, by sinking a Number of Piers as such Places ... as may best answer the Good purposes designed there from -- Resolved, that we approve of the above plan, and that we will Contribute thereto." Towards that end, Samuel Harrison, John Mickle, Joseph Low, John Sparks and Joseph Hugg of "Old Gloucester County" would participate "... in Viewing the Place and Sounding the Water, to discover where it may be most practicable to Sink the Above Works..."

While General George Washington was conducting a successful seige of Boston during the winter of 1775 and early spring of the following year, it was resolved in Philadelphia during January 1776 that David Rittenhouse, Daniel Joy, John McNeal and Samuel Morris Jr., be "appointed and required to make a Survey of the Jersey Shore from Billingsport to Newton Creek, and to determine what posts it may be necessary to fortify ..."

By February 2, 1776, Joy, Rittenhouse and McNeal had reported the following to "The Honorable the Committee of Safety for the Province of Pennsylvania:"

> "According to your request, we proceeded from hence into the Province of New Jersey, to the lower part of Billingsport on the River Delaware, and survey'd the shore from thence to the lowland near Mantua Creek. We determined the bearing and distance of the upper Pier at the Fort from thence, and likewise the breadth of the channel opposite Billingsport, which was readily done by means of the grounded Ice on each side of it."

It is interesting to note that the Rittenhouse Committee stated that if they might give their judgment "with regard to fortifying any part of the Jersey Shore, we are unanimous in our opinion, that it is not adviseable, because any part of Billingsport or Red Bank is at too great a distance from the Chevaux de Frize, for either Friends or enemys to annoy with certainty any Boats, etc., that may be stationed in them."

The general consensus was that "if a Fort were built at either of those places, the Enemy could land above or below it, without any difficulty, (unless a superior army could be collected before, on the spot to oppose them,) amd oblige our people to spike their Cannon and quit the Fort, or submit to be made

57

prisoners ..." Rather than fortify at Billingsport or Red Bank, the Rittenhouse committee suggested "a number of Guns, 12 or 18 lb'rs, mounted on strong Traveling Carriages, and previous to the enemy's approach, to raise Breast works at the most convenient places at Billingsport, Manus Hellem's, and other places, from whence those Guns, thus mounted, and well ply'd with Star and Cross Barr'd Shot ... will annoy the Enemy much ..."

Such an "Old Gloucester County" defense plan would harras the British "and if they should land and press hard, our people can retreat, and make a fresh stand at suitable places ... If the Enemy should land their whole force in the Jerseys, with an intent (as we may suppose) to bombard this City (Philadelphia,) in such case the Bridges, after our Cannon are retreated over them, should be destroyed ... and thus, if our cannon are well supported with Misquetry, every Inch of Ground may be disputed, with great inconveniency and ,loss to the enemy."

President Samuel Tucker of the Provincial Congress of New Jersey was increasingly concerned about British intentions along the Delaware River. He wrote to the Continental Congress: "(NJ) having taken into their serious consideration, the necessity of defending such parts of this Colony as are more immediately exposed to an invasion of the enemy, are of opinion" that:

"... the part of West Jersey, which is situate on the river Delaware, below Philadelphia, appears ... to merit great attention at this time. Opposite to Reedy Island, at a place called Elsenborough in the County of Salem, a landing might easily be effected."

In addition, President Tucker was aware of the economic and strategic value of "Old Gloucester" and Salem Counties. He pointed out to the Continental Congress that Elsenborough was "within forty miles of Philadelphia, in a county abounding with provisions; and from whence an army might easily make its way to Cooper's Ferry (Camden) in a very short time."

Tucker further informed the Continental Congress that "the interests of this Colony in particular being so connected with that of the United Colonies in general, as to render an invastion of New Jersey, a matter of importance to all; we humbly conceive, that the necessity of the occasion will induce the wisdom of your Honourable House to take into Continental pay two battalions and two companies of artillery, or such a body of forces as may be thought sufficient to answer the desirable purpose."

While New Jersey was facing up to the reality of a possible British invasion, the Philadelphia "Committee of Safety" passed two important resolutions on March 13, 1776, which concerned "Old Gloucester County:"

1. "RESOLVED, that Arthur Donaldson be employed to launch the Chevaux-de-Frize built at Gloucester, and that he be fully authorized to precure anything for that purpose, hire persons under him, on the best and cheapest terms ..."

2. "RESOLVED, that John Cobourn be employed to take the Chevaux-de-Frize, when launched at Gloucester, and sink them in their proper places near Fort Island ..."

On May 21, 1776, the Philadelphia Committee of Safety "Resolved that Mr. Owen Biddle be requested to procure 5 or 6 Waggons and send them to Doct'r Coxes' Iron Works in the Jerseys, to bring with all possible expedition, the Shot he made for account of this Committee." Reference was being made to the important iron works at Batsto, located in "Old Gloucester County" until the creation of Atlantic County in 1837.

Indeed, the iron works at Batsto became vital as it became obvious to realists in the 13 colonies that only an official "Declaration"' remained to make the struggle between the Americans and British a legal war. It was the Batsto Furnace which turned to producing articles of war for the Colonies. As Jack E. Boucher has so well phrased it: "cannon and ball, iron fastenings and fittings for caissons, waggons and ships ... and the countless other products required by the military" were produced in South Jersey at Batsto.

Also on May 21st, the Committee of Safety at Philadelphia notified the Continental Congress that in order "to give ... additional security to this Province and City and the navigation of the River and Bay of Delaware ... which must be of the highest importance to the Common Cause of the Colonies, this Committee ... are also of opinion that some military works should be erected on the Eastern Shore of the River Delaware, and particularly at a place called Billingsport."

Within weeks, the Continental Congress approved of the plan for fortifications in "Old Gloucester County" and General George Washington was notified that"

"By the Inclosed Resolution of Congress, your Excellecy will perceive there is an Intention of erecting some Works of Defense at Billingsport on the River Delaware ... As they are extremely desirous of rendering that important Post as strong as the nature of its situation will permit, a skilful Engineer should be on the spot to view the Ground and furnish suitable Plans. Our Deficiency in that respect, puts us under the necessity of applying to your Excellancy to furnish us with a proper Person for that purpose ..."

In South Jersey, a spirit of cooperation was in the air, for news was to come that was encouraging. In a letter from Batsto, dated "May 22nd, 1776, 2 o'clock, P.M.," John Cox advised the Committee of Safety at Philadelphia as follows:

"... the six waggons are new loaded and ready to start, and I expect will be at Cooper's Ferry (Camden) by tomorrow Evening. My manager sent off three loads this morning, and I am in hopes that my Overseer, who is gone in quest of teams, will return to-morrow with a sufficient number of waggons ..."

John Cox lauded the Committee for its wisdom in sending "Teams from Philadelphia, it being almost impossible to procure them here at this season of the year, most of the Farmers being busily engaged in planting, and those who make carting a business, all employed in transporting goods across from hence to Philada ... Brunswick and New York."

In Canada, the picture was exceedingly gloomy for the Americans as June 1776 began and in Sparks' "Correspondence of the American Revolution," one finds Brigadier General William Thompson notifying George Washington on June 2nd that "the prospect is rather unfavorable on ourside at present, but I hope will clear up ... I now begin to entertain doubt of our ability to keep the Province" of Canada. Thompson continued:

"... our Artillery is lost; and the New England Troops are so much infected with, or afraid of, the small-pox, as to almost prevent their doing duty. Could I have command of the Jersey and Pennsylvania regiments, I still believe, if I could not keep the country, it would require at least five thousand men to oblige me to evacuate ... and perhaps recover a little of the honor we have lately lavishingly thrown away."

During June, July and August of 1776, the American troops in Canada were to be forced out of that province, down Lake Champlain to Crown Point and ultimately to Fort Ticonderoga. The American loss on Long Island and the British capture of New York City made the plight of the valiant Americans, who had participated in "The Northern Campaign," very serious.

On August 5, 1776, Robert Smith, the Philadelphia architect responsible for sinking the "Chevaux-de-Frize," wrote the Committee of Safety from "Bellengsport" that he was "new ready to raise a Number of Frames, But the depth of the water opposite to where we have framed them, is not sufficient to bear them off, we must go lower down. The water there is deeper, but we have not room enough on the beach to raise them, I beg, Gentlemen, that this may be attended to, otherwise, I shall be hindered much, and the public business (the defense of the Delaware River) will lag behind."

Despite Robert Smith's deep concern, it appears that very little work was done at Billingsport during the fall of 1776. In fact, it is not until February 15th, 1777, that the Continental Congress authorized and directed the Philadelphia Council of Safety as follows:

"... to erect a Fortification at Billingsport ... and as it is necessary that some proper person be appointed not only to superintend the said Works, but to command such parties, whether regular Soldiers, Militia, or others, as may be employed to compleat and defend them; therefore, RESOLVED, that John Bull, Esq'r, be appointed Colonel commandant of the Fortifications at Billingsport ..."

Finally, the fortifications were underway at Billingsport and from the Pennsylvania Archives, it is learned that Joseph Rhoads submitted a report "... with Respect to the State of the Chevaux de Friezes at Billingsport" as of February 24, 1777. Rhoads noted that:

"there are Eight Frames finish'd & plank'd ... There are 42 Loggs at the Water side; and a Certain Woulfe, who lives at the place, informs that there are Several Loggs along shore ... There are 36 small Loggs on the ground, which will make floor Timbers ... The Spear Irons are all on."

On March 17, 1777, at the urging of David Rittenhouse of the Philadelphia Council of Safety, Governor William Livingston of New Jersey sent the following communication to Lt. Col. Josiah Hillman of the "Old Gloucester County" Militia:

"Haddonfield 17 March 1777

Sir:

I have received an application from the honorable the Council of Safety of the Commonwealth of Pennsylvaina for a number of our Militia to assist them in carying on the fortifications begun at Billingsport for the mutual Defence of both States. I think the request so reasonable in itself & so greatly conducive to the defence of the State against an Attack by the Enemy's Fleet that I cannot hesitate to recommend it in the strongest manner. They have also promised an addition to the pay allowed by the United States, to the detachment of our Militia that shall be so employed. I therfore desire you to wait upon the Honorable David Rittenhouse Esqr. Vice President of the said Council of Safety for the Terms proposed by them with the Number of Men wanted & then to procure that Number of Volunteers from the Gloucester Militia properly armed & equipped, whose Service in that Station shall be considered as in lieu of so much military Duty in any other part of this State. I am Your most humble Servant"

On the same date, Governor Livingston informed David Rittenhouse as follows:

"Haddonfield 17 March 1777

Sir:

Your Letter respecting my procuring a detachment of our Militia to assist in the works at Billingsport, I laid before our Assembly. It is mislaid by the Clerk of the house, or at lest missing a present; & I cannot precisely recollect the Terms mentioned in it. I have therefore sent Lieutenant Colonel Hillman one of the fittest Men among us (as I am informed) for procuring a Number of Volunteers of our Militia for the purpose intended, to wait upon you to know the Terms, & the number of our Men wanted to assist in the works ..."

Governor Livingston was writing from Haddonfield in "Old Gloucester County" because it served as the capitol of New Jersey during the period January 29 - March 18, 1777. The Assembly had had to flee to the safety of Pennsylvaina when the British troops drove General Washington's army over the Delaware River during the bleak days of December 1776.

Haddonfield served as the political capitol of New Jersey on two other occasions: from May 7 to June 7, 1777: and from September 3 to October 11, 1777. Of special significance is that during May, the "Great Seal of New Jersey" was received from a Special Committee and adopted" by the Assembly which held most of its meetings at the "Old Tavern House," known today as the Indian King Tavern. In addition, it should be noted that Haddonfield also served as the military headquarters for the South Jersey Militia during the American Revolution.

A recurring problem for the American Troops during the Revolution was a command one. On April 13, 1777, it is found that Colonel John Bull, in command at Billingsport, was disturbed because his authority was restricted to the confines of the fortifications. In a letter to Thomas Wharton, President and Commander in Chief in Pennsylvania, Bull stated:

"I was this Day favour'd with your Inteligence ... and shall Pay Immediate Attention to your Ex'cency's orders in Arming the men, which, While in Garrison at Billingsport, will only be under my Comand ... In answer to the ... Very Proper Question in asking, what I think of the Enemy Marching through Allentown, Croswix, Mount Holly, Haddenfield, &, to attack our fort, I will not pretend to say, But, Sir, I think I should be much Happier had I the Command of the men Now here when out of the fort, as well as while in ... but one Company of Jersey militia are with us ..."

To the north, the British Fleet in New York Bay, several hundred naval and support vessels, posed a constant threat to the New Jersey coast. In particular, the coasts of "Old Gloucester County" (present day Atlantic County), Cape May, Cumberland and Salem were vulnerable to possible British naval attacks. The severity of the danger is indicated in a May 20, 1777 letter from the Naval Board indicated that it was ready to comply with the Continental Congress in

61

providing weapons for the defense of South Jersey:

> "In consequence of a Resolve of Congress, we were directed to forward Six Guns to Cape May in the Jerseys, to be stationed there for the protection of our vessels &c., that may put in or run ashore in or near the said District ... As it is requisite this matter should be immediately attended to, we wish you would lend us 4 Four Pounders ready mounted on travelling Carriages ..."

On June 11, 1777, the Congress at Philadelphia resolved "that Governor Livingston be requested forth with to order out 500 of the Militia of the State of New Jersey to assist in compeating the Works now erecting at Billing's Port for the Defence of the River Delaware ..." These troops were to be from South Jersey and serve under the command of Brigadier General Silas Newcomb from Cumberland County.

In addition to the South Jersey Militia who were to proceed to Billingsport to aid in the completion of Fort Billings, it is learned from a letter of General George Washington to Major General John Sullivan, dated June 12, 1777, that Washington had been informed by New Jersey Governor William Livingston "that he had ordered the Militia of Gloucester, Salem and Cumberland to assemble at Mount Holly and that Col. Bowes Reed (Burlington) was to assemble his Regt. at Borden Town."

Even though the South Jersey Militia was destined for Billingsport, General Washington remarked to General Sullivan that those "Troops are much out of the way at either of the above places (Bordentown and Mount Holly). You had better order them to Cranbury or that Neighbourhood; they will then be ready to join you if the Enemy move intirely upon the direction of Princeton Road, or to oppose a Column should they advance one from South Amboy ..."

As for the defenses at Billingsport, the French engineer and Major General Philippe Tronson du Coudray observed that "as to the Situation, it is well chosen; it commands the River in the narrowest Part I have seen, and is the most capable of Defence." He further stated that:

> "As to the Plan or Projection, it is very bad. The object in view ought to have been to defend the Chain of Chevaux-de-Frize, which bar the River. For that purpose 30 or 40 Cannon well placed would have been sufficient ... To defend the Chain of Chevaux-de-Frize which bars the River opposite to the Fort, all dependence for the present must be on the Floating-Batteries and Gondolas ..."

Du Coudray suggested the building of two earthern redoubts by 1500 or 2000 laborers and that he would only risk "in those Redoubts only 4 or 500 men with 25 or 30 Pieces of Cannon, still observing that it is not upon them, but on the Floating Batteries supported by those Redoubts that the defense of the Chevaux-de-Frize depends." Even though General Washington came to think otherwise, Du Coudray felt strongly that the major defense position on the Delaware River ought to be constructed at Billingsport. While there are no visable remains of Fort Billings today, one may see the remains of some of the Billingsport Chevaux-de-Frize at Fort Mercer National Park, near modern-day Woodbury.

On June 14, 1777, Major General Benedict Arnold became the commanding officer in the Delaware Valley and the following resolution of the Congress at Philadelphia stated that:

"Major General Arnold be authorized to take upon him the Command of all the militia now at Bristol and on every part of the River Delaware to the Eastward of Philadelphia ... and that he be authorized to dispose of himself and the Troops under his command in such a manner as he shall deem best adapted to promote the public service."

Four days later, General Arnold sent the following to President Thomas Wharton of the State of Pennsylvania:

I have this minute received a Letter from His Excellency General Washington; as it in part respects the militia of your State & fortifying the Delaware, I have taken the Liberty of inclosing a copy of it for your perusal ... We propose to have them (the troops) arranged in the following manner Viz., Colonel Stewarts Battalion with one thousand militia at Red Bank, Fort Island & Billingsport, to compleat the works at those Posts; two thousand militia stationed between Corryells Ferry, & Bristol to fortify and guard the most accessable Passes on the Delaware ..."

On June 30, 1777, British troops under General John Burgoyne reached Fort Ticonderoga and by July 15th, the British were in complete control of Lake Champlain. The seriousness of the situation was reported to General Washington by Major General Philip Schuyler:

"My prospect of preventing them from penetrating, is not much. They (the British) have an army flushed with victory, plentifully provided with stores, cannon, and every warlike store. Our Army, if it should once more collect, is weak in numbers, dispirited, naked, in a manner, desitute of provisions, without camp equipage, with little ammunition, and not a single piece of cannon ..."

General George Washington, at this juncture, was not certain whether General William Howe would march up the Hudson River Valley to join Burgoyne, or whether Howe would sail for the Delaware Valley and attempt to take the American capital at Philadelphia. In a letter to Lord George Germaine, dated July 5, 1777. General Howe stated that "the embarkation of the troops is proceeding with the utmost dispatch, and I shall have the honour of sending your Lordship further information as soon as the troops are landed at the place of their destination."

The Pennsylvania Journal reported to its readers on July 4, 1777, that:

"YESTERDAY, being the first anniversary of the Independence of the United States of America, was celebrated in Philadelphia with demonstrations of joy and festivity. About noon all the armed ships galleys in the river were drawn up before the city, dressed in the gayest manner, with the colors of the United States and streamers displayed ..."

In addition, the Pennsylvaina Journal noted that "at one o'clock ... they began to celebration of the day by a discharge of thirteen cannon from each of the ships, and one each from the thirteen galleys, in honor of the thirteen United States ... The glorious fourth of July was reiterated three times, accompanied with triple discharges of cannon and small arms, and loud huzzas that resounded from street to street through the city ..."

On July 8, 1777, the Congress at Philadelphia passed the following resolution:

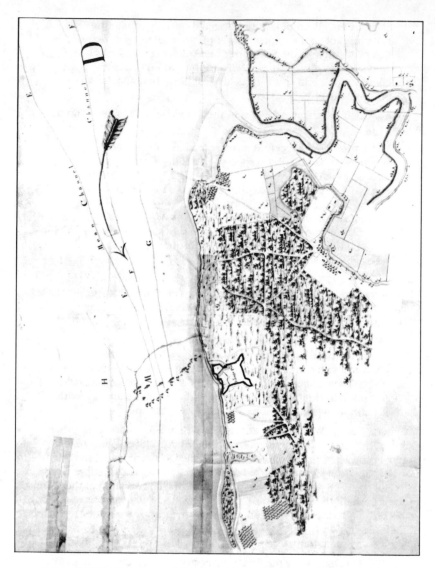

"RESOLVED, That General (Francis) Nash be directed immediately to repair with the North Carolina and Virginia forces now in and about Philadelphia, to Billingsport, there to remain till farther orders; and that these troops, with the militia from Pennsylvania and New Jersey already ordered to that place, be employed in compleating the works for the defense of the river Delaware."

On July 12, 1777, the Congress resolved "that the Governor of the State of New Jersey be informed, that the Continental Troops now at Billingsport are under marching Orders to join General Washington, and that it be warmly recommended to him to comply with the former Requisition of Congress, to send 500 of the Militia of the State of New Jersey, to assist in compleating the Works at that place."

Despite the threat of war coming to New Jersey, the Pennsylvania Evening Post of July 12 published the following notice:

"Notice is hereby given to the public that the COLLEGE of New-Jersey (Princeton) was opened on Tuesday the eighth instant. It is therefore requested that the under-graduates would repair to Princeton immediately, taking care to provide themselves with books, as none are to be had there."

The above notice was signed by the Rev. Dr. John Witherspoon, president of the College of New Jersey and also one of the signers of the Declaration of Independence from New Jersey. Incidently, it is not common knowledge that at the time of the Revolution, the state of New Jersey was the only one to possess two institutions of higher learning: Queen's College (Rutgers) and the College of New Jersey (Princeton).

As July wore on, the Americans were still in doubt as to British intentions and General Washington so informed the Congress on July 22: "We have been under great embarrassments respecting the intended operations of Gen. Howe, & still are, notwithstanding the utmost pains to obtain intelligence of the same. At present, it would appear, that he is going out to sea." Washington continued:

"As I observed before, their destination is uncertain & unknown, but I have thought it my duty to inform Congress ... that they may give orders to the Militia to hold themselves in readiness ... in case Philadelphia should be their object."

General George Washington was always a realist and he told the Congress that "Our situation is already critical, & may be rendered still more so, by inaccurate & ill-grounded intelligence." He thus requested there should be "a sufficent number of proper look-outs fixed at the capes of Delaware ... to make the earliest reports of the arrival of any fleet ..." In a post-script, Washington wrote: "I think the works at Billingsport well worthy of attention, & it expedient to effect their completion as soon as possible."

On July 23, 1777, the British Fleet sailed from New York Harbor and Captain John Hunn, in charge of observations at Cape May, was notified on July 24th that "By Intelligence re'd this Day from Shrewsbury, all the Enemys ships to the number of 240 & upwards, (including all sizes,) with Troops on Board, left Sandy Hook yesterday ... as it is of the utmost consequence that Gen. Washington have the Earliest Intelligence what part of the Continent they intend to land their Troops on ... request you to make the best of your way to the Sea shore and observe what course the Enemy's ships stear, & their numbers, and if they have Troops on Board; endeavor also to find out what part of the Continent they purpose to land on ..."

The greatest naval armada ever seen in the Americas was enroute down the New Jersey coast, destined as all thought for the Delaware River. The Board of War at Philadelphia was notified on July 24 by the Supreme Executive Council that it was "at a loss to know where to procure Cannon for the Works at Billingsport, and other places of defense, in case of Invasion."

On the same date, the Pennsylvania Board of War notified President Thomas Wharton of that state that "... Fort Island will be left without a Guard. We thought it our duty to inform the Honorable Council ... and beg leave to suggest the propriety of sending a Company of the Militia from Billingsport to mount Guard ... as the ordinance & stores there are of considerable value."

On the Atlantic Ocean side of South Jersey, there was much consternation regarding the destination of the British Armada of several hundred ships. Captain John Hunn, a watcher along the Cape May coast, dispatched a rider to Philadelphia on July 26, 1777, by whom he reported the following to President Thomas Wharton of the State of Pennsylvania:

> "We got to the Sea Shore at two o'clock yesterday Six Miles west of Little Egg harbour & Crossed over, & have Not Been able to Gain any Intellignece of the fleet. I Now am Going to the pitch of the Cape ... I am now at Capt. (Enoch) Stillwells, whare theares Mr. Slater, Master of the Roebucks tender with Six of his Men taken in there Boat with all arms ..."

On the same date, Colonel Nicholas Stillwell, commanding officer of the Cape May Militia, notified President Wharton that the Roebuck's tender "... came into Corson's Inlet, situate Between the Five Mile Beach and Pecks Beach ... and put into a small Creek by the Name of Chesapeake Fish, putting in at the West end of Pecks Beache in a Whale Boate under the Command of Thomas Slater & Roland Edwards chief Piolet ..." Colonel Stillwell also submitted "An Account of the Arms &c., taken from the Enemy on Friday July 25, 1777:

6 Musketts	6 Board Pistols
2 Swivels	6 Cutlashes & 1 Scabbard
1 Spie Glass	6 Cartarage Boxes, Compleat
1 Can, with Ball in	1 Worm, 1 Spung, 1 Rammer
1 Priemg Horne	1 Case with 5 bottles of Powder
12 Swivel Cartarages	1 Bottle Rum, & Two Empty Ones
1 Compass	5 Small Bundels of Muskett Cartarages
1 Whale Boate	1 Sale
6 Oars."	

While Captain John Hunn continued his vigil at Cape May, increased activity was taking place along the Delaware River and at the fort being constructed at Billingsport. Until a recent discovery was made in the Manuscript Division of the Historical Society of Pennsylvania, it was not known who the actual men were who contributed to the building of Fort Billings. Now, it is possible to identify at least 48 men who were at work on the fort during June and July of 1777. The following is a "Muster Roll of the Workmen on the fortifications at Billingsport, June & July 1777:

Henry Robinson	William Nicholson
Francis Goodwin	Charles Moore
Robert McNiel	Edward Levy
Samuel Barclay	Francis Gallagher
Michael Kain	Zechonias Connally
Thomas Bond	John McCallen
John Ferguson	James McCallen
John Leary	Richard Oliver
John Finemore	Joseph Meyers
Francis Elliott	George Meyers
Michael Hackett	George Morely
John Barrett	Alexander Bowers
Charles Finemore	James Sloan
Henry Mullen	Valentine Prock
Christopher Meyers	Hugh Wasson

August McDonnell	Killenure (Negro)
Mathew Morgan	William Buckett, Jr.
Samuel Donawine	Mark Ellis
Michael Frock	Nathanial Cardwell
Charles Daily	Tobias Fenemen
John Harkiness	Peter Homan
Duke Bedford	Daniel Meyers
Robert Scott	James McAllister
William Garrett	Martin Murphy."

In addition to the above workmen, the following contributed these items to the building of Fort Billings: "Hudson Springer furnished a 2 ox team and one Horse Cart; Thomas Thompson, one Horse Cart; Andrew Derrickson, one Horse Cart; George Bowers, one Horse Cart; Edward Kegan, one Horse Cart; Wm. Buckett, Sr., one Horse Cart."

While muster-rolls have not yet been located, it is possible to show that the following South Jersey Militia companies were stationed at Billingsport during July and August of 1777 and were under the command of Lt. Colonel Josiah Hillman of "Old Gloucester County:"

Capt. John Barker, Cumberland County Militia, 27 men
Capt. Cornelius Niewkirk, Salem County Militia, 40 men
Capt. David Paul, Gloucester County Militia, 29 men
Capt. Samuel Westcott, Cumberland County Militia, 59 men

As July 1777 ended, the Congress at Philadelphia resolved that "WHEREAS, the States of New Jersey, Pennsylvania and Delaware are in danger of an immediate invasion from the enemy's army, a powerful fleet being daily expected within the capes of Delaware ... That it be recommended to the executive powers of the States ... to cause the horses, waggons, carts, cattle, and other live stock contiguous to the bay and river Delaware, to be removed into the interior parts of the country whenever the arrival of the enemy's forces at the capes shall announce the necessity and propriety of such a measure."

At ten in the morning on the very day of the above resolution, the "necessity and propriety" of it became a reality, when Henry Fisher of Lewes, Delaware, directed the following intelligence to the State Navy Board at Philadelphia:

"By this Express you will be certain that the Fleet is in sight, and at this time about 4 Leagues from the Light House; ther is 228 (two hundred and twenty-eight) sail ..."

Later in the day, at five P.M., Captain John Hunn reported to President Wharton that "The Fleet is standing in a Gain, 45 sail in sight & more of Cors will be in Sight ... it appears to me they are bound up our Bay ... Mr. Jones come of to Morrow by way of Philadelphia as going through Menmouth (Monmouth) is attended with Danger of being Stopped, as the people heare inform Me." Indeed, Monmouth had long been one of the strongholds of Loyalism (Toryism) in central New Jersey.

In remarkably swift time, General George Washington had been informed of the British naval movements towards Delaware Bay. From Coryell's Ferry, (15 miles north of Trenton), he sent the following orders on July 31 to Colonel Elias Dayton, in command of the Third Regiment, Second Establishment, New Jersey Continental Line:

"I have this moment received information from Philadelphia that

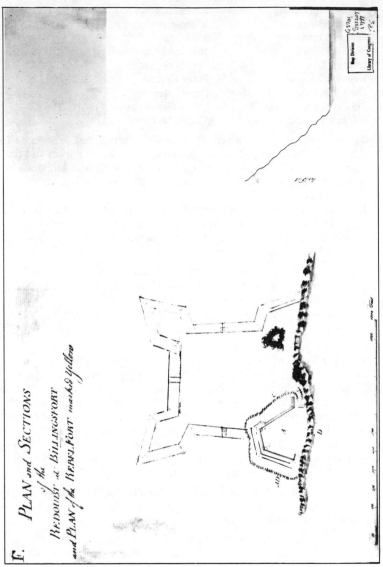

F.

PLAN and SECTIONS
of the
REDOUBT at BILLINGSFORT
and PLAN of the REBEL FORT mark'd Yellow

the Enemy's Fleet made their appearance at the Capes of Delaware Yesterday; you are therfore to march as expeditiously as you can with your own and Colo. Ogden's Regiment (First Regiment, Second Establishment, New Jersey Continental Line) to Philadelphia, by the way of Trenton, where Boats will be prepared to carry you across. You will take care and not over march your men. Come light, by no means over load yourselves with baggage."

Interestingly, the distance from Lewes, Delaware, to Coryell's Ferry is approximately 150 miles, thus Washington received the intelligence from Henry Fisher in twenty-four hours, "a creditable performance for men and horses." Immediately, General Washington reported to president John Hancock at

Philadelphia he had already "set the Army in Motion. One Division had cross'd the Delaware the day before Yesterday, and I am in hopes the whole of the Troops now here will be able to reach Phila. tomorrow Evening ... I propose setting off for your City as soon as I can get the Chief part of the Army over."

The entire movement by Washington's forces was expeditious and the General himself reached Philadelphia "about 10 o'clock p.m., on July 31. On the next day, Washington crossed back over the Delaware River to South Jersey to inspect the fortifications at Billingsport (Paulsboro) and Red Bank (National Park, near Woodbury). From Washington's "Expense Account," it is learned that he requested the "Exps. of a Trip to examine Mud Island, Red Bank and Billingsport $60^2/_3$ dollars. To Ditto incurred incurred in another trip to Marcus hook 86 Dollars."

After his observations at Billingsport, General Washington came to the conclusion that the fort would be in an untenable position if the British should be able to successfully land a substantial body of troops behind Fort Billings. In an August 10th communique to the Congress, Washington pointed out that if "the enemy were in possession of the commanding ground on the Jersey side," Fort Billings would not be able to hold out "more than fifteen or twenty days at most, at the end of which, we should be obliged with the loss of our cannon at least to abandon the defence, and leave it in the power of the enemy to remove or destroy the chevaux de frize at pleasure ..."

During September of 1777, General Anthony Wayne indicated to Washington that "the two Bastians at Billingsport to be enclosed and mounted with eight pieces of artillery and manned with about five hundred troops including one company of artillery."

At both of the South Jersey fortifications, there were military units from Salem County under the command of Brigadier General Silas Newcomb of Cumberland, who was the only South Jersey officer to attain the rank of general in the Revolutionary Army. On August 11, 1777, General Washington wrote to General Newcomb at Woodbury, noting that "as you have got so many of the Militia collected, I would think it highly impolitic to discharge them until we can with some degree of precision, explain the late extraordinary Movements of the Enemy, and determine the object of them."

General Washington further advised Newcomb that "in the interim my desire is that you order your Men to Red Bank to assist in completing the Works there ... The disagreeable Suspense we are now kept in, cannot possibly be of long duration, during which, your Corps will be doing a Service to their Country, at least equal to the pay they draw, which I am satisfied will be more agreeable to them than to remain idle."

"The "Disagreeable Suspense" continued to confuse General Washington, especially after General Howe's "departure from the Capes of Delaware and of the uncertainty we are in respecting his designs and operations." President John Hancock advised General Washington at this juncture that "...a large Fleet of Ships, consisting of upwards of two hundred Sail was Seen off Sinapuxon Bar ... Sinapuxon leeds to the Southward of the State of Delaware and forms an Inlet into Maryland. This is the first information we have had of them since they left Cape May, and I am now as much puzzled about their designs, as I was before ..."

On August 12, 1777, General Washington reported the following intelligence about the South Jersey troops to President John Hancock:

"General Newcomb having informed me, that he had collected a body of about five hundred Jersey Militia at Woodberry, I have desired him to endeavour to keep them together, while matters remain in their present uncertainty and suspense and to employ them in whatever works may be carrying on at Billingsport or Red Bank, for the defense of the river ..."

By August 23, the suspense was over and it was learned by the Congress at Philadelphia "... of the arrival of the British Fleet in Chesepeak Bay" and that it was "... preparing to land the army near the head of the Bay, with a view of penetrating the country this way ..." The British Army landed units at the head of the Elk River in Maryland on August 25th; they were under the command of General (Sir) William Howe and withing a month, the city of Philadelphia was to fall to the victorious British and the American Congress was forced to remove to Yorktown (York), Pennsylvania.

From Woodbury, General Silas Newcomb advised Governor William Livingston on August 25th that "having been frequently been informed, that a number of the inhabitants of Downs, in Cumberland county in this state, had made a practice of going on board the enemy's ships in Delaware Bay..., I issued orders to Major Ewing to detach from the militia a sufficient number" to "...apprehend the persons suspected to be guilty ..." Major Ewing was successful in apprehending fifteen suspected Tories, "twelve of whom were discharged by the civil authority, on taking the oaths of the state."

General Newcomb also reported to Livingston that "agreeably to your orders I am now at this place (Woodbury) with near 300 of the militia of my brigade, which number was furnished by the following regiments, and in the following proportions, viz.; Col. Hand's 60, Potter's 24, Holmes' 110, Dick's 20, Ellis' 55; the other regiments furnished none, nor have any appeared from Burlington as your orders intimated."

It is readily seen that the Militia at Woodbury consisted of a large number from Salem County, for Colonels Benjamin Holme and Samuel Dick were able to bring more of their men to Woodbury. It has been possible to ascertain that the following specific units from South Jersey served at Woodbury and Red Bank under the command of Brigadier General Silas Newcomb:

> Captain Jacob Browning, 2nd Regiment (Gloucester), 64 men
> Captain Jonathan Beesley, 1st Regiment (Cumberland), 73 men
> Captain Jacob DuBois, 2nd Regiment (Salem)
> 1st Lt., Ephraim Lummis, 1st Regiment (Cumberland), 73 men
> Colonel Bowes Reed, 1st Regiment (Burlington)

1st Lt., James Wright, 1st Regiment (Salem), 29 men. As Lt. James Wright was in Captain William Smith's Company of Salem Militia, it is thus possible to ascertain that Smith's unit was indeed at Woodbury, as suggested by Frank Stewart and others.

In addition to the South Jersey Militia companies which served at Woodbury and the area south to Mantua Creek during October-November 1777, one of the most important units was the West Jersey Artillery, commanded by Captain Samuel Hugg of Gloucester City. Men from most of the South Jersey counties served under Captain Hugg and from a September 1777 muster roll, located at the New Jersey Historical Society, it is found that in addition to Captain Hugg, the following men were present and probably formed the battery near Mantua Creek which harassed British warships off Billingsport:

> Lt. Benjamin Whitall, Sgt. Samuel Cole, Sgt. George Sparks and
> Privates John Telford, Benjamin Haines, Judiah Haines, Joseph Flint,

Thomas Langley, Thomas Heath, Thomas Magree, Daniel Laurence and Philip Peters.

From another remarkable document, albeit a xerox of the original, found at the Gloucester County Historical Society, it is possible to identify a larger number of the members of the West Jersey Artillery, no doubt the orignal men. The document, a deposition, was signed by Lieutenants Eli Elmer (Cumberland County) and David Moore (Gloucester County) on April 29, 1783. The importance of the deposition is that we now have what amounts to a substantial muster roll of the troops of Captain Samuel Hugg's West Jersey Artillery, a unit that saw service at Trenton, at the time of Washington's crossing, and at Princeton, where the great victory over the British was won at the expense of the life of General Hugh Mercer, for whom the fort at Red Bank was ultimately named.

In addition to Trenton and Princeton, Captain Hugg's West Jersey Artillery played an important roll in the defense of the South Jersey side of the Delaware River, as the British, attempted, after the capture of Fort Billings on October 1, 1777, to open up the Chevaux-de-Frize defenses of the river during October. It needs to be kept in mind that Fort Billings and Fort Mercer were to be the last obstacles in New Jersey to British control of the Delaware River; their elimination was vital to the British at Philadelphia, lest they have to withdraw because of their otherwise long and difficult problem of defending supply lines from Maryland to Pennsylvania.

The Elmer-Moore "Deposition" identified the following enlisted men of the West Jersey Artillery:

Jonah Garrison, Parsons Lummis, Andrew Peck, Joseph Lummis, Ephraim Dayton, James Horne, Andrew Cross, William Rawlins, John Brown, Nathaniel Diskell, David Diskell, David and John Cahill, George Barnett, John Booten, John Barber, Joseph Bennett, Lawrance Doerir, Nathaniel Price, McCalory Adams. Job Ryley, James Bright, William Barrot, Arthur McGinies, John Cann. James Dunwoody, William Johnston, Matthew Dugan, John Carlile, Michale Christian, Levi Albertson (Gloucester, killed at Princeton), Joseph Hugg, Matthew Parvin, Thomas Smith, Richard Colyer, Elijah Price, Thomas Goren, Thomas Legrange, Joseph Reve.

With the British on the march northward from Maryland to Philadelphia, it was necessary for General George Washington to call in units of the Continental Army and many of the militia from Fort Billings and Fort Mercer. On September 5, 1777, Colonel John Bull reported that there were at Billingsport: "30 Contin. Artillery; 50 City Militia (having only 8 days left to serve); and 50 Labours & Carpenters - mostly the latter." At Red Bank (Fort Mercer), Bull reported only the presence of "a few labourers." Indeed, if Washington were correct, the defense of the South Jersey side of the Delaware River had to be sacrificed if the British drive on Philadelphia was to be thwarted. No matter, it was requested at Philadelphia that "four pieces of cannon should be got to Billingsport for the present, if nothing more can be done."

In addition, the Supreme Executive Council at Philadelphia indicated to Colonel Jehu Eyres, commander of the First Artillery Battalion, on September 6, 1777 that there was "great reason to believe that the Enemys Ships will make an attempt to design to reach this city; whilest their army is endeavoring to penetrate the Country.

Colonel Eyres was further advised that "the Works at Billingsport, Fort, Island, Darby Creek and Bush Island, by orders of his Excell'y Gen. Washington, are left almost without Guards. You will therefore immediately report to these Works and Post the two Companies of Militia Artillery that are under your command ..." Indeed, by September 9, Colonel Eyre had moved quickly by placing one of his artillery companies at Billingsport and the other at Fort Mifflin. He then joined his other two companies to the command of General John Armstrong at Newport, Delaware.

A day earlier, General Armstrong had written to President Thomas Wharton of the State of Pennsylvania that his private opinion was "... that if Mr. Howe do not come on very soon, his intention is to re-embark on the Delaware, Cross over & land where he may think most convenient on the Jersey Shore, march up to the Shevar de frize" at Billingsport. Armstrong noted firmly that the "Jersey Militia shou'd immediately finish the Labour at Billings-port or rather take post on their own Shore."

The Congress at Philadelphia passed the following resolution on September 9, indicating that war was shortly to come to South Jersey:

> "Congress having received information from General Washington, that a great part of the enemy's fleet have sailed, with the intention ... to come round into the Delaware river; and whereas, General Washington hath requested that a proper lookout be kept up and intelligenece by sent him with as much dispatch as possible of the movements of the said fleet;
>
> Resolved, that the Executive Council of Pennsylvania be informed thereof, and that it be recommended to them to pay immediate attention thereto."

General George Washington apprised President Wharton of his own dilemma in the following communication from the American Headquarters at Germantown on September 13, 1777:

> "I wish it were in my power to turn any part of my present force to the completion of the Works upon Delaware; but in our present Situation, it cannot be afforded. Except General Howe can be checked upon land, the obstructions in the River will be of little avail; for if he can once totally defeat this Army, he will take possession of the Forts of course, and turn our own Guns upon our Ships, Gallies, and floating Batteries ..."

Washington's "present situation" was the defeat of his forces at Brandywine on September 11th and the subsequent retreat of his battered army. The carnage on both sides was severe and we learn from a letter of Henry Livingston to his father, the Governor of New Jersey, that while it appeared the Americans suffered badly, "you may be assured that (Brandywine) is the most unlucky affair that General Howe has yet encountered on this continent." Livingston estimated that the Americans may have lost as many as "five and six hundred at most ... The enemy sustained a much greater loss; you may at least rate is at the double of ours -- I myself a witness to the havock which General Maxwell (Maxwell's Jersey Brigade) made among them this morning ..."

Three days after the news of the British victory at Brandywine had reached Admiral Richard Howe at Elkton, Maryland, the British fleet weighed anchor and headed for Delaware Bay on September 14, 1777. Shortly, the citizens of Salem and "Old Gloucester Counties" were to see the great British Armada of more than 200 vessels at anchor off Reedy Island, where they were to await the British attempt to breach the Chevaux de Frize at Billingsport if Fort Billings could be taken from the Americans.

On September 15, Captain Charles Alexander, writing from the "Delaware Frigate off Billingsport," informed Robert Morris of the Congress that he had taken pains "to inspect the situation of our Forts and Chevaux de frize, and do acquaint you as my opinion that if some troops and Boats of Observation down the River is not, you may Soon expect to hear of the Enemy having Billings Port in Possession..."

Governor William Livingston of New Jersey, writing from Haddonfield on September 20, notified Brigadier General Silas Newcomb of Cumberland County, in command of the South Jersey Militia stationed at Woodbury, that if would be necessary to detach some of Newcomb's men to the main army in Pennsylvania. Livingston noted that he thought "it best those now collected at Woodbury should immediately march to join the militia under the immediate command of General Armstrong, and to reinforce the command of his Excellency, General Washington."

Aware that General Newcomb was a veteran of the French and Indian War, as well as the Battles of Long Island and White Plains, in New York, during the summer and fall of 1776, plus remaining with General Washington's retreating army until it crossed over the Delaware River into Pennsylvania, Governor Livingston tried to soothe General Newcomb's possible hurt feelings by assuring him that "this detachment, I am persuaded from your zeal for the cause, you would upon this important occasion be desirous of commanding in person. But as in all probability the enemy's fleet, should their land army meet with success, will attempt to ravage our coasts, and they may perhaps throw over some troops besides, I think your prescence will be more necessary in this state. You will therefore direct Capt. Potter to take command of the troops now at Woodbury, and to march them with all possible expedition as directed." Livingston was referring to Colonel David Potter of the Cumberland County Militia, who was later to become a prisoner of war in the vicinity of Frankford Creek on September 25, 1777.

After the defeat at Brandywine, the Americans fought a delaying action on the road to Philadelphia; however, by September 25, the British army was camped at Germantown, a short five miles from the American capitol. On the next day, Lord Cornwallis led approximately three thousand British and Hessian troops into Philadelphia and the Tories of the city rejoiced. Fortunately, the Congress had fled to Lancaster and then York, Pennsylvania, before the British took Philadelphia.

Continually conscious of the fact that supplies were in short supply, General Howe dispatched three thousand troops to Elkton, Maryland, to bring the material left there on the initial landing of his forces. Indeed, General William Howe and Lord Charles Cornwallis were keenly aware that the British Army could not be maintained at Philadelphia, thus the Delaware River had to be opened up to British shipping or the conquerors of Philadelphia would have to return to New York at great loss of face and man-power.

General George Washington and his officers learned that the British were about to send troops over the Delaware River, leaving less than ten thousand in the Philadelphia area. Washington's plan was to attack the remaining British and Hessians in force; however, before the Battle of Germantown took place on October 4, 1777, General William Howe ordered two regiments to the Jersey side of the Delaware. Their mission was the destruction of the American fortification at Billingsport, a step necessary if the British Navy was to breach the Chevaux de Frize.

Lt. Colonel Thomas Stirling was entrusted with this vital British operation on October 1, 1777. With the 10th and 42nd regiments under his command, Stirling crossed over the river and landed his men near the mouth of Raccoon Creek. It is from the Journal of the famous British spy, Major John Andre, that it is learned: "Lieutenant-Colonel Stirling marched from Germantown ... in order to take possession of some Rebel works at Billingsport below Mud Island on the Jersey Shore of Delaware."

From the same Journal, dated October 2, we learn from Andre that "Lieutenant-Colonel Stirling took possession of Billingsport; about 300 Militia who were in it having evacuated the work and spiked the cannon." Andre's entry is confirmed in Colonel William Bradford's report to President Wharton of Pennsylvania, dated October 3:

> "General Potter tho't it most adviseable to cross Delaware and get into Billingsport ... I there found Col. Will of the 4th Battn with about 100 men, & Capn. Massey Company of Artillery which was reduced by desertion to 12 men, after I got in was reinforced by 100 Jersey Militia & next day with about 40 more."

Colonel Bradford reported further to President Wharton that on "the first of October the Enemy landed a number of men near Raccoon Creek; various were the accounts of their number, tho' mostly agreeing that not less than 500, but many made them 1000. We kept a good look out that night, and dispatched 60 of the Jersey men in the afternoon to harrass them if they were on the march, but they did not move that Evening," thus Fort Billings still remained in American hands.

Bradford put his men on alert, "but could get no account from General Newcomb tho' Majors Marsh & Boys were sent off for that Purpose, but at last I had certain account that the Jersey men had retreated and the Enemy were advancing to the Fort ... I ordered the People into Boats ... spiked all the Cannon we could not carry off, and set the Barracks & Bake House on Fire ... We took off all the Amunition ... The Enemy ships are now coming up to Billingsport."

Some historians concerned with the American Revolution in the Delaware Valley have used Colonel Bradford's criticism of General Newcomb and the South Jersey Militia as gospel; however, now as the result of the discovery, at the Massachusetts Historical Society, of a letter from General Newcomb to Governor William Livingston, dated "Haddonfield Octr. 4th, 1777," it is possible to learn from Silas Newcomb what exactly transpired when the British landed at Raccoon Creek and marched towards Fort Billings.

In his letter to Governor William Livingston, Brigadier General Silas Newcomb noted that "after the Enemy took possession of Philadelphia, most of the detachment which I had sent over by your Excellency's Order, under the command of Col. Potter, returned. Colonel Potter himself being taken prisoner at Frankfort, 2 miles in the rear of his Battalion ..."

General Newcomb then proceeded to make his headquarters at Woodbury, where he utilized his slender forces in such a skillful manner as to destroy the John Jackson myth that Newcomb was a bumbling, incompetent officer. He reported the following to Livingston:

> "A guard of about 50 men at Big Timber Creek; with a Sgt's guard at

each of the ferries to serve as a picquet, & to prevent any boats going over to the enemy ... Three guard boats from Ancocus (Rancocas) to Gloucester; a guard of about 40 men at Thompsons Point, 4 miles below Billingsport."

In order to make Fort Billings more secure, Newcomb noted that he had sent the rest of his men, "about 150 ... to Billingsport to reinforce that garrison, reserving only a small guard at Woodbury." Taking Newcomb's own figures at face value, the total number of South Jersey Militia was approximately 300, hardly enough of a force for the challenge ahead for General Newcomb.

On the evening of October 1, Newcomb "was informed that a party of the enemy was landing on this shore, opposite Marcus Hook. Their number said to be about 400. I immediately called in my out guards & marched to a heighth, on the Salem road, about 15 miles below Philad. Gnel. Washington had written to the Commanding Officer at Billingsport (Colonel Bradford of Pennsylvania) that, if he thought it indefencible, he ought to evacuate it, and destroy the works; which accordingly was done; it being the unanimous opinion of the officers there that the place could not be defended against any considerable force."

General Newcomb noted in his report that "about 9 in the morning of the 2 of this month, the Enemy advanced within a few hundred yards of where we were drawn up, with 2 or 3 field pieces, when a pretty brisk fire from both sides ensued." At this moment, it was discovered that "they were not less than 1500 ... They (the British) detaching off strong flanking parties, by which we might have soon been surrounded, I thought it prudent to retreat, which we did in tolerable good order, keeping up a constant fire in our rear ..."

The British forces under Lt. Colonel Thomas Stirling advanced over Mantua Creek; however, according to Silas Newcomb, they turned back and took possession of Billingsport, not before the Americans removed "the stores to this place (Woodbury)."

As for casualties, General Newcomb reported: "I believe we had none killed, nor any badly wounded; several are missing, but I believe they are mostly, if not all, gone home. The enemy had 3 or 4 killed at Mantua Creek bridge. We still keep strong piquets at Woodbury, and at the ferries. I have at present not quite 300 men under my command ... it is impossible to get any more under the old Militia Law ..."

Lt. Colonel Stirling remained at Billingsport for three days, then on October 4th, he recrossed the Delaware River with all but 300 of his troops after reducing Fort Billings to ruins. The British were now faced with the breaching of the Chevaux de Frize in order to proceed against the relatively under-garrisoned Fort Mercer at Red Bank (Woodbury). While it is not completely clear why the British recalled Stirling's main force, it is agreed that the American move against Germantown was of greater intensity than the British had initially realized, hence Stirling's regiments were actually needed against the four-pronged American Attack on October 4. Silas Newcomb has given us this report of the beginning of the Battle of Germantown: "There has been all this morning (October 4) a heavy firing, both of artillery and musketry, in or about Philad. Now about 8 o'clock, it is a little abated ..."

On October 7, 1777, Colonel Bradford informed President Wharton of Pennsylvania that the British troops under Lt. Colonel Stirling had actually taken possession of Billingsport. The force "consisted of Highlanders and Marines from the Men of War, about Thirteen or Fourteen hundred in Number by the most Intelligent People that I have spoke with." Bradford merely confirmed the estimate made by General Newcomb to Governor Livingston three days earlier.

From Bradford, it is also learned that on October 4, the British "embarked all their men but 300, after making some Efforts to remove or weigh the Chevaux de Frize, which I believe they could not effect." Finally, on October 6, "the Enemy Set Fire to all the Works and Houses that were left at Billingsport, and embarked the (300) Men."

When the British evacuated Billingsport, Colonel Bradford returned and then informed President Wharton that he Had been "in Billingsport this morning, and every Thing that would take Fire is burnt, and most the Ambrusers destroyed. The Commodore is now sending down a Scow to bring off the Iron Work that is there ... We are pretty well off for Cattle ... and the Boats are just now going to fetch six Waggon loads of Flour that is at Timber Creek," no doubt part of the supplies that General Newcomb had so wisely moved to the Woodbury area.

Colonel Bradford was very "confident the Fleet cannot get up this River as we are now situated -- Tho' should they get Red Bank, where we have not one Man, I do not know the Consequences." Despite Bradford's confidence, the British Navy was intent on breaking through the Chevaux de Frize at Billingsport and on October 8, Bradford was forced to report that the Last two Chevaux de Frize "that were sunk to stop the Gap are removed higher and put on one side, so that a Ship May warp thro'. A Ship & Brig are now preparing to be sunk in the Gap, which, if we can Effect, will stop the Channel." In a postscript, Bradford optimistically stated that "The Commodore (John Hazelwood) is not under the least doubt of Stoping the Channel, and should they warp thro' he can destroy them."

Even so, the British continued their attempt to clear a channel through the Chevaux de Frize. Colonel Bradford and Commodore Hazelwood reported to President Wharton of Pennsylvania on October 11:

"The Enemy lays so near the Chevaux de Frize at Billingsport that we have not been able to sink the Ship I mentioned ..."

Fortunately, the American naval vessels off Billingsport, small as they might be, compared to the British men-of-war, were able to force the British to withdraw from their clearing operations. In addition, the effective work of Captain Samuel Hugg's West Jersey Artillery greatly aided Commodore Hazelwood's vessels as they kept the British fleet on the defensive.

By October 14th, the British had widened the gap in the Chevaux de Frize so that an approximately 100 foot passage existed. The Fleet was now free to move up the river to attack both Fort Mifflin on the Pennsylvania side of the river and Fort Mercer which was located near the mouth of Woodbury Creek in "Old Gloucester County."

B - Fort Mercer (1775-1777)

After the dust had settled and the serious implications of Lexington and Concord had been digested around the 13 British Colonies, plans were brought into being which were to provide land and water defenses should Great Britain decide to punish any further defiance by the colonials, including those of the Delaware Valley.

As early as July 1775, Benjamin Franklin, as President of the Philadelphia "Council of Safety" had crossed the Delaware River to Red Bank in "Old Gloucester County." Franklin, members of the Committee and engineers, chose the Red Bank site for possible fortification to prevent any future British naval action against the city of Philadelphia.

During the rest of 1775 and until March 17, 1776, military activities between the Americans and British took place around the city of Boston, thus the "war" was far removed from the Delaware Valley. When the British evacuated Boston, General George Washington removed his forces to New York City and Long Island.

The American defeat at the "Battle of Long Island" and General Washington's string of reversals on Manhattan Island and in Westchester County, New York, did not prompt further work on the future Fort Mercer at Red Bank. Even Washington's retreat over New Jersey to Trenton and his crossing of the Delaware River on December 8th, 1776, did not stir activity at Red Bank.

At this point, General Washington sent General Israel Putnam to Philadelphia to serve as that city's Military Governor and to "superintend the Works (Fortifications) and give the necessary directions" to their construction. As for Red Bank, it does not appear that any difinitive plans for construction existed prior to December 1776.

Finally on December 23rd, Major Thomas Proctor, an Artillery officer from Philadelphia, sent the following communication to the "Council of Safety:"

> "I waite on General Putnam to Fort Island yesterday, in order to view the works and the adjacent ground, and gave it as his opinion that works should be formed on Red-Bank to prevent the enemy takeing advantage of the situation; and the Block houses at the Fort should be removed to Red-Bank, to be fixed as redoubts, and form lines of Communication to each other and their flanks ..."

Two days later, Major Proctor informed the "Council of Safety" that he had "Twice ... rec'd the General's Instructions to prepare myself, and a party of Artillery under my command to go with him into the Jersey with all possible Despatch in my Power ..." This urgency was dictated by fear that the British might march south to the Red Bank area and attempt a crossing of the Delaware River to Philadelphia.

General Israel Putnam acquired the services of the Polish engineer, Thaddeus Kosciuszko, and under the General's order, Kosciuszko began the defense fortifications at Red Bank in "Old Gloucester County." Indeed, it was the Polish patriot who drew "the plans and directed the laying of the foundations of this fort during the winter of 1776-7."

By early April of 1777, Colonel John Bull began earnest work on the fortifications at Red Bank. When completed, it would become known as Fort Mercer, in honor of General Hugh Mercer of Virginia who had commanded the "Flying Camp" and who was killed during Battle of Princeton on January 3, 1777.

By June, a considerable amount of work had been completed on Fort Mercer. At that juncture, General George Washington thought it expedient to send Philippe Charles Trouson du Coudray, a French artillery expert, to view the fortifications under way in the Delaware Valley. In his official report, Du Coudray commented that Fort Mercer was "better conceived, directed, and executed than either" Fort Billings or Fort Mifflin.

Du Coudray, whose official title was Inspector of Ordnance and Manufactories under General Washington, stated that the good work being done on Fort Mercer did "the more Honour to Colonel Bull, as he had no other assistance than natural good-sense unenlightened by theory ... There are indeed Faults in the Plan ... but, they do not render it useless as the two former forts. If we may judge by the proportion of the work already finished, it is reasonable to expect the whole will be in a state of Defence in the Courst of a Fortnight."

Israel Putnam

In his concluding remarks, Du Coudray advised that it was necessary "to preserve Colonel Bull's Fort (Fort Mercer)." He continued:

"The cannon at this Fort might partly serve for the Batteries at Billingsport. I would not, however, advise to demolish the Battery at Red-Bank. But to leave there two or three of the poorest of the cannon."

By preserving "Colonel Bull's Fort," the British would be induced to believe that they would have:

"... a second Line of obstacles to encounter after they had surmounted the first; and besides for another Reason, which appears to me a very important one, especially in the present Circumstances of Affairs, the Government would escape the Censure of Inconsideration and mistakes, which the evil minded are always ready to pass, and the People to adopt, when they see works which have been erected with much Labour and Expense, pulled down..."

With the completion of Fort Mercer in early June, Colonel John Bull sent most of the unknown builders of the fort back to Philadelphia; however, a small detachment of troops were left behind to guard the installation. From John Jackson's "Fort Mercer: Guardian of the Delaware," it is learned there were left behind at the fort:

"...one captain, lieutenant, ensign, three sergents, drum and fife, and fifty privates...It cannot be determined when this small garrison was withdrawn, but it apparently occurred within a few days..."

On August 11, 1777, General George Washington wrote to Brigadier General Silas Newcomb as follows:

"Your favour of Yesterday from Woodbury I have this Moment received. As you have got so many of the Militia collected, I would think it highly impolitic to discharge them ... my desire is that you order your Men to Red Bank to assist in completing the Works there ... The Officer Commanding will take orders from General De Coudray or whoever he has left there to Superintend them..."

The next day, General Washington informed President John Hancock of the Continental Congress:

"General Newcomb having informed me, that he had collected a body of about 500 New Jersey militia at Woodbury, I have desired him to endeavour to keep them together...and to employ them in whatever work may be carrying on at Billingsport or Red Bank, for the defense of the (Delaware) river..."

Writing from his camp at "Neshamini, August 21, 1777," Washington reported to John Hancock:

"Since I wrote to you on the 12th instant, on the subject of the Militia under the Command of Genl Newcomb, I have recd another letter from him...By this it appears, that the Men were not employed in any way while they were at Red Bank, and that they are now anxious to get home to their farms, as they see no immediate occasion of their Services...In my opinion they had better be suffered to go home, than be kept discontented, as they will turn out with more spirit when they are wanted again."

The arrival of the British Fleet and Army at Elkton, Maryland, on August 23rd, should have inspired the stationing of American troops at Fort Mercer; however, General George Washington for unaccountable reasons chose not to do do, for Colonel John Bull's report of September 5th indicated that there were only "a few labourers" at Red Bank. It became apparent then that Fort Mercer was not garrisoned during July and August of 1777, as well as the first week of September.

By September 11th, the Americans were defeated at Brandywine and by the 26th, the city of Philadelphia was in British hands. Earlier in the month, General Anthony Wayne advised George Washington:

"Red Bank being a post of consequence it will be necessary to enclose the two bastains and place therein five hundred men which with the assistance of the militia of New Jersey after cutting the banks and dams and breaking up the Bridges over the creek will greatly retard if not totally prevent the enemy from penetrating that way."

The day after the American defeat at Brandywine, President John Hancock sent the following urgent communication to Governor William Livingston of New Jersey:

"It is the earnest Desire of Congress, and I have it in Charge to inform you of it, that you will immediately order out four Thousand of the Jersey Militia to reinforce the Army under General Washington with all possible Expedition. If you should not be able to call out that Number, it is the Request of Congress, that you will call out as many as possible in this critical State of our Affairs..."

Writing from Haddonfield on September 19th, Governor Livingston reported to Charles Stewart, commissary general of issues in Philadelphia, that he had:

"Issued orders to our Militia at Woodberry to assist in transporting the Stores from Philadelphia to New Jersey. As to impressing Waggons, have no Authority for that Purpose, the Assembly is now about passing a Resolve to authorize the Measure..."

Colonel Joseph Ellis, commanding officer of the "Old Gloucester County" Militia, took his troops over the Delaware River to assist in removing military supplies to New Jersey. His troops "were empowed to impress wagons, horses, and oxen if necessary." There is no doubt that this successful mission by Ellis and his militia helped prolong the defense of Fort Mercer.

With the fall and destruction of Fort Billings on October 1st and the ultimate clearing of the Chevaux de Frize by the British, it had become obvious, even to General George Washington, that Fort Mercer was going to be the last bastion of defense for the Americans on the Delaware. Indeed, Alexander Hamilton noted that the British attack on Fort Mercer, when it came, would be "...sudden & violent as they are hardly in a situation to delay a matter so essential to them..."

It will be recalled that as late as October 7, 1777, Colonel William Bradford was officially reporting that there were no American troops at Fort Mercer. Fortunately, there were men at Red Bank under the command of Colonel Elijah Hand of the Cumberland County Militia. It is not clear at this writing as to who ordered them there or how long they were stationed at this important post.

On October 9th, General George Washington had decided to replace the militia at Fort Mercer with regular Continental Troops. The following orders were sent to Colonel Christopher Greene of the First Rhode Island Regiment:

"I have directed General Varnum to send your regiment and that of Colonel Angell's to Red Bank, by a route which has been marked out to him...You will find a very good fortification at Red Bank, but if anything should be requisite to render it stronger...you will have it done. The cannon you will stand in need of, will be furnished from the galleys at Fort Mifflin, from whence you will also derive supplies of military stores."

Washington finally awakened to the importance of Fort Mercer urged Colonel Greene to "not lose a moment's time in getting to the place of your destination and making every preparation for its defense. Any delay might give the enemy the opportunity of getting there before you, which could not fail of being most fatal in its consequences."

Greene was also advised by General Washington that he had:

"written to General Newcomb, of the Jersey militia, to give you all the aid in his power, for which you will accordingly apply when necessary. Upon the whole, sir, you will be pleased to remember that the post with which you are now entrusted is of the utmost importance to America...The whole defence of the Delaware absolutely depends upon it; and consequently all the enemy's hopes of keeping Philadelphia and finally succeeding in the object of the present campaign..."

Colonel Christopher Greene was to command Fort Mercer from October 9 to November 20, 1777, at which time, the Americans would be forced to withdraw in the face of an expected attack by more than 5,000 British and Hessian regulars under the command of Lord Cornwallis.

Colonel Greene, who had been a British prisoner of war in Quebec, Canada, was a worthy choice to command Fort Mercer. He reported his arrival in "Old Gloucester County" via a letter to General Washington from "Fort at Red Bank 14 October 1777:

"I arrived here on Saturday last with my regiment. They were much fatigued with the march, as I forced thirty-five miles one day. They are now in high spirits, and go to their duty with the greatest cheerfulness...I saw General Newcomb last evening. He informs me that the small number (of militia) now on duty expect to return home in a day or two; those that relieve them expect to be relieved in three days."

It was remarkable that the Americans won their revolution against Great Britain, for there were command problems, resulting usually from faulty communications. For example, Colonel Greene believed that the South Jersey Militia were to remain at Fort Mercer, whereas General Newcomb believed otherwise. According to Greene: "The General (Newcomb) thinks your Excellency's intentions were, for the militia only to help complete the fort; after that, to fall on the rear of the enemy, in case of an attack."

Colonel Greene very soon was aware of the insufficiency of the troops under his command, thus he commented to General Washington as follows:

"Could your Excellency give us the assistance of Colonel Angell's regiment, I doubt not that this post would be secure without dependence on militia. If they are to be relieved in the manner I understand they are, it is my opinion they will do us no service. General Newcomb gives very little encouragement of any to supply the place of those that are going off the ground."

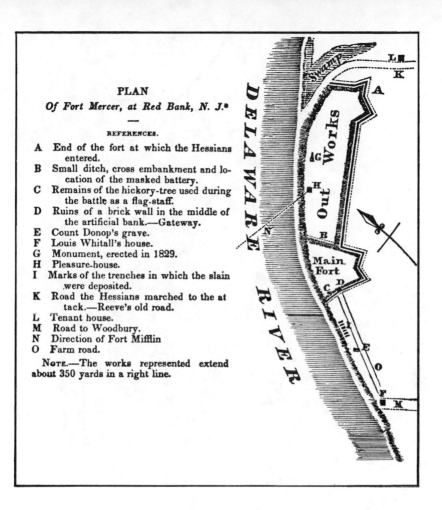

The Battle At Red Bank

When Colonel Christopher Greene arrived at Fort Mercer on October 11th, he realized that "Colonel Bull's Fort" was far too large to defend, thus he informed General Washington that he had found "it necessary to contract the fort." In addition, Greene realized that he needed capable artillery men to man the cannon already present at Fort Mercer. General Washington responded by ordering Captain Mauduit to Red Bank to serve as commanding officer of Artillery.

Captain Mauduit was a French volunteer who had gained valuable artillery experience as an aide to Brigadier General Henry Knox. Greene and Mauduit quickly came to the conclusion that Fort Mercer was much too large to defend with the forces available. As many as 1500 would be required to man the works. In addition, as John Jackson has noted, Colonel Greene was dispirited because "no barracks, hospital, magazine or other buildings had been constructed to receive a garrison" of troops.

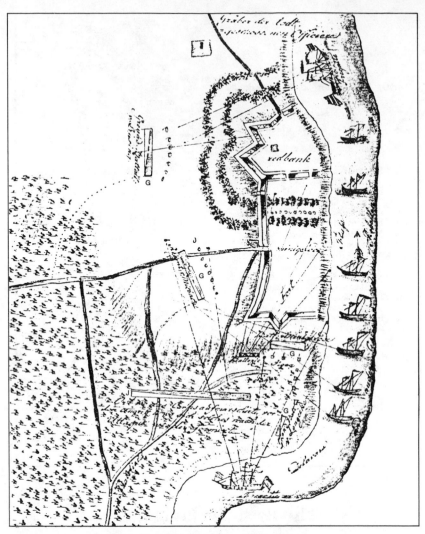

Capt. Ewald's sketch of Fort Mercer

By October 15th, work had begun on what would really be a new Fort Mercer and when completed, the new fortification was approximately 60% the size of Colonel Bull's works. Captain Mauduit had sufficient cannon at hand, thus he placed fourteen of them in strategic places to guard any land approach to the fort.

In reality, the reconstructed Fort Mercer was "a fort within a fort" and was surrounded on the land side with an Abatis, "a defensive obstacle formed by felled trees with sharpened branches facing the enemy." Mauduit also constructed a moat around the land approaches to the fort. Mines were also placed on the main approaches to Fort Mercer, making it a formidable obstacle to any possible British attack.

From the "Diary of a Common Soldier in the American Revolution, 1775-1783- Military Journal of Jeremiah Greenman," it is learned that the long awaited

Colonel Israel Angell and his 2nd Rhode Island Regiment were enroute to Fort Mercer. Greenman wrote on October 17th that the troops had "crossed the Delaware at Burlington where we drew sum Provision...about 11 o'clock we proceeded on to Mount Holley where we drew sum Lequor and pushed on till day Break..."

On the 18th, Greenman wrote that "this day pushed on to Hattonfield where we halted and drew sum Provision...then pushed on to Red Bank at Fort Mercey (Mercer)...we lodged in our tents, & very cold." This arrival of Angell's troops was to cause severe over-crowding at Fort Mercer, for on October 21st, Samuel Stelle Smith tells us in his "Fight For the Delaware, 1777," that:

> "In the Ft. Mercer garrison on the 21st, there were 101 men of Col. Greene's Rhode Island regiment (150 were at Ft. Mifflin), 284 men of Col. Angell's Rhode Island regiment, 63 men of Capt. Cook's artillery company, 16 men from the New Jersey militia, serving as artillerists, plus a Virginia regiment 'reduced to 150 men.'"

Outside the fort were several hundred militia from Brigadier General Silas Newcomb's South Jersey Brigade, which included units of the "Old Gloucester County" Militia. All told, the defenders of Fort Mercer, the regular army Continentals and the South Jersey Militia, numbered approximately one thousand.

On October 20, 1777, General George Washington was advised that the British "had sent a large body of troops across the Delaware with the intention no doubt to storm or invest Red Bank." Two days later, unaware that the "Battle at Red Bank" was to ensue that day, General Washington wrote to Silas Newcomb, pointing out that "the Enemy seem determined to possess themselves, if possible, of the Forts on the River...For this purpose, it is confidently said, that a pretty considerable Detachment crossed the River Yesterday morning." It was Washington's hope that Newcomb's South Jersey Militia would be "able to fall on their Rear with such a respectable number...as to make them decline the project." It would appear from this statement of General Washington that Newcomb was following the order "to fall on the rear" of the British, thus they had to be out of the fort.

Washington concluded his communique to Newcomb with the following postscript:

> "I cannot forbear observing to you, and the Inhabitants of Jersey, the dreadful consequences that must follow should the Enemy keep possession of Philadelphia, and that if they get Red Bank into their hands, a considerable force must...be kept there by them...this I hope will stimulate the Militia to a speedy and vigorous opposition."

Meanwhile in Philadelphia, General Sir William Howe was advised by his staff officers that it was now possible to attack Fort Mercer, thus on the evening of October 20th, twelve flat-bottomed boats were loaded with approximately two thousand crack Hessian troops under the command of Count Carl Emil Ulrich Von Donop. Their destination, unknown to Colonel Greene at Red Bank, was Fort Mercer and in the afternoon of October 21st, Von Donop's troops arrived at Cooper's Ferry, now Camden. The Hessians marched to Haddonfield where they were to spend the evening in bivouac and in making themselves obnoxious to the citizens of this predominantly Quaker village.

Colonel Christopher Greene at Fort Mercer had been alerted to the fact that

British or Hessian troops had crossed over into New Jersey, but he still was not aware that their destination was Red Bank. He had sent out a scouting party under the command of Captain Oliver Clark, but before Clark's expected return, 16 year old Jonas Cattell, the "Paul Revere of South Jersey," arrived from Haddonfield with the news that the Hessians were enroute to Fort Mercer. Incidently, Captain Clark was captured by Von Donop's troops approximately three miles from Fort Mercer, thus it was to Jonas Cattell that Greene was greatly in debt.

Colonel Greene sent Captain Felix Fisler of the "Old Gloucester County" Militia towards Big Timber Creek with instructions to destroy the bridge, near today's Westville. Ultimately this act was to delay the Hessian approach to Fort Mercer and allow the Americans more time to prepare for an attack on the fort.

Shortly after 12 noon, advance units of the Hessians arrived before Fort Mercer. After more than two hours of reconnaissance and staff meetings, it was decided to send a flag of truce to Colonel Greene. From the Diary of Jeremiah Greenman, it is possible to learn exactly what transpired on October 22, 1777:

> "this morning are informed that a party of the Enemy crossed Cooper fery last Evening and was on their way thro Haddonfield for this Fort. Came a crost this morn from Fort Mifflin, had scarce an opportunity to git into the Fort, before a Flag came to Colo. Green, who commanded the Fort threatning to put the Garrison to (death?) if he did not surrender it immediately. Colo. Green answered with disdain, that he would defend it 'till the last drop of his Blood.'"

With the return of the flag, Von Donop opted to attack Fort Mercer and by approximately four in the afternoon, the Hessians began a cannonade against the Americans to no avail. Jeremiah Greenman tells his very poignant story about the Hessian attack:

> "...as soon as the Flag had returned they oppined 7 field peaces & 2 Howitzers on the fort and played very smartly for about ten moments; then they rushed on a very Rash that even success could not justify its temerity...they attacked on the North & South Sides, the North Side was a breast work within another which we cut off and made the Fort small as we had but few men to man it especially the Bigness it was when we first arrived...the Parapet was high the Dikes deep, a row of strong pallesaids sallied out from the parapit on the gate on the South Side...we had a small place big enough for eight men to fight in which overlooked all the ground round the Fort which was surrounded with a double abattis..."

Greenman has confirmed that Fort Mercer really was a fort within a fort. This had been the plan of Captain Mauduit and it worked a great success, for the Hessians were thoroughly confused and suffered a large number of dead and wounded. Greenman noted that the Hessians "advanced as far as the abbatis, but they could not remove it (tho sum few got over) being repulsed with great loss...they left their Command'g officer dying on the Ground in his glacis, and retreated with a hurry & Confusion..."

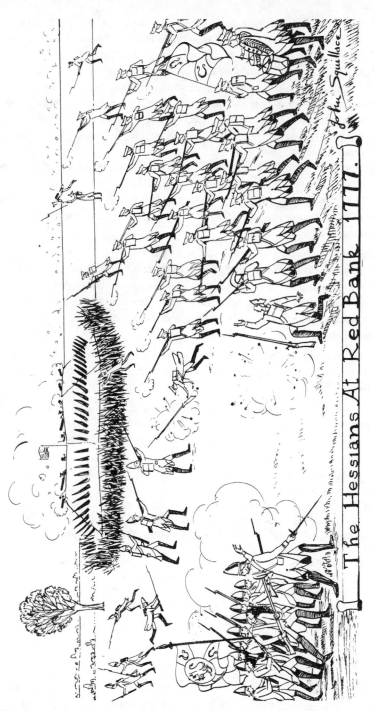

The Hessians At RedBank 1777.

John Squillace

The Hessians marched over Clements Bridge enroute to Haddonfield and from the Diary of Quaker John Hunt, it is learned that "them Hessians that were at Haddonfield had a battle with ye Americans and were beaten and Returned back to Phil. ye 23 of ye 10 mo." The Hessians actually arrived at Coopers Ferry at noon and were taken over to Philadelphia by the waiting flatboats.

At Red Bank, Colonel Christopher Greene was not aware of the extensive carnage the Hessians had suffered, thus on the morning of October 23rd, the Americans emerged from Fort Mercer to find dead, dying and wounded Hessians everywhere. Jeremiah Greenman noted in his "Diary" that the Americans spent "the fore part of this day implying ourselves in burying the dead 73 buried in one grave 4 or 5 in (an) other..."

The total Hessian casualties probably will never be known; however, it would appear that a fair estimate, derived from American, British and Hessian sources, would be approximately 500 killed and wounded. In addition, as many as 60 to 100 Hessian soldiers deserted. Archibald Robertson, a British officer and engineer, noted in his Diary that:

> "Early this morning (October 21) Colonel Donop with 3 Battalions Hessians Grenadiers Regiment of Merbach and Jagers passed the Delaware into the Jerseys to take possession of Red Bank opposite Mud Island where the Rebels had a work. They attacked it...but wre repulsed with the loss of about 25 officers and 300 men killed and wounded."

The Rev. Nicholas Collin of "The Old Swede's Church" at Swedesboro was asked by the Hessians to come to Red Bank to minister to them after the battle. He noted in his Journal:

> "...I went to the wounded Hessians, prayed with them and comforted them as much as I could, using the German language, especially as they asked for my assistance, when they heard a clergyman was at hand. Here was a pitiable sight."

Indeed, the Rev. Collin wrote that about 200 Hessians "were lying on straw in two large rooms, some without arms and legs (outside of the house lay two piles of arms and legs) and others again with their limbs crushed like mush by langrel; some floated in blood, and told me that some had died for lack of something to bandage their wounds with. While I was there several men died in great agony and convulsions..."

The Whitall Mansion, an imposing brick edifice, stood very close to Fort Mercer and prior to the arrival of the Hessians, Colonel Christopher Greene used it as his headquarters. It is not likely that its owners, the pacifist Quaker Whitall family, approved of the use of their home for military purposes; however, when the wounded Hessians were brought to the house, Ann Whitall "was on hand with bandages that evening" and "the house was filled, even the attic was crowded. That night she was an angel of mercy to the wounded and dying, but when some of them fretted because of the noise, she reminded them that they 'must not complain, who had brought it on themselves.' She administered to their needs, this being clearly within the line of duty --'to care for the ill and dying and direct their minds to a solemn commemoration of the approaching period of life.'"

American losses were 14 killed and 23 wounded. Jeremiah Greenman wrote

The Whitall Mansion at Red Bank

that in the Hessian attack on Fort Mercer, "...we lost 7 of our Regiment killed and 14 wounded...(one) of the killed proved to be my Capn. Shaw who was shot thro the Neck." In any event, it was a great victory for the Americans, one that is given too little attention by many historians of a consensus nature.

Closely related to the decimation of the Hessians is the great naval activity which occurred off Fort Mercer on October 23rd. The British Navy was supposed to support the Hessian attack; however, due perhaps to faulty communications, the fleet did not move far enough up the Delaware River on the 22nd to be of any assistance.

From Jeremiah Greenman, it is learned that "about 9 o'clock the Ships Eagle, Summersit, Isis, Augusta, Pearl Leverpool & Several Fregates with a Galley, came up to the Chevaux de frize 500 yards from the fort, at the same time the Land Batteries & our gallies, & the British Squadron engaged and one of the Most Solumest Actions commenced, that may be seen by a soldiers eye...the Spectacle was magnificent, to see at once, the river covered with Ships, four great fire ships, in a blase, floating on the Water..."

Greenman was describing a major naval engagement which was taking place off Fort Mercer in "Old Gloucester County," one which was to see the destruction of the 64 gun Augusta and the 22 gun Merlin. Both of these vessels had run aground and could not be floated. Vice-Admiral Viscount Richard Howe reported the situation to London:

> "...the Augusta and Merlin unfortunately grounded some distance below the second line of chevaux de frize, and the fresh northerly wind which then prevailed greatly checking the rising of the tide, they could not be got afloat on the subsequent flood."

Howe noted that "the Rebels, discovering the state of the Augusta and Merlin in the morning of the 23rd, renewed the fire from their galleys, works and floating batteries...the Augusta by some accident, not otherwise connected with the circumstances of the action but as it was probably caused by the wads from her guns, took fire abaft and it spread with such rapidity that all endeavours to extinguish it were used in vain...In this state of the proceeding it was necessary to withdraw the frigates for securing them from the effect of the blast; and as the Merlin could not be protected from the same injury I judged it requisite to give order for the sloop to be evacuated and destroyed. The other ships dropped down nearer to Billingsport."

Jeremiah Greenman provides us with a very poignant American report of the action off Fort Mercer:

"Likewise one of the floating Batterys & either by chance or good luck one of these shot set (afire) the Augusta, a 64 gun Ship, the nearest to the Chevaux de frize...(She) suddenly took fire at the stern, and in a moment She was in a blase, & soon after blew up, with a thundering noise, before the enemy could take out all their hands...a Moment after the Merlin, a 22 gun Frigate ran a shore below the Agusta nigh to this shore...and as she could not be moved from the explosion, took fire & also blew up...the other ships frightened by the fate of those two retired below hog island..."

Indeed, the defeat of Von Donop's Hessians, the British loss of the Augusta and Merlin, and the removal of the British fleet to Billingsport, were important morale builders for the Americans. The British had been unable with a superior navy to open up the Delaware River to Philadelphia, where food supplies were in serious short supply.

On October 31st, nine days after "The Battle at Red Bank," Count Von Donop died from wounds he received. Jeremiah Greenman made the following entry in his "Diary:"

"this day buried the Hasan Cole (von Donop) who said previous to his Death, I fall a victem to my own ambition & to the avarice of my prince; but, full of thankfulness for the good treatment I have received from my generous Enemy...he was buried with the Honours of War."

Jeremiah Greenman wrote on November 1st that "this day we hung two who piloted the hasans (Hessians) to this fort (Mercer)..." Orders for the hanging had been issued on October 31st and read as follows:

"At a Court Martial held by Order of Cole. Greene of which Lt. Col (Jeremiah) Olney was President, Jno. Mucklewain, and Dick Ellis, were tried for conducting ye Enemy thro the Country, for being Spies & Traitors...found guilty of ye former Charge, & sentenc'd to suffer ye pains of Death...The Colo. approves ye above Sentences of ye Court Martial, and orders that Jno. Mucklewain & Dick Ellis...be hang'd tomorrow Morning 10 o'Clock...A Gallows will be erected this afternoon for that Purpose...The Garrison will attend the execution of the Criminals...under Arms at ye time appointed..."

Postscript

Historically in the minds of many American historians, The American Revolution has been recorded as a "white man's war." The records indicate to the contrary, in that upwards of five thousand Black Americans served in the army and the navy before the war was completed.

H.M.S. AUGUSTA, 1777.

In view of the above, it does not seem strange then that over the centuries since October 22, 1777, historians have been at odds as to whether or not Black Americans were involved in the Battle at Red Bank. According to Isabella C. McGeorge's paper, "The Heroine of Red Bank," read before the Gloucester County Historical Society on January 11, 1904, the fallen Count von Donop was taken to the Job and Ann Whitall house by "those Rhode Island negroes, who tenderly lifted him out from the encumbering carcasses." The Black Americans were indeed soldiers of the 1st Regiment from Rhode Island commanded by Colonel Christopher Greene. In addition, the remarks made by Persifor Frazer, found later in this work, were directed at these same troops when Frazer

Battle Monument at Fort Mercer

In Barber and Howe's history, they tell us that "Fort Mercer was nothing more than a 'good earthen rampart raised to the cordon a fosse and an abattis in front. They constituted the whole strength of the fort --in which wre 300 men and fourteen pieces of cannon. This corps was from Rhode Island, and mainly negroes and mulattoes, who were in a ragged destitute condition.'"

In 1845, Isaac Mickle published his "Remininscences of "Old Gloucester or Incidents in the History of the Counties of Gloucester, Atlantic, Camden, New Jersey." Mickle drawing upon the notes of an aged man who was at Fort Mercer after the defeat of the Hessians informs us that "...of the men under Col. Greene in this action, many were blacks and mulattoes. He was in the fort on the morning of the twenty-third of October, while the garrison was burying the slain, and cannot be mistaken as to this point."

Frank Stewart in his 1927 "Battle of Red Bank" takes up the cross for the old belief that it was presumed "...that the swarthy complexion of these Frenchmen (at Red Bank) gave origin to the report that there were some Negroes under Colonel Greene."

It ought not to appear strange that Blacks were among the troops at Red Bank, for as Benjamin Quarles noted in his "The Negro in the Making of America," New England, despite its relatively small black population, probably furnished more colored soldiers than any other section." Indeed, an observer reported that in Massachusetts in 1777, he found no New England regiment without "A lot of Negroes."

John Jackson in his "Fort Mercer: Guardian of the Delaware" is cautious in his verdict about Blacks serving at Red Bank:

"Local tradition has placed many black Americans in the garrison at Fort Mercer. Unquestionably there were some Black men serving in the 1st and 2nd Rhode Island regiments. However, neither Greene nor Angell's regiments were the heroic all black 3rd Rhode Island Continental Line."

Jackson misses the point, for it is the 1st and 2nd Rhode Island regiments that are of concern here. Both were involved in the engagement with the Hessians at Red Bank an October 22nd, 1777, and as Quarles informs us: "The Rhode Island First Regiment enrolled from 225 to 250 colored men," thus, there is no doubt about the composition of Colonel Christopher Greene's regiment.

As for the third Rhode Island Regiment, it was created in February 1778, while Greene's and Angell's regiments were at Valley Forge. Due to casualties, both were highly depleted, thus we find Jeremiah Greenman writing on January 8th, 1778 that "Colo Greens turn'd into colo Angells . . . all ye spayr officers sent home to recruit a nother regiment . . . "

It would appear then that it is not possible to refute evidence which does indeed indicate that there were Black Americans in the ranks at Red Bank and that they participated in one of the important battles of the American Revolution.

Fort Mercer: The Final Days

With Fort Mercer secure in American hands, there developed friction between leaders of the South Jersey Militia, for General Washington had ordered Major General David Forman to proceed to Red Bank with men under his command from Tom's River. Arriving in the Woodbury area, General Forman gave orders on October 26 "to several of the Militia officers of This part of the County to Assemble their men." Washington had failed to notify Newcomb of a change in Militia command.

Forman reported to Washington that "the lower militia and a Genl. Newcomb have not as yet produced a single man. As being elder in command than Newcomb I take the liberty this day to issue orders for their immediate assembling, and will from time to time do everything in my power to assemble them." It was unfortunate that General Foreman was abrasive towards Silas Newcomb and his loyal militiamen, for they were in "Old Gloucester County" and stationed at strategic points.

With the defeat of the Hessians fresh in their minds, the British were determined to open up the Delaware River before the onset of winter, thus on the morning of October 26th, they sent 200 soldiers and 100 marines over the river to Billingsport. A redoubt was constructed on the site of Fort Billings to insure safe passage up the river for British warships still at anchor below the Chevaux de Frize.

On October 28th, George Washington ordered Brigadier General James Varnum to West Jersey: " You are immediately . . . to proceed to Woodbury with the Brigade under your command . . . You will probably find General Foreman at the head of a body of Jersey Militia, in the neighborhood of Red Bank; as he is there for the same end that you will be, a co-operation between you and him will also be requisite."

A day later, General Forman continued his attack apon Silas Newcomb by advising George Washington that "from the best information I can Collect, he (Newcomb) has at no time given any assistance either to The Garrison or the fleet -- particularly in The late Attack on Red Bank he neither harrassed The Enemy in their Advance, During the Assault or in Their retreat."

Fortunately, General Varnum arrived at Woodbury on November 2nd and his report to Washington, dated November 7, 1777, is interesting in terms of the Forman-Newcomb controversy:

> "I have not seen Genl Forman, nor can I learn where he is. There are about sixty of his Militia at Red Bank. Genl. Newcomb is still here, & his Troops may amount to two Hundred. I cannot tell their number exactly, and believe he cannot. They are badly provided, and can be of little Service in any serious Operations."

Brigadier General Varnum was unable to find General David Forman because he had left Woodbury, no doubt disgusted with the command problems which existed between Militia commanders and the Continental officers sent to Gloucester County by George Washington. It is learned from a letter from New Jersey Governor William Livingston to General George Washington, dated November 9, 1777, that "General Forman has to my great concern, & contrary to my warmest sollicitations, resigned his Commission, upon some misunderstanding with the Assembly."

With David Forman gone from the scene, General Varnum was able to report to George Washington a day earlier that he had "placed the Continental and Militia Guards, upon Timber & Manto Creeks. In a word, I am perfectly satisfied with the different arrangements, & the universal spirit, which apparently pervades the whole."

Indicative of the cooperation, Silas Newcomb informed General Varnum that he had about 500 Militia at Woodbury; however, Varnum reported to George Washington that Newcomb's men were "principally without ammunition. They are good men, & have many good officers with them. It is a pity they cannot be properly furnished." Again on November 10, Varnum reiterated the sorry state of Newcomb's South Jersey Militia around Woodbury: "It would be serviceable to furnish the Militia with Ammunition, or discharge them..."

Recently, it was possible to obtain a valuable document, one apparently unknown previously to South Jersey historians, from the Massachusetts historical Society. This document, a muster roll, informs us that on November 12, 1777, Brigadier General Silas Newcomb, commanding officer of the South Jersey Militia, had six hundred and sixty six officers and men stationed at strategic points in "Old Gloucester County." Their disposition was as follows:

Side of Mantua Creek	Capt. John Peterson (Salem) 40
Mouth of Mantua Creek	Capt. Richard Cheesman (Gloucester) 50
	Capt. Joseph Thorn (Gloucester) 27
Mantua Creek Bridge	Capt. John Barker (Cumberland) 57
	Capt. John Cousins (Gloucester) 40
	Capt. Elisha Davis (Cumberland) 55
	Capt. David Mulford (Salem) 20
Coopers Creek	Capt. Jacob Browning (Gloucester) 37
Gloucester City	Colonel Ephraim Lummis (Cumberland) 60
Woodbury	Capt. Abner Pentor (Salem) 19
	Capt. Joseph Dickinson (Salem) 49
	Capt. Robert Brown (Gloucester) 58
	Capt. David Elwell (Cumberland) 26
	Capt. George Pierce (Gloucester) 16
	Capt. Charlton Sheppard (Salem) 39
	Lt. Ludlam (Cape May) 36

As the British were expected to cross the Delaware River to the general area of Billingsport, General Silas Newcomb committed seven companies of his Militia to Mantua Creek and environs. Seven companies were kept in readiness at Woodbury to aid in the defense of Fort Mercer or to move to any point of British invasion of Gloucester County. Cooper's Creek was guarded by 37 men and a larger force of 60 was stationed at the important area around the ferry at Gloucester City.

It is noteworthy that companies were present from Cape May, Cumberland, Gloucester and Salem Counties, a tribute to General Silas Newcomb, thought by many of his peers to be too cantankerous and old, albeit he was only 54.

On November 15, 1777, the Americans "opened a Battery of two Guns, near (the) Tench Francis House, against the Somerset of 64 (guns), the Isis of 50" and several additional British warships. The South Jersey Artillery kept the British at bay and come nightfall, the "Ships droped down" the river. This action, of course, took place near the mouth of Mantua Creek; however, the Americans were to suffer the loss of Fort Mifflin, leaving only an out-numbered American Navy and the troops at Fort Mercer as deterrents to a complete British victory in the Delaware Valley.

Colonel William Bradford reported to President Wharton of Pennsylvania on November 16th that "...Fort Mifflin is fallen. What will become of our Fleet? I know not. To lay under Red Bank is impossible. If they retreat to LADS Cove, a Battery or two on League Island will reach them. I suppose we shall have Ships up again today."

On November 17th, Colonel Christopher Greene, the commanding officer at Fort Mercer, reported to General George Washington that the situation was worsening:

"Our fleet here are now moving as fast as possible to Timber Creek. The river is so open to the enemy's shipping, that top sail and other vessels are now passing between Mud Island and Providence Island to the Schuylkill, unmolested. Fort Mercer is tolerably secure

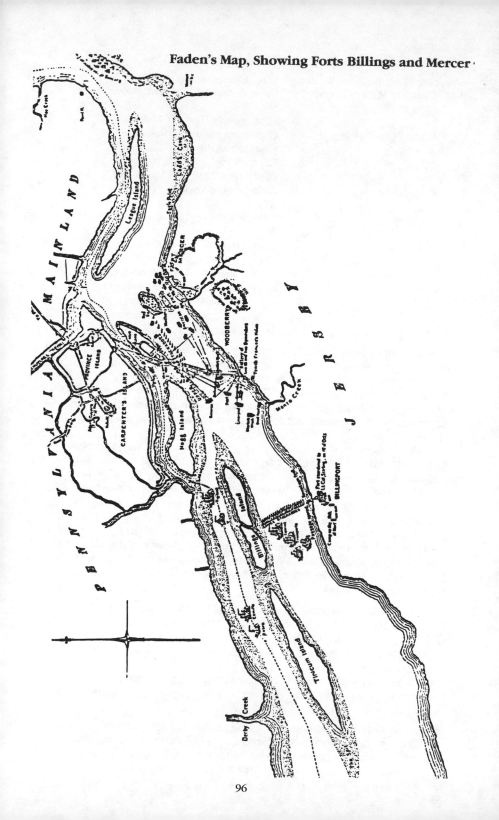

A True Return of the number of Officers and Privates in General Newcomb's Brigade in Service & Stationed at Woodbury November 12 1777

Names of Captains	Captain	Lieutenant	Ensign	Sergeant	Corporal	Drum & Fife	Privates	The place where each Company are Stationed
Capt Chesman	1	1		3	3		50	Stationed at Woodbury or Town
Capt Thorn	1	1	-	2	2	-	27	at the Mouth of ...
Capt Browning	1	1	1	2	3	---	37	Cooper Creek
Capt Ashers	1	1	1	3	3	--	37	Mantua Creek Mouth
Capt Pintors	1	1	1	4	2	--	19	at Woodbury
Capt Dickinson	1	2	1	4	4	1	49	Do
Capt Shepherd	1	2	1	3	3	1	39	Do
Capt Brown	1	2	1	4	4	1	58	do
Capt Elwell	1	1	1	3	-	2	26	Do
Capt Pierce	1	1	-	1	1	-	16	Do
Lieut Ludlam	1	1		2	2	-	36	Do
Capt ... Rochie	1	2	.	4	4	-	57	at Mantua Creek Bridge
Capt ...	1	2	.	4	4	1	40	Do
Capt Davis	1	2	1	4	4	1	55	Do
Capt Mauford	1	1	1	3	3	--	20	Do
Col ... Battalion	2	4	2	6	6	1	60	at Gloster
	16	25	12	52	46	8	626	
Capt Pierson	1	1	1	3	2		40	Jn Smith Big Island
Total	17	26	13	55	50	8	666	

Newcomb's Return of November 12, 1777

against a storm only."

With the fall of Fort Mifflin, Colonel Greene informed General Washington the "the communication to Red Bank, by water, is nearly intercepted; and should a party of the enemy invest this fort by land, our whole supply would be cut off; and, should they erect bomb-batteries on the land side, they would be able to throw shot to us on all sides."

On the same day, Brigadier General James Varnum noted in a dispatch from Fort Mercer to General Washington that:

"A considerable Number of Shipping have moved up this Day & anchored off Billingsport. It is probable they may intend landing the Troops from New York which in Addition to those already there (I mean Billingsport) may be such as to put it out of my Power to prevent a Siege."

Indeed, as it came to pass, on November 18th, upwards of 5,000 crack British troops under Lord Cornwallis were to land at Billingsport to begin the invasion of "Old Gloucester County." If they could not be contained and were able to march successfully northward, the Americans at Fort Mercer would find themselves totally outmanned. In addition, Varnum told George Washington that if the "Enemy should attempt crossing Timber and Manto Creeks at the same Time, Woodberry will be a more ineligible Situation than Haddonfield, as it will throw my Troops between the Enemy's Front and Fort Mercer."

At 8:30 P.M. on November 18, 1777, Brigadier General James Potter reported to George Washington that the British were "all Imbarked on Bord their ships and gon over to the Jarsey -- Redbank must now fall." At 9:30, Colonel Joseph Reed gave Washington more specific information on the British movements towards "Old Gloucester County:"

"...the Troops began to embark at 11 oclock this Morning & past over to Billingsport with their Cannon, Waggons &c. --they made no Secret of their Intentions to attack Red Bank --They gave out their Number was 5000."

From the Journal of the British spy, Major John Andre, it is learned that "Sir Thomas Wilson with the Troops from New York, viz. the 7th, 26th, 83rd, two Battalions (German) of Anspach and Corps of Jaegers landed on the Jersey shore at Billingsport. They were joined there by Lord Cornwallis." Andre also noted on November 18th that "the Rebels appeared busy in landing cannon or other navy stores at Red Bank."

The British Engineer, Archibald Robertson, noted in his Diary on November 18th that the British troops "Embark'd in small Craft and flat Boats and in the Evening we all Landed at Billings Port." On the morning of the 19th, Lord Cornwallis began to prepare for the march to Woodbury and Fort Mercer. From Robertson, it is learned that on the "19th employ'd in getting Waggons, etc., for our march. Went up to Manto (Mantua) Creek to reconnoitre...This night 2 Companies Light Infantry were landed the other side of the mouth of Manto Creek to see if the Battery was evacuated." This was, of course, the two gun battery located on the Tench Francis farm near modern Paulsboro. It was manned by the West Jersey Artillery and one of the officers present was a great Gloucester County patriot, Captain Franklin Davenport.

At 5 P.M. on November 19th, Brigadier General James Varnum, the senior American officer present at Woodbury, sent the following intelligence to George Washington:

"My Videts have just informed me from Manto Creek Bridge, Sunton (Mount Royal), that the Enemy moved three Hours since with about one Thousand towards that Bridge, but as it was taken up...I imagine their Principal Manoeuvre was filing off from their Rear to their Right, in Order to cross five Miles above, where the Creek is easily fordible..."

It is important to remember that the South Jersey Militia fought the British advance, tooth and nail, from Fort Billings (Paulsboro) to Woodbury by destroy-

ANDRÉ

Major John Andre, Noted British Spy of the American Revolution

LORD CORNWALLIS.

Lord Cornwallis - Commander of British Troops at Woodbury, November 1777

ing bridges and by constant attack upon the British flanks. Infact, Major John Clarke, Jr., an intelligence officer for General Washington, reported back to Delaware at 8 A.M. on November 20th that the Americans and British "were skirmishing yesterday at 4 P.M., between the advanced (British) parties at Mantua Creek & Woodberry; today I expect the matter decided."

Archibald Robertson has provided us with a more complete British point of view on the same action:

> "20th early in the Morning other 2 Companys were sent over and found the Battery evacuated and a 24-Pounder unspiked...This day the 1st Light Infantry were advanced to the Bridge at Sand Town (Mount Royal) over Manto Creek...and repaired the Bridge which was Broke in the Centre, the Creek about 25 Yards broad."

When one considers that the main American force was stationed at Fort Mercer and around Woodbury, it is the more remarkable that the greatly outmanned South Jersey Militia was able to delay the 5000 man British Army as long as it did. Infact, Brigadier General James Varnum, writing from Haddonfield, at 11 A.M. on the 20th, reported to George Washington that it did not appear that the Americans could further contain the advancing British and that the commanding officer at Fort Mercer, Colonel Christopher Greene, had given "Orders for an Evacuation. The Powder by Capt. Duplisses was strewed over the Fort."

The authority for the potential evacuation and destruction of Fort Mercer was contained in a communication from Generals A. St. Clair, Baron De Kalb and Henry Knox to James Varnum. It was their opinion that because the invading

British force was superior to the American defenders, Varnum should remove his troops to the other side of Big Timber Creek. If that came to pass, Fort Mercer was to be blown up. This is an important point to remember, for later Varnum was to come under heavy attack for withdrawing from Fort Mercer and Woodbury.

As for Varnum, he assured General Washington that the Americans at Fort Mercer and Woodbury had "bro't off many Stores; a large Number of Waggons have gone this Morning for the same Purposes. I believe possession will be ours 'till we can get away every thing valuable, except the heavy Cannon, or till a strong Force might again be sent in." As will be seen an approximately 2000 man force under Major General Nathaniel Greene arrived in New Jersey too late to save Fort Mercer.

Jeremiah Greenman noted in his "Diary" on November 18th and 19th: "we hear a number of the Enemy is marching for this post (Fort Mercer), at 10 oclock at night we received orders to march and struck our tents, loading them into waggons & took what provision we liked...destroyed the remainder, then proceeded on to Haddon Field where we made a halt."

On November 20th, Greenman wrote that the Americans were "continuing in Haddonfield...a party of men sent back to ye fort with a Serjeant to stay there till ye enemy appeared then to blow ye fort up...Sum waggons ariv'd this afternoon with sum clothes...a quanterty of flower came in from the fort..."

From Archibald Robertson, it is learned that by daybreak of November 21st, the British Army "march'd by the Bridge over Manto Creek...The 7th and 63d Regiments were posted here to keep up the Communications with Billingsport and to Collect Cattle. The rest of the Army went to Woodbury where they were encamp'd (3½ miles) on very advantageous ground round the Village. The 1st Light Infantry took Possession of Red Bank and the Bridge over Timber Creek which was Broke up" by the retreating Americans.

While the British remained encamped at Woodbury, Colonel Joseph Ellis, commanding officer of the Gloucester County Militia, reported to Major General Nathaniel Greene that "Lord Cornwallis quarter'd at Mr. Coopers." This house was the home of John Cooper, the noted "Old Gloucester County" patriot and politician.

Fortunately, the Americans were able to withdraw from Fort Mercer and Woodbury in fairly good order. Brigadier General James Varnum, now at Mount Holly with his troops, reported the situation to George Washington on November 21, 1777:

> "Last Evening Fort Mercer was evacuated. Some of the Shipping burnt this Morning. Most of the Stores bro't safely off. The Enemy, part at Billingsport, part between Manto & Timber Creeks, and some at Fort Mercer."

Varnum, despite the loss of Woodbury and Fort Mercer, remained optimistic, for he notified Washington that "General Huntington has already joined me. General Greene is at Burlington. The Militia amount to Twelve Hundred. Three Hundred here, seven Hundred at Haddonfield...Two Hundred at Coopers Ferry and Gloucester...With the great Force you have ordered, we shall be superior, I believe, to the Enemy in the Field." Interestingly, Varnum noted that the South Jersey Militia "'dont like the Manoeuvre.'"

There was to be much controversy surrounding the surrender of Fort Mercer and the evacuation of the American troops to Haddonfield and Mount Holly.

Major-General Nathaniel Greene

Perhaps none expressed the bitterness more strongly than Colonel William Bradford's comments from Burlington to Pennsylvania President Thomas Wharton on November 22nd:

> "It is astonishing to think of the Precipiate retreat from Fort Mercer; they seemed determined not to see the Enemy. How General Varnum will account for this, others must judge. There was at the Fort and at Woodbury at least 1800 men. Thursday, General Huntington with 1200 crossed...going down to their assistance, but were turned back yesterday by General Varnum, and are all now at Mount Holly."

The long awaited Major General Nathaniel Greene was enroute from Burlington with "2000 men, also on their way to Red Bank, so that had the Fort made a small show of Resistance, a relief would have come and a noble Fleet had been saved," lamented Colonel William Bradford.

Writing from Mount Holly on November 23, 1777, Colonel Christopher Greene sent Governor William Livingston his official report of what transpired at Red Bank:

"On the 19th early in the Morning having information of a very large body of the Enemy passing Manty Creek, & being previously informed by a Number of General Officers from Head Quarters that a Seige (was possible) Red Bank could not be speedely Raisd from Hed quarters, it being their Sentiment that the Fort (Mercer) could not hold out 24 hours in a Seige -- and that it be evacuated before we were shut in by the Enemy."

Colonel Greene stated further that "at 4 oClock in the Morning with the unanimous Voice of the Officers put up what Stores we had (and) Teams to (bring) off, & March (ed) past Timber Creek, leaving only a Guard to blow up the Magazine (after they should receive my particular Orders.) But finding my patrole had given false information concerning the Movements of the Enemy, I returned to the Fort with 250 Men & had Time to git out the Ammunition & Stores and most articles of Particular Service, with some of the Cannon, which were bro't to Hadenfield...the Magizine was on the 21 instant Blown up..."
Greene concluded with great optimism:

"General Greene with his Division & with several Reinforcements, with General Varnum's party & (the) Red Bank Garrison are now in this Place which in the whole make up a very respectable Command, sufficient I hope to Turn the Tables in the Gerscys and that very soon I expect we shall pay the Enemy a Formal Visit..."

As for the tragic burning of the American Fleet, the Continental Navy Board notified General George Washington from Bordentown on November 23 as follows:

"It is with the greatest concern that we inform you of the total destruction of the Continental Fleet at Red Bank; having been burned by our own Officers in Consequence of a Determination of a Council of War."

Some of the small American vessels sailed further up the river towards Bordentown, but as the wind was light, the heavier vessels, "the Continental Brig Andora Doria, Xebechs, Repulse and Champion, sloops Race Horse & Fly, with the Province (Pennsylvania Navy) ships and two Floating Batteries," were set on fire. According to Colonel William Bradford, the firing and burning of the American vessels "made a most terrible conflagration, to the great joy of our cruel & wicked enemies, and much to the depression of my spirits."

From the Philadelphia side, Robert Morton noted in his Journal that he had "walked down to the wharf and see all the American Navy on fire coming up with the flood tide, and burning with the greatest fury...They burnt nearly 5 hours; 4 of them blew up." Elizabeth Drinker noted in her diary that the "Americans had set their whole Fleet on fire...We had a fair sight of ye blazing Fleet from our upper windows."

Captain John Montresor, a British officer, noted in his Journal that the Americans had "burnt 15 Topsail vessels and 15 galleys got up the river...Rebel Fleet here cost five hundred thousand pounds Sterling currency." An unconfirmed rumor of the day, connected with the burning of the American fleet, was that the British "had burnt Woodbury."

Much mystery remains as to what happened to Brigadier General Silas Newcomb, commanding officer of the South Jersey Militia, during the British march
to Woodbury and the destruction of Fort Mercer. On November 15th, Brigadier
General Varnum had reported to George Washington that "the Militia are without a Command," but he did not indicate that this was a permanent situation. In
any event, it appears that Newcomb returned to his home in Cumberland
County and that Colonel Joseph Ellis of the Gloucester County Militia assumed
command, for in a letter dated November 24, 1777 from Haddonfield, Ellis sent
Major General Greene a report of the militia under his command: "about 400
effectives at this place, and about 100 in the neighbourhood below Manto
Creek."

Colonel Ellis also reported to Major General Greene on the positioning of the
British troops in "Old Gloucester County:"

> "...their main strength is at Woodbury, and their lines extend from
> Manto Creek, to Little Timber Creek, an extent of six or seven
> miles; their whole force about 5000, consisting of British, Hessians,
> and Marines; The Marines are employ'd in destroying the Works at
> Red Bank; when that is effected they give out, they intent moveing
> their Army upwards, to Burlington and Mount Holly; Their Post at
> Woodbury is advantageous & difficult to attack...The Enemy have 8
> or 9 Field pieces on the different Roads near Woodbury..."

Nathaniel Greene was disturbed about the comments from Colonel Ellis that
"The Hospitals in the Jerseys are greatly complained of -- they prove a grave for
many of the poor Soldiery -- principally oweing to the Negligence of the Sur-
geons who have the care of the hospitals." Greene asked General George
Washington to send "good trusty Officers to inspect the Management of the
Hospitals & to remain there until regularly relieved."

While the main force of the British Army remained at Woodbury, small detachments were sent into the countryside in search of livestock, which the British planned to take back to Philadelphia as soon as they had secured the area
around Gloucester City.

On November 24, 1777, the name of the young French nobleman, the Marquis de Lafayette, appears in a communique from Brigadier General George
Weedon of Virginia to General Greene: "We only arrived here a few minutes
ago. Some of our parties have taken 9 prisoners...From them we have had I
believe a pretty exact account of their numbers, which the Marquis (Lafayette)
will enclose you a particular account of." Weedon noted that the British force
he had observed amounted to "4250, 60 pieces of Artillery and 100 Light
Horse."

From the Diary of the British Engineer, Archibald Robertson, it is learned that
the British troops under Lord Cornwallis began to evacuate Woodbury early in
the morning of November 24th: "At daybreak the Army marched from Woodbury and encamped between Little and Great Timber Creeks by which both
flanks were secured." By daybreak of the 25th, Robertson noted that the "3 Regiments from Red Bank joined us and the whole marched to Gloucester (City),
where we encamped between Newton and Little Timber Creeks."

Confirmation of the British troop movement is confirmed by Brigadier
General Weedon in this intelligence report to General Greene: "They have...ad-
vanced on this side Great Timber Creek with their Main Body, and have pitched
on this side of Little Timber Creek also -- Some of the prisoners were taken

Major-General LaFayette led American Troops against the British at Gloucester City during November 1777

within two miles of the town (Gloucester City) -- They have no troops at Red Bank, and but few at Billingsport. The prisoners say they intend crossing the Delaware at Cooper's Ferry (Camden.)"

At this point, an unknown Gloucester County heroine was sent on an intelligence mission behind the British lines. From a communique from Colonel Adams Comstock to General Greene, dated November 25, 1777, it is learned:

"This moment I arrived from a reconnoitering tour near Little Timber Creek Bridge, sent a smart young woman who had a sister in Gloster as a spy to Gloster; she has returned and I believe has received no other damage than receiving a kiss from the Hessian General (This is as she says.)"

The girl reported to Comstock that "a very large number of British & Hessian troops are in Gloster, that they are embarking in boats & going to Philadelphia, and that her sister there informed her they had been embarking over since early in the morning." Both the senior British and Hessian officers "asked the young woman where the Rebels were? She answered, she could not tell -- she had seen none of them."

There was extensive contact between the American and British troops in the area of present day Gloucester City, as the British attempted to send over their troops and the live-stock foraged from the farmers of Gloucester County. Comstock reported to General Greene that "Seven prisoners just arrived here (Haddonfield) from the Enemy taken by the Militia, about 3 miles from this place on the road to Glos'ter...The Prisoners...say the Main Body Lye about 4 miles from this on the Gloster Road encamp'd that their Line form a Tryangle, that they are to wait there till they have embark'd all the Stock for Philadelphia...& that the Army expects to embark tomorrow and go into winter Quarters..." Comstock in great heroic passion concluded: "O how I want to give em a Floging before they Leave the Gersey."

On the evening of November 25th, Archibald Robertson noted in his Journal that "the Jagers were attacked. They had 1 officer and 4 or 5 killed and about 20 wounded and 1 officer. The loss of the Rebels uncertain." Captain John Montresor reported in his Journal that "In our attack in the Jersey under Lord Cornwallis, we lost 31 Jagers killed, wounded, and missing."

The attack on the Jagers and Hessians was led by the Marquis de Lafayette in command of 300 men, including 150 of the South Jersey Militia and 150 of Morgan's Rifles. Fortunately a letter survives from Lt. Azariah More of the Second Battalion of the Cumberland County Militia. More wrote to his brother:

"We have had an engagement with the party of the Enemy this evening (November 25th) near Little Timber Creek, in which we have lost Lieutenant Mulford, as brave a man as ever lived...We have no other loss in our company except Thomas Harris who had his arm broken..."

Lt. More told his brother that "we have ten or twelve prisoners with three artillery horses branded G.R. Our light horse took three grenadiers yesterday with no loss on our side. We have Morgan's Riflemen with us. I believe as fine a body of men as any on earth."

Lieutenant Azariah More of the Cumberland County Militia also reported to his brother at "11 o'clock at night, 25th of November 1777," that the Americans had "been expecting re-inforcements several days, sufficient for a general action...and it is now reported and I am ready to believe that the enemy are crossing the river at Gloucester Ferry." More said hopefully that it was "expected that we shall have none of them (the British) in Jersey by to-morrow morning. If it should be true I shall conclude that they have taken fright at our torpedoes."

Actually Lord Cornwallis did not dare chance a full-scale confrontation with the seasoned, regular troops of Major General Nathaniel Greene, a general officer often compared with the brilliant Benedict Arnold and with the commander-in-chief, General George Washington. In addition, Cornwallis had been led to believe that Greene had a much larger troop concentration than actually existed, hence he hoped to ferry over to Philadelphia all the confiscated "Old Gloucester County" livestock and then his troops before Greene arrived at Gloucester City.

Writing to General Washington from Haddonfield, at 4 P.M. on November 26, 1777, Nathaniel Greene lamented that he was "sorry our march will prove a fruitless one -- the enemy have drawn up to cover the troops -- there is but one road that leads down to the point." Greene pointed out that "on each side the ground is swampy, & full of thick underbrush, that it makes the approaches impracticable almost."

Major General Greene realized that the British fleet would cut his men to pieces, as it was "so posted as to cover the troops, and this country is so intersected with creeks, that approaches are rendered extremely difficult, and retreats very dangerous." Even so, Greene proudly told Washington that he had "a fine body of troops & in fine spirits, & every one appears to wish to come to action" against the British.

The Marquis de Lafayette also dispatched a communique to General Washington from Haddonfield on November 26th about his encounter with the British and Hessians in "Old Gloucester County" a day earlier. Lafayette had marched his men down the road from Haddonfield towards Gloucester City. When he was two miles from town, he encountered a 350 man force of Hessians, including artillery, which was posted there to prevent the Americans from impeding the transporting of the livestock and British troops to Philadelphia.

Lafayette's troops, Morgan's Rifles and units of the South Jersey Militia, drove the Hessians from their position, forcing them to retreat within one mile of Gloucester City itself. Lord Cornwallis, apprehensive that General Greene was about to make a full-scale attack on the embarking British forces, marched out to cover the retreat of the harassed German mercenaries. As Lafayette proudly phrased it: "We pushed the Hessians more than half a mile...and we made them run very fast; British reinforcements came twice to them, very far from recovering their ground, they went always back."

The Marquis informed General Washington that he "had ten light horse with Mr. Lindsey, almost a hundred and fifty riflemen, under Colonel Butler, and two piquets of militia, commanded by Colonels Hite (Haight) and Ellis: my whole body was not three hundred." Despite the intensity of the American attack, casualties were rather light, for Lafayette reported: "We left one single man killed, a lieutenant of militia, and only five of ours were wounded." This confirms Lt. Azariah More's report to his brother of the death of Lt. David Mulford of the Cumberland County Militia during the Battle of Gloucester City.

At this point of research, it has been possible to identify some of the South Jersey Militia who participated in the late November 1777 action against the British and Hessians in the areas around Big and Little Timber Creeks and Gloucester City. In addition to Colonel Joseph Ellis of the Gloucester County Militia, it has been learned that Captain Robert Brown of Swedesbor saw action, as well as Captain Jacob Browning of Waterford Township and Private Zadock Bowen of Galloway Township. While the above mentioned were from "Old Gloucester County," Lt. Colonels Benjamin Holme and William Shute, as well as Captain Jacob DuBois were from the Salem County Militia. Captain Levi Preston, Lt. Ephraim Lummis and Private Samuel Westcott from the Cumberland County Militia have been identified as participants against the British and Hessians. Without doubt, with additional research, it will be possible to expand the list of South Jersey Militia-men who engaged the British and Hessians from the moment they landed at Billingsport and embarked for Philadelphia from Gloucester City.

As for the Hessians who encountered Lafayette on the Haddonfield-Gloucester City Road, the Marquis noted that he understood they "had between twenty-five and thirty wounded, at least that number killed...we got yet, this day, fourteen prisoners..." Of the Americans, he told General Washington: "I never saw men so merry, so spirited, so desirous to go on to the enemy, whatever forces they could have...I found the riflemen above even their reputation, and the militia above all expectations I could have." At long last, the South Jersey Militia under the command of Colonel Joseph Ellis of "Old Gloucester County" received favorable plaudits.

From Major General Nathaniel Greene, it is learned that once Lord Cornwallis and his British and Hessian troops had departed "Old Gloucester County," the main American troops were also able to cross the Delaware River at Burlington in order to join forces with General George Washington at the temporary headquarters at White Marsh in Pennsylvania:

> "I purpose to leave General Varnum's Brigade & the rifle corps at this place (Haddonfield) for a few days, especially the rifle men who cover the country very much...My division, Huntington's & Glover's Brigades will proceed with all despatch to join your Excellency -- I could wish the enemy might leave the Jersies before us."

In a communique from Mount Holly, dated November 27, Major General Greene informed George Washington that "the greater part of the troops returned to this place last night and marched early this morning to cross the Delaware -- I staid at Haddonfield myself with General McDougal's division to give the necessary Orders to the Militia -- I have left the rifle Corps at Haddonfield and Capt's Lee's troop of light Horse to encourage the Militia and awe the enemy."

On November 27th, Jeremiah Greenman noted in his Diary: "this morn we marcht from the woods...came to morestown ware our tents was...ordered to be in readyness for a march." And finally on the 28th, he wrote: "this morn at ye beet of ye genl (General) struck our tents...came as far as burlington ware we made a halt...then crost ye Diliware..." Little could Greenman have known what a winter the Americans would have to endure at Valley Forge.

As a portent of things to come at Valley Forge during the winter of 1777-1778, Greene now at Burlington on November 28, told Washington that it was "with the most difficulty we can get bread to eat -- the Commissary of purchase of flour is very ill managed -- there is no magazines of consequence, and the army serv'd from hand to mouth."

At last, Nathaniel Greene was able to inform his commander-in-chief that "Three Brigades are now on their march for Head Quarters, my division & Glover's Brigade -- General McDougall's division is not yet come to town (Burlington) -- they had orders to march at four this morning...I am afraid the want of provisions has detained them this morning -- Mr. Tench Francis an uncle of Col. Tilghman was brought to me as a Prisoner this morning...he was taken at Glocester -- he said Lord Cornwallis's detachment consisted of about 6,000 that none embarked untill yesterday (November 27th)."

From the November 27th entry in the Journal of the British spy, Major John Andre, the intelligence given the Nathaniel Greene by Mr. Tench Francis from Billingsport is confirmed: "Lord Cornwallis having sent over his baggage and cattle, crossed from Glocester...The Rebels had assembled in his rear and began firing on the last Troops who embarked, but the Vigilant, a galley and an armed schooner having brought their guns and cross their fire upon the places where they were collecting, dispersed them."

Of this last large scale operation against the British in "Old Gloucester County" during 1777, the British Enginner, Archibald Robertson, reported that Lord Cornwallis "had only 4 men slightly wounded" during the final evacuation at Gloucester City. In commemoration of the American-British-Hessian encounters around Big and Little Timbers Creeks during the last week of November 1777, a small memorial tablet may be located near the Holiday Inn on Route 130.

The British response to their victory in the Delaware Valley during November 1777 is well expressed by Lt. Col. William Harcourt in a letter from Philadelphia dated November 29th:

"The reduction of the Forts upon Mud-Island and Red Bank having at last given us possession of the navigation of the De Lawarr, our campaign draws near to a conclusion; and though we may still affect to hold the language of driving the Rebel Army over the River Susquehannah, I am inclined to think our Operations will be confined to little more than the procuring such supplies of Provisions and Forage, as will enable us to pass our time somewhat more at ease than during the last Winter."

Recently a remarkable document has been located at the Massachusetts Historical Society, in which Colonel Joseph Ellis, commanding officer of the South Jersey Militia, gave a full report of the military situation to Governor William Livingston on December 6, 1777. Writing from his military headquarters in Haddonfield, Ellis said:

"I take the liberty to acquaint you of the present State of the Army at this Post, which is composed of Militia from Different parts of this State, amounting to between two & three hundred men, the most of whose times will expire in a few days. Some new draughts coming out of this (Old Gloucester) & the lower countys; what number is very uncertain, but in all probability shall be very weak considering that an extent of country has been exposed to the Depredations of the Enemy from their Shipping alone."

Colonel Ellis pointed out that "...If a few Continental Troops can be obtained, it would be of Singular advantage to act with the Militia here, or if that cannot be obtain'd, some of the Militia from the Eastern part of this State will be absolutely necessary, as there still remain a very considerable quantity of Stock such as Cattle, Hoggs...Near the River, which cannot possibly be drove off without being Entirely lost to the owners for want of Means to Subsist them. In the Enemy's late Rout through part of this State vizt. from Byllings-Port to Gloucester, it is Suppos'd they took off near 2000 Hogs and a great quantity of cattle..."

In praising the oft maligned South Jersey Militia, Ellis said: "To the Honour of what few Militia we had...in the Field, I must needs say they have been the means of Saving a considerable quantity of Public Stores and Much Private Property by constantly keeping near the Enemy and preventing Small Parties from Plundering without their lines."

Colonel Ellis told Governor Livingston: "We are in great Want of Ammunition & Flints; a number of the Militia coming in from the Lower countys of this State Entirely unprovided. Should be glad to know where to apply for these articles." It was imperative that the Militia have the means to defend themselves, for as Ellis reported: "The Enemy keep their Post at Byllings-port where they are fortified. I have posted a few men at Swedesborough and a party at Woodberry who I hope will be able to keep them pretty close in their Quarters." Indeed, the Revolution was far from over for the residents of "Old Gloucester County" and the existence of a British fortification at Billingsport was a constant reminder that they must pay constant vigilance or perish at the hands of the British and their Tory supporters.

Another important issue addressed by Colonel Ellis was that of money for his Militia. He told Governor Livingston that "we are likewise under a disadvantage for want of a paymaster, the pay being difficult to come, it causeth much grumbling among the Men; some of them having two months pay due. If a proper Person were appointed for that Purpose, residing handy to this place it would have a good Effect, as most of the Men serving in the Militia are (needful?) for their money when due."

The New Jersey Council of Safety met at Princeton on December 12th and the first two items on the agenda concerned the troops of Colonel Ellis. It was stated that "Application was made to the Board for the payment of the Money due to the Militia in the County of Gloucester under the Command of Col. Ellis." It was then agreed "That Col. Ellis be informed by Letter that the Legislature have directed the Delegates to obtain from Congress the sum of 120,000 for discharging the debt due to the Militia of this State, and the proportion of 16,000 dollars when obtained will be paid into the Hands of Thomas Carpenter for the payment of the Militia of Gloucester & Salem."

At Princeton on December 13th, the Commander-in-Chief of the New Jersey Military Forces, Governor William Livingston, requested "that every Captain or Commanding Officer in the Militia of this State, do forthwith make a return of the number of men in his company, and of their accoutrements and ammunition, to the Colonel or Commanding Officer of a regiment belonging to the brigades of Generals Forman and Newcomb, make return of the condition of his regiment..."

It is interesting that Governor William Livingston still considered Brigadier General Silas Newcomb in command of the South Jersey Militia, for Newcomb had resigned on December 4th, and was officially replaced by Colonel Joseph Ellis of "Old Gloucester County."

From the "Diary" of Jeremiah Greenman, it is learned that General Washington's troops arrived at Valley Forge on December 19th: "this morn ye hold camp moved about 6 miles & stoped in a thick woods ware a corn field stud by...about 10 acres not gathered...in 5 minits it was all gethered & sum of it to the fire."

On December 20th, Greenman wrote: "Continuing near vally forg...we drawed axes to build huts for ye winter...we began our huts...order'd to build them with logs 14 feet one way & 16 ye other...Continuing building our huts..."

The New Jersey Council of Safety agreed on December 22nd "...that Col. Ellis be authorized to remove any Cattle, Sheep & Hogs (excepting Milch Cows) from any places of greater security." As the winter of 1777/78 wore on, the livestock of "Old Gloucester" and Salem counties would be increasingly coveted by the British as supplies diminished on the Philadelphia side of the Delaware River.

Chapter VII
Foraging in South Jersey, 1778

Prologue

With the capture of Fort Billings in early October 1777 and the destruction of Fort Mercer during late November 1777, the Delaware River, even though not adequately cleared of the Chevaux de Frise, was now open to British shipping and the British Army and Naval commanders believed thay could look forward to a very comfortable winter in Philadelphia. Indeed, as John Jackson has written in his "With The British Army in Philadelphia, 1777—1778," the morale of the British and the civilians of Philadelphia was:

"revived by the colorful spectable of the supply ships, merchantmen, victuallers and transports that lined the city wharves. Supplies and provisions were arriving in quantities sufficient to ease any immediate distress . . . "

In addition to the improved supply lines into the city by ship. many residents of Burlington, 'Old Gloucester" and Salem counties were to become increasingly the "market people," gaining hard British coinage for their beef, mutton, pork, butter, cheese and vegetables. It was, as John Jackson has pointed out that the "farmers were willing to risk running the American blockade to sell their produce for English specie (hard money), a preferable alternative to the almost worthless Continental currency."

Of course, the absence of any significant American military units on the Jersey side of the Delaware River aided the "market-people" in this subversive work, even though Colonel Joseph Ellis and his "Old Gloucester County" Militia valiently attempted to control the flow of trade from South Jersey to the British over the river.

In all fairness, it needs to be pointed out that many of those from South Jersey who trafficked with the British did so for the sheer survival of themselves and their families; however, as Jackson notes: "Loyalists in significant numbers were evident throughout southern Jersey. Gloucester County alone tried,in person or absentia, over one hundred of the most active British partisans . . . "

Governor William Livingston in his letter of November 25th, 1777, to Isaac Collins of the New Jersey Gazette strongly indicated his feelings about the trade with the British in Philadelphia:

"BEING informed that numbers of people, under various pretences, are passing from the state of New-Jersey into the city of Philadelphia, and returning back into New-Jersey, without permission required by law for going into the enemy's lines. To prevent such delinquents from pleading ignorance whenever they may be apprehended, I would acquaint them, thro the channel of your paper, that by an act of this State, it is felony without benefit of clergy, in a man; and in a woman, three hundred pounds fine, or one year's imprisonment . . . "

General George Washington, writing from Valley Forge on December 31st,

1777, urged Governor William Livingston of New Jersey to have potential supplies of food for the British troops and forage for their animals removed from the Jersey shores of the Delaware River and Bay, lest they fall into British hands. Towards this end, Governor Livingston wrote to Colonel Joseph Ellis on January 8th, 1778:

> "You are directed to remove all the horned Cattle, Sheep & Hogs and all the Cowes which do not give Milk from the Vicinity of the Jersey Shore in the Counties of Burlington, Gloucester and Salem, that may be within reach of the Enemies foraging Parties . . . "

This order to Colonel Ellis did not include all of the comments found in the minutes of the New Jersey Council of Safety, namely that " . . . the Genl (Washington) be informed that the powers lodged in the Council of Safety are inadequate to the requisition of having the Forage removed, & that it be recommended to him to exercise his own authority in having it effected . . . "

Following the orders of the Council of Safety, Governor Livingston, writing to General Washington from Springfield on January 8th, commented as follows:

> "Your Excellency will observe that the Council of Safety have no Authority to order the removal of any other Articles save those mentioned on the orders to Colonel Ellis. So that with respect to Forage & Provisions your Excellency must recur to the Powers vested in you."

A week later, on January 15th, Governor Livingston is found writing to General Washington, pleading with him. as it were, to help put an end to the illegal trade of the "market-people" from Cooper' Ferry (Camden) to Philadelphia. Actually, General Washington did not have the man-power to comply with Livingston's request and he did not have access to the Delaware River waterfronts and the Jersey shore.

To compound the problem, Colonel Joseph Ellis had indicated that his small number of "Old Gloucester County" Militia could not possibly guard every part of territory from Burlington to Salem. As he was to tell General Washington on February 8th: " . . . my troops never exceed 500. The coast is very extensive, and I fear it will not be in our power to Guard every part effectively," thus it was that the British would continue to be partly sustained by South Jersey meat and produce, as well as fire-wood and hay for the British horses.

All during the first weeks of January 1778, living conditions and food shortages were the order of the day for the desperate Americans at Valley Forge. Little hope was in the hearts of many of the officers and men for a better day Gloom and doom were everywhere.

Christopher Marshall in his "Diary" entry of January 18th wrote:

> "My mind seems anxiously concerned on account of our distressed friends and acquaintance, with our brave Gen. Washington, as he and his army are now obliged to encounter all the inclemency of this cold weather, as they with him are living out in the woods with slender covering . . . "

Marshall also felt great compassion for the Americans trapped in Philadelphia. Of them, he wrote:

> "Our poor friends in town, many of them in want of fuel and other necessaries, while our internal enemies, under the protection of

that savage monster Howe, are revelling in luxury, dissipation and drunkenness, without any feelings for the distress of their (once happy) bleeding country. Here I must stop, as the theme is too melancholy and distressing . . . "

A — Valley Forge

From December 19th, 1777 to June 18th, 1778, what remained of General George Washington's Continental Army attempted to endure the ravages of a severe Delaware Valley winter. Indeed, in his "Valley Forge," Harry E Wildes has painted this gloomy portrait:

"Never in the entire Revolution had the men felt so despondent, so weary, or so helpless. Defeat at Brandywine had left them disappointed but still confident . . . failure at Germantown had seemed an accident of weather . . . but now, at Valley Forge, the men were losing hope . . . "

Private Joseph Plumb Martin from Connecticut, a soldier who endured the winter at Valley Forge wrote in his "Narrative of some of the Adventures, Dangers and Sufferings of a Revolutionary Soldier," that the Army prior to leaving Gulph Mills for Valley Forge on the morning of December 19th "was now not only starved but naked. The greatest part were not only shirtless and barefoot, but destitute of all other clothing, especially blankets."

After first reaching Valley Forge after an eight hour march covering a short six miles, Martin tells us that the soldiers were " . . . in a truly forlorn condition — no clothing, no provisions and as disheartened as need be . . . we were now absolutely in danger of perishing, and that too, in the midst of a plentiful country. We then had nothing and saw no likelihood of any betterment of our condition."

Poor Joseph Plumb Martin continued his "Narrative:"

I lay here two nights and one day and had not a morsel of anything to eat all the time, save half of a small pumpkin which I cooked by placing it upon a rock, the skin side upper most, and making a fire upon it. By the time it was heat through I devoured it with as keen an appetite as I should a made of it in some other time."

As difficult as the situation was for the American troops at Valley Forge, it was equally as bad for loyal American civilians in and around Philadelphia. In his "Diary," Christopher Marshall wrote on December 28th, the British were "revelling in balls, attended with every degree of luxury and excess in the City; rioting and wantonly using our homes, utensils and furniture; all this (and) a numberless number of other abuses we endure from that handful of banditti . . . headed by that monster of rapine, General Howe."

In addition to the unhappy scene in Philadelphia, Marshall has given us a vivid insight into conditions in the country:

"Add to this their frequent excursions round about for twenty miles together, destroying and burning what they please, pillaging, plundering men and women, stealing boys above ten years old, deflowering virgins, driving into the City for their use, droves of cattle, sheep (and) hogs; poultry, butter, meal, meat, cider, furniture and clothing of all kinds . . . "

Marshall was very bitter about conditions and he lamented that "all this is done in the veiw of our Generals and our army, who are careless of us, but carefully consulting where thay shall go to spend the winter in jollity, gaming and carousing."

He concluded his entry as follows:

"O tell not this in France or Spain! Publish it not in the streets of London, Liverpool or Bristol, lest the uncircumcised there should rejoice, and shouting for joy, say 'America is ours, for the rebels are dismayed and afraid to fight us any longer!' O Americans, where is your virtue? O Washington, where is your courage?"

Fortunately, General George Washington was possessed of great courage, even in the face of the ugliness encountered at Valley Forge, where he had under his command approximately 11,000 Continentals and Militia when the "wintry ordeal" began. Included in the number of troops were those of Brigadier General William Maxwell's Brigade from New Jersey. The commanding officer of the Second New Jersey Regiment, under Maxwell, was Colonel Israel Shreve, originally of Deptford Township in "Old Gloucester County."

One of the most rewarding sources of information about South Jersey troops at Valley Forge is the "Diary" of Ensign Georg Ewing of Cohansey in Cumberland County. He tells us that at least some of the soldiers of the "Jersey Camp" got into their crude tents as early as January 10th, 1778. Ewing wrote the following on January 29th:

"This day I was on fatigue building a breast work to defend the Middle line of the camp . . . had the pleasure to meet with Mr. David Sayre (a soldier from Salem County) . . .

On the next day, Ewing noted that he had "visited and dined with Lieuts Bowen & Elmer of the Train." Both of these men were officers in Colonel Israel Shreve's 2nd Regiment of Maxwell's Brigade. On February 4th, Ewing wrote happily that he had obtained "a furlough of B.G. Maxwell and prepared to set out in the morning for Cohansey." By the 7th, he had arrived at the "Blue Ball," a tavern on the vicinity of today's Mullica Hill. There he "breakfasted with Major Maskell and Mr. Tomlinson and had the pleasure to ride in Company with them to Roadstown."

George Ewing was fortunate and did not resemble Dr. Albigence Waldo's, a surgeon fom Connecticut, description of an American Soldier at Valley Forge:

"There comes a soldier. His bare feet are seen thro his worn out shoes. His legs nearly naked from the batter'd remains of an only pair of stockings; his breeches not sufficient to cover his nakedness; his shirt hanging in strings; his hair dishevell'd; his face meagre; his whole appearance pictures a person forsaken & discouraged."

The British were well apprised of conditions affecting the Americans, for we learn from the January 21 entry in the "Diary" of the Hessian Captain Friedrich von Muenchhausen, an aid to General William Howe, that:

"The Rebels, we are told, do not like the huts they have built in the hills of Valley Forge nor do they like the lack of rum and clothing. Hence they do not only have many sick but also much desertion far back into the country."

It has been estimated that more than 3000 Americans deserted at Valley Forge, while another 3000 were found "unfit for duty because they are bare foot and otherwise naked." The Marquis de la Fayette wrote sadly that the American "soldiers were in want of everything; they had neither coats, hats, shirts, nor shoes; their feet and legs froze till they had become almost black, and it was often necessary to amputate them" under hospital conditions which were often barbaric and inadequate.

Such were the times that "tried mens' souls" and the Revolutionary Spirit was to continue at a very low ebb. The men were exhausted and there was a constant need for medicine and proper medical care, as well as mere rest, something nearly impossible to obtain because of the cold and snow. As always, there was constant hunger.

Thousands of pounds of flour were needed for bread and there was increasingly little to be found at Valley Forge, even though 1000 barrels were at Reading in February. As John F. Reed had indicated in his "Valley Forge: Crucible of Victory," some of the flour "was shipped down the Schuylkill until falling water put an end to the business. The balance remained at Reading, since wagoners could not be found to undertake the journey."

As the winter wore on, fresh meat was unobtainable, as food animals were to be found neither at Valley Forge, nor in the immediate vicinity, for both the British and the Americans had foraged the area literally to the very bone. Many of the cattle had been driven far from the area by the frightened farmers of Bucks County; however, Joseph Plumb Martin tells us in a humorous manner of one of the poor cows that fell into American hands:

VALLEY FORGE

GEORGE WASHINGTON, ESQUIRE,

GENERAL and COMMANDER in CHIEF of the FORCES
of the UNITED STATES OF AMERICA.

B Y Virtue of the Power and Direction to Me efpe-
cially given, I hereby enjoin and require all Perfons
refiding within feventy Miles of my Head Quarters to
threfh one Half of their Grain by the 1ft Day of February,
and the other Half by the 1ft Day of March next enfuing,
on Pain, in Cafe of Failure of having all that fhall remain in Sheaves after the Period above mentioned, feized
by the Commiffaries and Quarter-Mafters of the Army,
and paid for as Straw

G I V E N *under my Hand, at Head Quarters, near
the Valley Forge, in Philadelphia County,* this 20th
Day of December, 1777.

G. W A S H I N G T O N.

By His Excellency's Command,

ROBERT H. HARRISON, Sec'y.

LANCASTER: PRINTED BY J O H N D U N L A P

(After an original in the library of the Historical Society of Pennsylvania.)

"We stayed at the quartermaster general's quarters till some time in
the afternoon, during which time a beef creature was butchered for
us. I well remember what fine stuff it was; it was quite transparent. I
thought at that time what an excallant lantern it would make. I was,
notwithstanding, very glad to get some of it, bad as it looked."

To further complicate the deteriorating American situation at Valley Forge,
the British were still able to find food, forage and wood, due in great part to the
"market-people" of South Jersey and the farmers of southeastern Pennsylvania.
As General George Wahington phrased it: " The quantity of

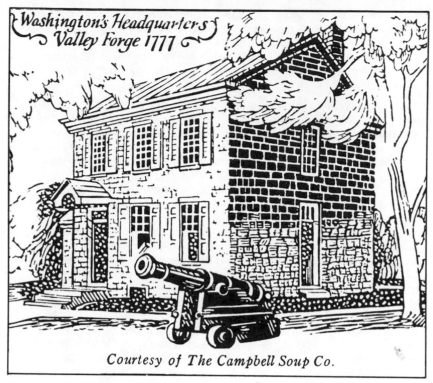

Courtesy of The Campbell Soup Co.

provision . . . carried into Philadelphia . . . is by all accounts so great that the British Army is well supplied with almost every Article needed to survive the winter."

In addition to the food and clothing shortages at Valley Forge, soldier illness continued to sap the Continental Army. Wildes tells us that " . . . three thousand men were reported unfit for duty in the first sick roll at Valley Forge. Within a month, eleven hundred more were added to the list. One day, more than a third of all the soldiers were ordered sent to the hospitals."

It has been estimated that more than 3000 soldiers died "at or as a result of Valley Forge," where upwards of 400 men a month perished. Dr. Benjamin Rush, surgeon general of hospitals, Middle Department, until his resignation in late January 1778, commented that the American military hospitals "robbed the United States of more citizens than the sword," and by far, small pox was the greatest offender, followed by typhus, typhoid, pneumonia, gangrene and severe powder burns. In addition, due to the lack of medical knowledge, a soldier seriously wounded by gun or cannon fire would almost certainly perish.

As for small-pox, Joseph Plumb Martin gives us this poignant comment:

> "When I was innocculated with the small pox, I took that delectable disease, the itch (scabies); it was given us, we suppose, in the infection. We had no opportunity, or at least we had nothing to cure ourselves with during the whole season . . . I had it to such a degree that by the time I got into winter quarters I could scarcely lift my hands to my head . . . "

Fortunately, Martin had "acquaintances in the artillary and by their means," he noted, "procured sulpher enough to cure all that belonged to our detachment, Accordingly, we made preparations for a general attack upon it (the itch)." In his humorous way, Martin concluded: "we killed the itch and we were satisified, for it had almost killed us. This was a decisive victory, the only one we had achieved lately."

A victorious day was to come to the ill and wounded soldiers at Valley Forge, for General Washington commisioned Colonel Bodo Otto to build a military hospital at Yellow Springs, approximately eight miles from the encampment. This hospital, which was to specialize in the treatment of contagious diseases, constructed by Dr, Otto and his collegues became the main Revolutionary hospital and was "the only hospital specially designed for soldier use." Interestingly, Dr. Otto was the father of Colonel Bodo Otto, Jr., a colonel in the "Old Gloucester County Militia" and whose house still stands in Mickleton, New Jersey.

This hospital, which became known as Washington Hall, was a three-story building, some one hundred feet long and thirty-six feet wide. Porches were attached on three sides so that on warm days, the soldier-patients could be taken out into the fresh air. It is of record that more than thirteen hundred typhus cases were handled at Washington Hall, most of them successfully.

In New Jersey, however, poor hospital conditions existed and continued through the fall of 1777 and well into the spring of 1778. Governor William Livingston wrote to Henry Laurens of the Continental Congress that "too many of the Sick are crowded together." He lamented further that the sick were "unprovided with Hospital Sheets, Shirts, and Blankets, and obliged to lie on Shirts and Blankets they have worn during the whole Campaign."

In the American hospital at Princeton, Livingston told Laurens that fifty soldiers a day were dying and ". . . should the same Number be kept up till the first day of April," at least 4500 would perish. Livingston was especially concerned that there were at least 5000 wounded and ill soldiers in hospitals in New Jersey and Pennsylvania, whereas "General Howe by the best information . . . has only one Thousand in all the hospitals in Philadelphia."

British medical officers were constantly faced with soldier hygiene problems, however John Jackson has written in his "With the British Army in Philadelphia, 1777-1778," that:

"Not withstanding the Great Care and attention that has been paid to Render the state house Barracks particularly Clean and Comfortable, some of the men have been so beastly as to ease themselves (urinate) on the Stairs and Lower area of the House between doors . . . the Centry . . . is to put a stop to such scandalous behaviour . . . "

Soldier hygience was also a problem with the American Army at Valley Forge; however, with training and with the advent of Washington Hall, there was a decided improvement on the medical level. Not so with the food situation, for General Washington was constantly being reminded by his officers that something had to be done in early February, 1778.

Washington called in the "only commisionary in camp, and with him this melencholy and alarming truth, that he had not a single hoof to slaughter and not more than twenty-five barrels of flour." General Washington then noted: "I am convinced beyond a doubt that unless some great and capital change suddenly takes place . . . this army must inevitably be reduced to one or the other of these three things — starve, disolve, or disperse in order to obtain subsistance."

Brigadier General Jamed M. Varnum of Rhode Island notified Washington that his troops had "been destitute of bread; two days we have been entirely without meat." In additon, Varnum told General Nathaniel Greene, now the American Quartermaster General, on February 14th, that "in all human probibility the army must dissolve."

On February 17th, Colonel John Laurens, an aid to General George Washington, pleaded: "We have lately been in a alarming state for want of provision." A week later, general Nathaniel Greene wrote to General Henry Knox:

> "The army has been in great distress since you left . . . the troops are getting naked. They were seven days without meat, and several days without bread . . . We are still in danger of starving. Hundreds of horses have already starved to death."

At this sorry moment in the fortunes of the suffering Americans at Valley Forge, General George Washington ordered General Anthony Wayne to proceed to Wilmington, Delaware, where he was to seek passage over the Delaware River to Salem County. As John F. Reed wrote:

> "Washington detached Wayne to New Jersey with 550 men picked for their physical condition and the comparative excellence of their equipment and clothing."

The Wayne expedition to South Jersey was to be a fruitful one in terms of the animals and forage collected for the suffering army at Valley Forge.

B - The Great Cattle Drive

Of all the Revolutionary War contributions of General Anthony Wayne and Captain John Barry that have relevance to South Jersey and "Old Gloucester County," perhaps none exceed in importance than their joint mission to Salem County, which began on the morning on February 19th, 1778. It occurred during the intense winter at Valley Forge, where the starving remnants of General Washington's decimated army were on the brink of capitulation.

In a last ditch attempt to obtain food and forage, Washington hoped that Wayne would be able to obtain passage over the Delaware River for his 550 troops. Fortunately, General Wayne was directed to Captain John Barry who transported Wayne's force over the river on the available vessels, row galleys and others. Wayne notified General Washington of the expedition as follows:

> "I landed in New Jersey the 19th and prepared to Salem the same evening. The next morning I sent out several detachments to collect cattle . . . It was difficult to meet any cattle altho the country abounded with them; however, I have got together upwards of one hundred and fifty head . . . Upon hearing that the Enemy were about to land at Burlington, I attempted to pass the cattle over at New Castle, but this failing have sent them by way of Mount Holly."

General Anthony Wayne

Captain John Barry

General Anthony Wayne remained in Salem County for three days and was only slightly successful in obtaining cattle and forage. By February 21st, "The Great Cattle Drive" began at Mannington and moved no more than eight miles a day, according to Dr. William D. and Ruth Timmins in their, "The Great Cow Chase, 1776—1976."

It has been generally agreed by historians that Wayne collected no more than the 150 cattle he reported. These came from the area from Elsinboro to Mannington and from the western side of Alloway's Creek; however, all of the Salem County farmers were not cooperative with Wayne and hundreds of animals were hidden in the woods and tall swamp grass.

It is possible to document the lack of cooperation by turning to a primary source Salem County Inquisition, dated August 26, 1778. It is found that Samuel Bacon, perhaps a Tory, did not wish to sell his livestock to General Wayne. It was said in that Inquisition that:

> "When General Wain (Wayne) came to Salem, some of his men went to said Bacon's and asked respecting two pare of oxen. Said he had none. They said you killed them? He said he had and that he sold the meat to poor people."

On the other hand, it was said in the Inquisition that "when the Detachment of the King of Brittian Army under the Command of Colonel Mawhood came down to the town of Salem, some of them went to the house of said Bacon. Bacon told them that he had beefe which was the beefe of oxen afore said."

In order to insure the safety of their mission, Wayne and Barry decided after a "Council of War" that all of the hay in Salem and "Old Gloucester" counties, which they could not transport to Valley Forge, would be purchased from farmers and burned at the river's (the Delaware) edge.

General Anthony Wayne, in a letter dated "Salem 23d Feb/y 1778," wrote to Captain John Barry as follows:

> "You are to pass up the River with your Boats, and burn all the Hay along the shore from Billings Port to this place, taken an acc/t of the Persons Names to whom it belongs together with the Quantity."

Wayne's intelligence was quite specific, for he told Barry that "on one John Kellys place at the Mouth of Rackoon Creek, there is near one hundred tons and up Mantua Creek, there is a Considerable Quantity," thus the hay of "Old Gloucester County" farmers was considerable. In addition, a large number of the highly coveted cattle might be added to the herd enroute to Valley Forge.

General Wayne's informed Captain Barry that it was General Washinton's wish "to deprive the Enemy from receiv/g the Benefitt of the Forage, and at the same time for such persons as are friends to this County — to receive a recompense at a future day — for altho, it is a Maxim that Private property must be sacrificed to Publick Good," it was not General Washington's "Intention to Distress the Individual for the benefit of the Public; but when Prudence & Policy, joined to necessaty will Justify the Measure — and not even Then, but with a full intent that Restitution be made to that Individual."

In order to facilitate future restitution, Wayne told Barry: "You will by the first oppertunity Transmitt to Head Quarters, the Names of the Persons, together with the Quanity of Forage belong/g to each that you may have distroyed, persuant to this order — by his Excellencys Command/d."

Beginning at Mantua Creek in "Old Gloucester County," Captain John Barry and his men ignited hay-stack after hay-stack down the Jersey side of the Delaware River as far as Salem Creek. On February 26th, 1778, Captain Barry dispatched the following report to General George Washington at Valley Forge:

"According to the orders of Gen. Wayne I have destroyed the Forage from Mantua Creek to this Place; the Quantity Destroyed is about Four Tons and should have Proceeded farther had not a Number of the Enemies Boats appeared in Sight and Lining the Jersey Shore Deprived us of the Oppertunity of Proceeding Farther on the same purpose."

As ordered by General Wayne, Barry assured General Washington that he would "Remit to Your Excellency the Names of the Persons Whose property was Destroyed and Likewise the Quantity of Each; have thought Proper to detain four of Your men to assist in getting the Boats away as some of My Men are Rendered Incapable of Proceeding thru Fatigue."

The British in Philadelphia had been alerted to the fact that Wayne and Barry were in Salem County. Hugh Cowperthwaite, a man friendly to the British garrison at Billingsport, is said to have been the Tory informant; however, the hay-burning efforts confused the British so much that the smoke and flames from the burning hay delayed the crossing of the British troops for a day, thus insuring initial success for "The Great Cattle Drive."

It was not until February 25th that approximately 2000 British troops crossed the Delaware River to the Billingsport area of "Old Gloucester County." They arrived too late to intercept Anthony Wayne, the cattle and the forage enroute to the hungry Americans at Valley Forge. The actual route of the cattle was up the King's Highway via Sharptown, Swedesboro, Woodbury, Haddonfield, Mount Holly, Burlington and Trenton.

The late arriving British troops were under the command of Lt. Colonel Robert Abercrombie and were to march from Billingsport to Salem County to search out General Anthony Wayne and the cattle. The "Diary" of Captain Friedrich von Muenchhausen has this February 24th entry:

At 12 o'clock the two English battalions of light infantry under the command of Colonel Abercromby received orders to march at once. They were embarked on flatboats at one o'clock and were landed at Billingsport. The intention of this operation is probably to have a slap at General Wayne, if possible."

According to Frank Stewart's "Foraging for Valley Forge," General Anthony Wayne informed Governor William Livingston of New Jersey on February 26th "that the enemy forces amounting to about 2000 men had been split at Billingsport and that 1500 of them had proceeded to Salem . . . and about 500 had gone up to Haddonfield, where they were joined at dawn of day on the 26th by about 1300 more men, who had crossed from Philadelphia to Cooper's Ferry at 2 o'clock in the morning with the expectation of capturing the forces under Wayne and Ellis."

It is learned from the Rev. Frederick Schmidt of the Moravian Church on the King's Highway near Oldman's Creek that Lt. Col. Abercrombie's troops passed by his church enroute to Salem County to head off General Anthony Wayne and the cattle.

From the "Journal and Biography" of the Rev. Nicholas Collin of the "Old

Swede's Church" at Swedesboro, it is learned that there were some exciting moments in "Old Gloucester County," for Collin noted:

"On this last of February the American general Vain (Anthony Wayne) passed through here with a detachment of 300 men, of whom the greater part were miserably clothed, some without boots, others without socks. He himself did not arrive until 12 o'clock at night and took up his quarters in my house. Just as he was about to go to bed, the sentries fired warning shots but nothing happened, however."

The Rev. Collin said that General Anthony Wayne was "a well-bred gentleman" and showed Collin "great respect." Wayne departed Swedesboro the next morning and according to Collin "at 11 o'clock, a regiment of English infantry came to attack him, but he had then already escaped. These troops had come in a running march the last (Swedish) half mile, and the militia in Swedesborough had hardly time to escape."

The English infantry regiment that marched through Swedesboro appears to have been the one that split off from Abercrombie's main force at Billingsport in order to join the other British forces at Haddonfield. The American militia stationed in Swedesboro area were undoubtedly under the command of Colonel Bodo Otto of the first Regiment of the "Old Gloucester County" militia.

Regarding the activity in the Haddonfield area, the Hessian Captain von Muenchhausen reported in the February 25th entry of his "Diary" that: "When reports came on late this evening that 500 to 600 militia were assembled at Jersey in Haddonfield, seven miles from here, Colonel (Thomas) Sterling with his 42nd regiment of Highland Scots consisting of two battalions and (John) Simcoe's Provincial Corps, were ferried across to take possession of Haddonfield." The militia were commanded by Colonel Joseph Ellis, who was under orders to aid General Anthony Wayne to insure the safe passage of the 150 Salem County cattle and the 85 collected in "Old Gloucester County" by the militia.

On March 4th, Anthony Wayne advised General George Washington that he had "received intelligence that the Enemy had Detached themselves in small parties and were collecting cattle, forage, etc., in the vicinity of Haddonfield, Coopers and Timber Creeks." Even though he had relatively few troops, Wayne decided to "make a forced March and Endeavor to . . . cut off some of their parties."

The British intelligence reports indicated that Wayne had a very large force, "being exaggerated to thousands," said Wayne. Colonel Thomas Stirling retreated to Cooper's Ferry and then over the river to Philadelphia, "leaving waggons, horses, cattle, etc., behind which he had stolen from the inhabitants who have since claimed and received their property."

The Wayne success in "Old Gloucester County" was due in great part to his skill and tactics; however, the militia of Colonel Joseph Ellis and the calvary of the Polish Count Casimir Pulaski, stationed at Trenton, played important roles in insuring the success of "The Great Cattle Drive." As for Pulaski, Governor William Livingston reported to General George Washington that Pulaski "shewd the greatest activity on the late irruption of the Enemy into this State, by marching down with all the calvary that could be collected in the neighbourhood on the first intelligence of their landing & a rencounter with them at Coopers ferry . . . "

As for the Abercrombie expedition to Salem, General Wayne reported to General George Washington that:

> "Mr. Abercrombie, who commanded the detachment that went to Salem — hearing that the militia were collecting in great numbers — and that we were advancing from Mount Holly — also took the horrors and embarking on board his boats and got safe to Phila . . . leaving all his collection of cattle, etc., behind."

On March 5th, Wayne advised Washington that he would begin his "March for Camp . . . it was not in my power to move until I could procure shoes for the troops almost barefoot." When Wayne left New Jersey for Valley Forge, an additional 100 cattle had been collected in Burlington County, making a South Jersey herd of 335 head. At last, by the middle of March, the 112 mile "Great Cattle Drive" was over and the troops at Valley Forge would have beef again.

One is forced to agree with Frank Stewart who wrote that "The Wayne Expediton is an important bit of American history . . . Washington's army was rescued from a serious famine as a direct result of Wayne's success, caused to a considerable degree by the unstinted co-operation of the troops under Colonel Joseph Ellis . . . " of "Old Gloucester County."

C — The Affair At Quinton's Bridge

After Lt. Colonel Robert Abercrombie's relatively unsuccessful incursion into into Salem County in search of General Anthony Wayne from February 25th to the 28th,1778, British intellegence became more keenly aware of the fact the ample supplies of cattle and forage were in South Jersey, and that there were Tories in "Old Gloucester" and Salem Counties who were ready and willing to help the King's troops obtain supplies from their friends and neighbors, as they had done even earlier.

An examination of "Old Gloucester" and Salem County Inquisition Statements bears out the prior Tory support of the British Army, thus it is possible to understand why the Britisn would attempt a second invasion of South Jersey, this time primarily for cattle and forage. For example, an early case is worth our attention, for on "or about the Second Day of October one thousand seven hundred and Seventy Seven, a detachment of the army of the King of Great Britain being landed at Raccoon Creek in the County of Gloucester," William Miller, "being asked, he then being one of the Captains of the Militia in Penns Neck . . . if he did not intend to call out the Militia Company under his Command to oppose them; he replyed no; it is best for us all to hide our arms and the officers to keep out of the way 'till such times as we should see whether the English would conquer." Miller further said that "he thought it best for the people here in general to trade with the Enemy Shipping and then they would not hurt and ransack us and when the Enemy was gone, then take our arms again . . . " The Miller episode occurred when Fort Billings fell to the British. William Rawson of Upper Penn's Neck in Salem County landed there on December 18th, 1777, in company with some British soldiers. In his Inquisition, it was stated that "Rawson swore at the said doldiers for taken his Sheep and said I am your head Pilot both by Land and water . . . " Rawson seemed to be "angry but then advised them to (go) up the road and by a Certain Stone House to a wooden house, for there was a Dam'd Rebel Capt. livid there and plunder Iiiiii . . . "

In an "Old Gloucester County" Inquisition Statement taken at Sandtown (Mount Royal), Peter Johnson formerly of Woolwich Towship was accused of joining " the Army of the King of Great Britton" on or "about the twenty fifth day of January in the year of One Thousand Seven Hundred & Seventy Eight" and "hath since assisted in taking the good citizens of this State Prisoners, destroying & taking away their property . . . "

Despite the assistance of the Tories, as the winter of 1777-78 wore on, the British in Philadelphia were growing short of food. In addition, Captain John Barry operating out of Port Penn, Delaware, was reeking havoc on British ships enroute to Philadelphia. Captain von Muenchhausen noted in his "Diary" entry of March 11th that:

> "Reliable news has it that two of our ships and one sloop of war of 10 guns have been taken at New Castle. The enemy has in this region, galleys, armed boats, and small armed vessels, which need only shallow water. They lie close to the banks and also in the smaller rivers and creeks . . . When they see something on the ground, or unarmed merchantmen, transports, or provisions ships to which they believe to be a match, they come out and take it."

The next day, Christopher Marshall noted in his "Diary" that "the inhabitants on the sides of our river Delaware had, within (a) few days past, taken three ships bound up to Philadelphia. One of them mounted ten guns. They were loaded with rum, sugar, dry goods, ammunition, some soldiers and wheat flour. It's said those (American) boats were commanded by Captain Barry . . . "

On March 13th, 1778, Captain von Muenchhausen wrote in his "Diary" that "three English regiments and Simcoe's Free Corps, altogether 1400 men, embarked under the command of Colonel Mawhood. It is said that they will disembark farther down the Delaware in Jersey to gather provisions, of which we have been having only a scant supply lately."

From the "Diary" of the British Engineer, Archibald Robertson, it is learned that the invasion forces destined for "Old Gloucester" and Salem Counties actually left Philadelphia on March 12th:

> "The 17th (New Jersey Volunteers), 27th and 46th Regiments and Queen's Rangers being embarked in transports, sailed under the command of Colonel Mawhood . . . to get forage down the River Delaware."

This second invasion of South Jersey was mainly amphibious operation at the onset, for all of the troops had to be ferried to Billingsport and later to Salem Creek. Three British warships, the Roebuck, the Camilla and the Pearl, were the big troop carriers, while more than 60 smaller vessels were sent to bring back to Philadelphia the hoped for forage.

Major John Graves Simcoe, commander of the highly specialized "Queen's Rangers" has written in his "Journal of the Operations of the Queen's Rangers" that his troops debarked at Billingsport, where horses were obtained for the Hussars in "old Gloucester County." Simcoe wrote that he "had assured the inhabitants that they (the horses) should be returned, or paid for, if they (the people around Billingsport) did not appear in arms, in a few days."

The main British Army under the command of Colonel Charles Mawhood arrived at Salem via the river on March 17th. As Archibald Robertson informs us: "Got into our boats at 3 in the morning and at 7 we landed in Salem Creek and marched directly to Salem. A few shots were fired by some Militia."

As for Major Simcoe and the "Queen's Rangers," it has been said that after their arrival at Billingsport, the warship "Pearl" took them to the area near present day Finn's Point National Cementary, from which place they marched to Salem, arriving early in the afternoon. Colonel Mawhood then conferred with Major Simcoe and orders were given to begin the forage on March 18th.

The objective of the British mission was to obtain horses for the calvary and staff, the army being very deficient in this branch of the service." In addition, Mawhood was to later claim that the British "got all the cattle they wanted for the supply of the troops in Philadelphia," which were increasingly short of food and forage.

Due to information obtained by Colonel Mawhood from Salem Tories, it was learned that cattle, forage and horses abounded on the eastern side of Alloway's Creek. Access over the creek could only be accomplished by crossing at Thompson's, Quinton's or Hancock's Bridges. These bridges were in the hands of small numbers of Cumberland, Salem and "Old Gloucester County" Militia, although the alarm had been sounded and more of the South Jersey Militia were momentarily expected.

On the morning of March 18th, Colonel Mawhood sent three foraging parties of 50 men each in the direction of the three bridges over Alloway's Creek. As Simcoe phrased it: "the rebel militia was posted at Hancock's and Quintin's, the nearest bridges, which they had taken up, and defended by breast-works." Of this operation, Archibald Robertson stated that "Two partys of 50 men went out different routes to drive in cattle; one by Penns Neck, the other by Quinton's Bridge on Alloes (Alloway's) Creek. Here this party was opposed by a party of the Rebels who were intrenched on the opposite side of the Bridge."

At this point the British realized that a considerable American force was gathering at Quinton's Bridge, a number that soon reached approximately 400. Colonel Elijah Hand, commanding afficer of the Cumberland County Militia, had arrived with his troops and two cannon. In addition, Captain John Barker of the "Old Gloucester County" Militia had arrived with his company of 29 men to augment the troops now under the joint command of Colonel Benjamin Holme of Salem County and Colonel Elijah Hand.

Prior to the arrival of Colonels Holme and Hand, Colonel Charles Mawhood brought 200 of the Queen's Rangers from Salem. Robertson noted that "the Rangers were concealed in a wood so that the Rebels might not know of the reinforcements." The British then "laid an ambuscade of 20 men in a house and about 60 behind a rail, 200 yards from "a house."

Captain William Smith of Salem County was the officer in charge at Quinton's Bridge. He was under orders from Colonel Benjamin Holme to only defend the bridge, not to assume an offensive posture. Seeing such a small number of British on the other side of Alloway's Creek, Smith had planks laid and ordered a number of his troops to cross and put the British to rout. At this juncture, as told by Archibald Robertson, Colonel Mawhood then ordered 50 of his men to retreat, "upon which the Rebels began to pursue with great eagerness, thinking to hang upon our rear by which means about 40 of them that were left in their front fell into our snare (the ambuscade). About twenty were killed and 12 taken, 4 of them wounded . . . We then returned home (to Salem)."

Fortunately for the Americans at Quinton's Bridge, Smith and most of his troops made it back safely to the east side of Alloway's Creek, where Colonels Holme and Hand had arrived with much needed reinforcements. Major Simcoe wrote the Rangers were "ready to force the bridge, if ordered . . . Colonel Mawhood thought it useless to pass it." Quinton's Bridge remained in American hands and the livesstock still eluded the British.

Archibald Robertson reported that a third British party "had been sent towards Hancock's Bridge . . . likewise found the Rebels posted and entrenched. on the opposite side. We got some cattle . . . " In addition, the British were to obtain small quantities of cattle and hay from the Elsinboro and Penns Neck areas of Salem County and when they left on their return to Philadelphia, they took with them "300 tons of hay besides oats and Indian corn."

Without being overly patriotic and romantic, it is possible to conclude that the affair at Quinton's Bridge," while not a major military encounter, was a major disappointment to General William Howe in Philadelphia. Instead of having large quantities of beef for his troops, after their intrusion into "Old Gloucester County" and Salem Counties, food became increasingly scarce. In addition, a few hundred raw militia-men from South Jersey had stood their ground before some of the most formidable British troops

It might be said that Quinton's Bridge was merely a place where " . . . embattled farmers, snared into a trap, had lost the fight and left their fellows killed, wounded or captured on the north side of Aloes Creek." But as Joseph Sickler has noted: "the creek itself was still uncrossed and the British in their failure to reach across it, had won but a 'Pyrrhic' victory."

In conclusion, according to the Tory newspaper, The Pennsylvania Evening Post, dated April 3, 1778. when the British Troops under under the command of Colonel Charles Mawhood entered Salem County, "none was found to oppose or impede them from collecting forage, except for a few, who had been prevailed upon to abandon their houses, and on the third after the landing of the troops, to shew themselves in arms, but the number being insignificant, they were easily crushed, and the whole killed or taken prisoner." Indeed, the South Jersey Militia who stood their ground at Quinton's Bridge present a strong historical rebuttal to Tory journalism of the Revolutionary War period.

D — The Hancock's Bridge Massacre

Had the British been able to send a large foraging expedition over Alloway's Creek at Quinton's Bridge on March 18, 1778, it is highly likely that the "massacre" at Hancock's Bridge would not have occured on March 21st, for with the arrival of Colonel Elijah Hand and more of the Cumberland County Militia, Colonel Charles Mawhood's force of approximately 1500 British troops was put on the defensive. Indeed, in the "Diary" of Christopher Marshall, he noted in his April 1st entry: "News today that the Jersey Militia had surrounded fifteen hundred English troops near Salem Creek, who had gone on shore to plunder, and that Capt. John Barry near Reedy Island had taken twelve boats belonging to the English and some prisoners."

On addition, on March 20th, Captain Barry reported to General George Washington that the British had " . . . forty sail vessels up Salem Creek, and about thirty more on the Delaware abreast of the Creek. They have, from the best information I can collect about fifteen hundred men landed and am

the Alliance

satisfied their intent is for stock and forage . . . "

Without doubt, the Hancock's Bridge mission was not one of foraging, but for destroying the South Jersey Militia thought to be there. if they could be reduced, the British would then have full access to the cattle and hay on the east side of Alloway's Creek, both at Quinton's and Hancock's bridges.

British intelligence indicated that there were approximately four hundred Salem, Cumberland and "Old Gloucester County" Militia at Hancock's Bridge. In Major Simcoe's "Journal of Operations," he presents the rationale for the proposed attack:

> "The rebels still occupying the post at Quintin and Hancock's bridge, and probably accumulating, Colonel Mawhood determined to attack them at the latter, where, from all reports, they were assembled to near four hundred men . . . "

The mission was assigned to Major John Simcoe and Colonel Mawhood joined him on an intelligence patrol opposite Hancock's Bridge. Simcoe tells us he then: " . . . ascended a tree and made a rough sketch of the buildings, which, by conversing with the guides (local Tories), he improved a tolerable plan of the place, anf formed his mode of attack accordingly."

Fortified with this new intelligence, Major Simcoe was dispatched to deal with the Americans. Again with the aid of Salem County Tories, Simcoe "embarked on the 20th at night, on board the flat boats . . . " and " . . . was to be landed seven miles below Aloes (Alloway's) creek" on the east bank of the creek. From that point, Simcoe planned to march under the cover of night and surprise the Americans early in the morning.

Due to a heavy tide running out to the Delaware River, Simcoe was unable to proceed as far up Alloway's Creek in the flat boats as planned, thus, he then "determined . . . to land on the marshes at the mouth of Aloes creek."

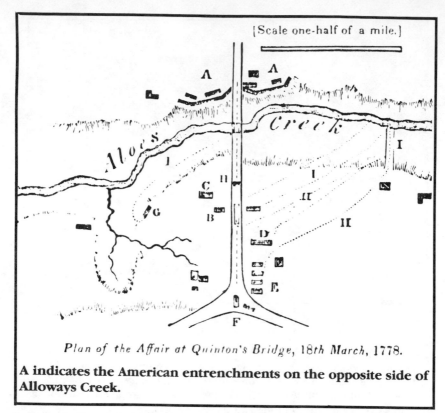

Plan of the Affair at Quinton's Bridge, 18th March, 1778.

A indicates the American entrenchments on the opposite side of Alloways Creek.

Fortunately, Simcoe had brought heavy planks which were used to march over the marshes and swamps until they arrived "at a wood upon dry land." Simcoe's forces were then formed for the march and attack on the Hancock House and the buildings adjacent to it.

By chance or counter-intelligence, the main body of the South Jersey Militia was not at Hancock's Bridge when Major Simcoe's troops arrived before dawn on March 21st. Figures vary as to the number of Militia and civilians present and sleeping when the attack began on the unsuspecting Americans. It is a generally accepted American figure that there were no more than "50 raw militia" at the Hancock House, when the front and rear doors were forced in by the British soldiers.

Major Simcoe recorded that "the surprise was complete, and would have been (more)so, had the whole of the enemy's force been present, but fortunately for them, they had quitted it the evening before, leaving a detachment of twenty or thirty men, all of whom were killed" by bayonet. He tells us that "some very unfortunate circumstances happened" at the Hancock House, for "among the killed was a friend of the Government (a Tory), then a prisoner with the rebels, old (William) Hancock, the owner of the house, and his brother."

Realizing the severity of the slaughter of the old and infirm Judge William Hancock, Major John Graves Simcoe emphasized that he "had made particular enquiry, and was informed that he (Hancock) did not live at home, since the rebels had occupied the bridge . . . " but "unfortunately returned home at night;

129

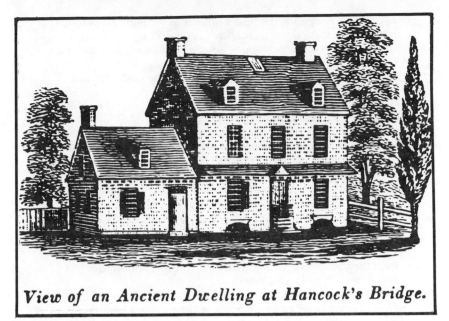

View of an Ancient Dwelling at Hancock's Bridge.

events like these are the real miseries of war . . . "

Frank Stewart in his "Salem County and the American Revolution" quotes a report of Reuel Sayre who was present at Hancock's Bridge when the Simcoe attack took place. According to Sayre:

"When the British were in Salem County, they came upon us (at Hancock's Bridge) by surprize; the guard was taken and every man killed or taken prisoner but myself. We were stationed at the Bridge; we had guards up and down the creek; they came through the marsh on the back of us at night . . . All were killed, left for dead or taken prisoners . . . I had one brother killed and one taken prisoner in this night affair."

After their victory at Hancock's Bridge, the British had the bridge repaired and "Major Simcoe communicated to Colonel Mitchell that the enemy were at Quintin's Bridge." Simcoe indicated that he had "good guides to conduct them" to Quinton's Bridge by a private road. Mitchell indicated that his troops were "much fatigued by the cold, and that he would return" to Salem as soon as the troops joined."

Almost magically, Simcoe tells us that " Lieutenant-Colonel Mitchell, finding his men in high spirits, purposing to march to Quintin's bridge; but going informed of the enemy's patrole, it was thought best to return" to Salem. There, Colonel Charles Mawhood, "in public orders, 'returned his best thanks to Major Simcoe and his corps, for their spirited and good conduct in the surprize of the rebel posts.'"

Unsuccessful in defeating the main body of American troops and in crossing over Alloway's Creek, the British, at Salem, had about given up any hopes of a real victory, but Colonel Charles Mawhood thought it appropriate to try his hand at psychological warfare by sending Colonel Elijah Hand his infamous ultimatum of March 21, 1778:

"Colonel Mawhood, commanding a detachment of the British Army at Salem, induced by motives of humanity, proposes to the military at Quintin's bridge and the neighborhood, as well officers as well as private men, to lay down their arms and depart each man to his own home. On that condition, he solemnly promised to re-embark his troops without delay, doing no further damage to the country; and he will cause his commissaries to pay for the cattle, hay and corn, that have been taken, in sterling money."

Colonel Charles Mawhood then indicated what he would do if the patriots of Salem County did not do his bidding:

"If, on the contrary, the militia should be so far deluded and blind to their true interest and happiness, he will put the arms which he has brought with him into the hands of the people well affected, called Tories, and will attack all such of the militia as remain in arms, burn and destroy their houses, and other property, and reduce them their unfortunate wives and children, to beggary and distress . . . "

On the same day that Mawhood sent his communication to Colonel Hand, Colonels Benjamin Holme and Hand communicated from the "Glassworks (Allowaystown)" to Governor William Livingston. They reported as follows:

" . . . on Tuesday last a large number of the enemy landed at Salem Town, as near as we can learn about of between two of three thousand and are advancing into the Country and plundering very fast; we have had two or three skirmishes with them and have lost on our side as near as we can yet learn about twelve killed and near forty taken prisoners; the lost of the enemy's side we cannot as yet positively learn, however, we are well assured we have killed some of them."

Holme and Hand stated: "we have made our stand on Alloways Creek, the lower side at Hancock's Quintin's or Thompson's Bridges, but last night the enemy landed out of their boats below all the aforesaid bridges and surrounded our guard at Hancock's Bridge and took and killed almost all of them . . . we fear they will advance over all these all these lower counties (as we find our numbers at present are not large enough to make a proper stand against them) except you Sir by some means can help us to some relief . . . "

On the next day, March 22nd, " . . . at Headquarters at Quintin's Bridge, " Colonel Elijah Hand replied to Colonel Charles Mawhood in a measured and dignified manner:

"I have been favored with what you say humanity has induced you to propose. It would give me much pleasure to have found that humanity had been the line of conduct to your troops since you came to Salem. Not only denying quarters, but butchering our men who surrenderedd themselves prisoners in the skirmish at Quintin's Bridge last Thursday, and bayonetting yesterday morning at Hancock's Bridge, in the most cruel manner in cold blood, men who were taken by surprise, in a situation in which they neither could or did attempt to make any resistance, and some of whom were not fighting men: are instances too shocking for me to recite and I hope for you to hear . . . Your proposal, that we should lay down our arms, we absolutely reject."

Colonel ELijah Hand continued: "You mention that if we reject your proposal you will put arms into the hands of the Tories against us; we have no objection to the measure, for it would be a very good one to fill our arsenals with arms. Your threats to wantonly burn and destroy our houses and other property, and to reduce our wives and children to beggary and distress, is a sentiment which my humanity almost forbids me only to recite and induces me to imagine I am reading the cruel order of a barbarous Attila . . . "

In a most remarkable manner, the letter of Colonels Holme and Hand reached Governor Livingston by express riders in a very few hours. On the very next day, March 22nd, he wrote to George Washington at Valley Forge that indeed he had and was transmitting the Holme-Hand missive and that he was ordering out a considerable number of militia to aid in Salem. Livingston noted that "considering how slowly the Militia generally collect, I fear they will not be able to give any seasonable relief; & both Salem & Gloucester are miserable infested with Tories." Livingston thus asked General Washington to give what assistance he might "in addition to Colonel (Israel) Shreve's Regiment, for which you have my hearty acknowledgments . . . ."

On March 23rd, Governor Livingston responded to a message from Colonel Shreve:

"I think it would at present be best to march with all Expedition to Haddonfield, & join the Militia under Colonel Ellis. The Enemy are at present at Salem, to the number I suppose of 1200."

Governor Livingston informed Colonel Shreve that "Colonel Ellis has been directed to order two classes from the Militia of Burlington, Gloucester, Salem and Cumberland. So that in a few days you will I hope have a respectable Body to frighten away the Enemy. I mean both of you together because I believe the Enemy is as much terrified at our Militia as they are at your troops . . . I have already written to General Washington on the State of Affairs below (at Salem), and if he can spare a Brigade & sees it necessary, he will doubtless order them over" to New Jersey.

Colonel Joseph Ellis reported to Governor William Livingston on March 23rd that he was having a difficult time obtaining troops:

" . . . I have repeatedly call'd on the Colonels at Burlington but without Effect; not a single man of them appears, nor do I hear there is any motion of the kind among them. We can get but very few from Salem or Cumberland as they plead the necessity of guarding their own Coast which I think not unreasonable."

As for "Old Gloucester County" at that great time of travail, Colonel Joseph Ellis further commented:

"Gloucester of late is little better, they being discouraged at the Weakness of the Post in part, & partly for want of their Pay, which with some Company's is several months in Arrear. Colonel Ottos Battalion have chiefly revolted to the enemy & have made prisoners of a number of their Officers, those who have eskaped dare not stay at their homes; Colonel Somerss Battalion upon the last call for two Classes have not sent twenty men."

Colonel Ellis wrote that "on the Enemy's first embarking to go down the River I received intelligence of their design which was to forage in Salem & Cumberland County's . . . They have since landed at Salem and are ravaging that part of the Country . . . I could just beg leave to remark that without some standing force we have little to expect from the Militia who being alone not sufficient to prevent the incursions of the Enemy . . . which will I hope be remedied on Colonel Shreves arrival."

Governor William Livingston was at Trenton of March 23rd, from which he dispatched Colonel Joseph Ellis' report of the dire situation in Salem County. In his communique to the Commander-in-Chief at Valley Forge, Livingston requested that the Jersey Battalion be sent to South Jersey. Unfortunately, Washington replied that he could not provide any additional regular or Continental Troops for the relief of the suffering soldiers and citizens of South Jersey.

Governor Livingston admitted that it was true that part of New Jersey's " . . . Misfortunes, that of not providing pay for the Militia is our own fault. Yet it is (a) pity that the Country should be ravaged upon that Account. I know that your Excellency will do what is proper . . . Colonel Shreve is this night at Burlington. I have advised him to proceed to Gloucester upon his addressing me upon the Subject of his Movements. I hope he will soon be joined by our Militia from those parts. Nor do I believe the Enemy in Gloucester and Salem is so numerous as was first represented . . . "

Fortunately for the American cause, Colonel Charles Mawhood's main force remained at Salem from March 21st to the 27th, contenting themselves with further foraging. This is learned from "Diary" of the British Archibald Robertson in which he wrote that on March 25th, the British "foraged on Penn's Neck." On the 26th, they "foraged from Fyn's Point . . . and the Waggons return'd to Salem." Finally, it is learned from Robertson that on March 27th: "All the Detachments embarked at Salem Creek without any Molestation."

On March 29th, Robertson wrote that the British encountered a "very hard Gale. Anchored at Billings Port." Finally on the 30th, Robertson reported his safe arrival in Philadelphia and that the expedition to Salem netted "about 300 Tons of Hay besides Oats and Indian Corn. We had 63 Small Craft besides 11 belonging to the Artillery."

Robertson's comments are partially confirmed by an entry in Captain Friedrich von Muenchhausen's "Diary" entry of March 28th: "The detachment of 1400 men under Colonel Mawhood, which had been foraging in Jersey down-river near Salem arrived . . . with 300 tons of hay." Neither man reported the arrival of cattle or other livestock in Philadelphia.

All told, Colonel Charles Mawhood's troops were in South Jersey for ten days, March 17th to the 27th, and it is noteworthy that the British failure to completely over-run Cumberland and Salem Counties was a bitter blow to their morale, as well as their supply problems. Without doubt, the South Jersey Militia, represented by men from Cumberland, "Old Gloucester" and Salem Counties contributed much more than they probably relized to the ultimate victory over the British at Yorktown, Virginia, on October 19th, 1781.

Over in Philadelphia, the Pennsylvania Gazzette of April 3rd, 1778 played down the business at Hancock's Bridge by editorial comment:

"The rebels never afterwards appeared in force, so that the troops collected the forage without any interruption and the inhabitants from all quarters flocked to them, bringing what cattle, provisions, etc., they could spare, for which they received a generous price; but lamented much that the army was to depart and leave them again to the tyranny of the rebel faction."

The Tory newspaper continued to give its readers a untrue representation of the attitudes of the mass of South Jersey people:

"If it is said that the King's troops evacuated the place, before the

133

militia could be collected, it will stand the test; for it is an uncontrovertable fact, that in a circuit of upwards of sixty miles, three hundred men could not be mustered; the people being fully sensible of their error, and heartily tired of the petty tyrants who have galled and broke their spirits . . . "

The true situation in South Jersey after the events at Quinton's and Hancock's Bridges was best expressed on March 28, 1778, in a letter from Roadstown to Governor William Livingston: "That plunder, rapine and devastation in the most fertile and populous part of these counties widely marked their footsteps wherever they go. That they are spreading disaffection. They are using every possible means to corrupt the minds of the people . . . "

The letter, signed by Colonels Benjamin Holme, Elijah Hand, as well as 19 other civil and military officers, continued to point out that the South Jersey people were "in no state of defense. That we are so exposed by reason of our situation that some of our officers civil and military have moved out of these counties for safety . . . That the extent of our country is so great, that our small number of men fatigued out, indifferently armed and without field pieces cannot defend it. That as Delaware runs along these counties we are liable to be attacked in numberless places."

The citizens of South Jersey realized the importance of their territory along the shores of the Delaware River and the letter pointed out:

"That the acquisition of these counties would be of great advantage to the enemy. That they could nearly maintain their whole army a campaign by the plunder, forage and assistance they could draw from them . . . it might perhaps be advisable to defend them to prevent the advantage the enemy might receive from them. That our riches and former virtues make us prey to an enemy 'whose tender mercies are cruelties'"

The men at Roadstown had not yet learned that Colonel Mawhood and his troops had departed from Salem Creek, thus they pointed out to Governor Livingston that:

"although the present detachment may be fled and gone before relief reaches us, yet a body of troops are necessary for our protection as long as the enemy possesses Philadelphia."'

Relief in the form of troops from General George Washington never came to South Jersey and fortunately, there was never another invasion of Salem County, for the fortunes of the American Revolution were to be such that the British would be forced to evacuate the City of Philadelphia almost three months to the day that Colonel Charles Mawhood, John Graves Simcoe and the British Army sailed out of Salem Creek.

E — The British Exodus From Philadelphia
A — Billingsport and Environs

With the demise of both Forts Billings and Mercer during October and November of 1777, plus the winter occupation of Philadelphia by the British from September 26th onward, the citizens of "Old Gloucester County" during the late fall of 1777 were relieved to know that the physical violence of war was gone, or so they believed; however, on October 28th, it is learned from the "Diary" of the Hessian Captain Friederich von Muenchhausen that the British were back: "with 400 men, we again occupied Billingsport in Jersey, which we had razed. They have orders to construct a redoubt there."

This British return to "Old Gloucester County" was a brief one, for as noted in the November 10th entry in "The American Journal" of Ambrose Serle:

> "The Post at Billingsport was this Day withdrawn. There is some Reason to fear that the Rebels, now having it in their Power, for this advantageous Ground & Red Bank (Fort Mercer) will be troublesome to Ships in their Passage on the River, and that it may cost us again some Labor to retake them in the Spring."

In view of the fact that the British still did not have control of the Delaware River on November 10th, it would seem that they would not leave a vital nerve center such as Billingsport unmanned for very long, especially as the clearing of the "Chevaux de Frize" was far from complete. This reasoning is borne out, for on November 18th and 19th, 1777, approximately seven thousand British Troops landed at Billingsport, and stationed there, as Samuel Stelle Smith tells us in his "Fight for the Delawawre, 1777," "...was a small British garrison...to guard the passage through the lower cheveaux." It is not plausible that the British Major General Thomas Wilson would land approximately 4000 troops at Billingsport if the area were not secure for the debarking of three English regiments, two Hessian Anspach battalions, the 17th regiment of Light Dragoons and two companies of Hessian Jaegers. The same reasoning applies to Lieutnant General (Lord) Charles Cornnwallis and the 3000 men he brought with him to Billingsport on November 19th.

In addition to Samuel Stelle Smith's comments about a British garrison at Billingsport, Joseph Plumb Martin confirms that at the time of his arrival at Woodbury, approximately October 22, the British "...had also a fortification on the shore opposite their shipping, at a place called Billingsport."

With the destruction of Fort Mercer, it is generally accepted that all British troops, including those at Billingsport, were withdrawn to Philadelphia for the winter. In view of the fact that General George Washington's Army was about to camp at Valley Forge and the South Jersey Militia was in shambles, there was no sense of danger to the British cause from the Jersey side of the Delaware River.

It is not possible at this writing to firmly establish exactly when the British re-occupied Billingsport during the early spring of 1778; however, there is a hint that British troops were there at the time of the John Barry-Anthony Wayne "Great Cattle Drive" of late February, for as the Timmins suggest:

> "As Kings Highway proceeds north, the distance between the road and the river narrows. Near Billingsport noted before as the British Jersey stronghold, it gets quite close. At this point, Wayne interposed most of his regulars between the cattle and the river...At Billingsport were the only British troops in the area..."

It is also of record that Lt. Colonel Robert Abercrombie crossed over to Billingsport during the early morning hours of February 25th. He remained in Salem and "Old Gloucester" Counties until his arrival back in Philadelphia during the afternoon of March 1st, at which time, Captain von Muenchhausen laconically noted that "...the two battalions of light infantry crossed over again."

By the time of the beginning of the expedition of Colonel Charles Mawhood on March 17th, 1778, which resulted in the incidents at Quinton's and Hancock's Bridges, Billingsport was firmly in British military hands, for as Major John Graves Simcoe noted in his "Journal":

"On the passage (to Philadelphia), the ships waiting for the tide, Major Simcoe had an opportunity of landing at Billings Port, where Major Vandyke's corps were stationed, and examining it, they arrived in Philadelphia, March the 31st."

As for the British forces stationed at Billingsport, Captain von Muenchhausen wrote in his "Diary" on March 24th:

"I forgot to mention that the day before yesterday, the 22nd of March, 80 Provincials or to be more exact Jersey Volunteers, were ferried to Billingsport. An engineering officer is with them to throw up earth works at Billingsport again, in which these volunteers will stay for the time being."

On April 4th, 1778, Archibald Robertson confirms von Muenchhausen's intelligence: "The Jersey Volunteers have take Post at Billingsport about ten days ago."

It is further learned from the "Journal" of Captain John Montressor that on April 2nd, "Lt. Sutherland Engineer returned after having completed the Defences of Billingsport which the Jersey volunteers now Garrison." Without doubt, the area between Swedesboro and Billingsport in "Old Gloucester County" was to take on a new importance, for the presence of British troops and New Jersey Loyalists there was to result in outbreaks of violence and military confrontation with the South Jersey Militia of Colonel Joseph Ellis.

April and May of 1778 were to see many unfortunate events take place in "Old Gloucester County" and it is from the "Journal and Biography of Nicholas Collin," minister of the Old Swede's Church in Swedesboro, that we learn of many of these happenings. He wrote that "the English soldiers are undisciplined and cannot always be controlled." This contributed to the very slight success of the British in South Jersey "because often both friend and foe were robbed in the most despicable manner, and sometimes with the permission of the officers."

Ambrose Serle noted in his April 24th entry of his "Journal" that he had "walked on Shore at Billingspot, where about 200 Provincials have refortified the Post, though very frequently disturbed by the Rebels. In an Excursion, yesterday, they had one man killed & two or three wounded." These "excursions" took the form of foraging parties and attacks on the homes and persons of men serving in the militia of "Old Gloucester County."

During the spring and "until the end of June when the English army left Philadelphia," Collin noted: "...Conditions here (in Swedesboro area) were in a rather wretched state. It looked as though America would soon be conquered." He continued: "...the people around here began, as early as last autumn, to trade with the English in order to obtain specie coin, as well as sugar, tea, syrup," as well as other needed items not available because of the war.

A great amount of information may be located in primary source documents of the period January to June, 1778. Such documents are usually found in county historical societies and in the archives of South Jersey Court Houses. For example, in a Salem County Inquisition Statement dated July 21st, 1778, it was written that the Tory James Clark of Pilesgrove (today's Woodstown area) "...did supply the adherents of the King of Great Brittian with provisions." Further, it was stated in this document found in the Salem County Courthouse that Clark.

"did supply...the enemys of this State...the army of the said King
with some furrage such as oats and swore by God that no man
should have his oats but Howe, meaning General Howe and on or
about the 17th Day of February above said, when the Detachment
of the aforesaid King's army came down the Salem Road through
Pilesgrove, (he) went and met them and marched with them some
distance through Pilesgrove aforesaid...it is turn about, the
Continental troops chased us yesterday for our horses and we will
chase them now and at an(y) other time; said he wished
Howe...had all the Head Rebels meaning the officers of government
of Pilesgrove in Philadelphia in prison.

On or about the tenth of March, 1778, the Inquisition continued, James Clark
did " . . . go to one Job Rees in order to get a boat to go to Philadelphia to get
an armed force to take Robert Clark out of the hands of the good people of
this State...and on or about the twenty-eighth of the above said March when
hearing that Capt. Beatman (Bateman) Lloyd was taken prisoner, a person saying
to the said Clark, I am sorry that the said Lloyd and others was taken prisoners;
said Clark said, Dam them that are sorry! I am not, and wish all the Dammed
Rebels (meaning all the good People of this state) was with them..."

Another Salem County Inquisition Statement, dated the 27th of July 1778,
deals in great part with Billingsport and "Old Gloucester County." It was noted
that Thomas Coatsutton, late of Pittsgrove, "on or about the twenty fourth day of
February one thousand Seven Hundred and Seventy Eight went to give notice to
sundry disafected Persons (Tories)...to wit Richard Mead, Jacob Vanmeter and
others when their would be Boats Ready to take them over to Philadelphia to
join the army of the King of Great Britian."

The Inquisition further stated that on April 10th, 1778, "Abdon Abitt, Jr., and
James Sutton two fugitives then belonging to the fort at Billings in the County of
Gloucester, then in possession of the army of the King of Great Brittian came to
the house of the said Thomas Coatsutton in the night; says Coatsutton, in the
name of God...the Militia has just been here; go to the head of the Seder Swamp
near my Meadow and I will bring you Vittles there; they went and he brought
Bread and Meat their; and then advised them to return to Billingsport and try if
they could bring down from thence an armed force sufficient to subdue
Pittsgrove...to obedience to the King of Great Brittian..."

In the military record of Captain Cornelius Nieukirk of Pittsgrove Township,
contiguous to "Old Gloucester County," it is learned that Nieukirk and his
militia company were "in service at Haddonfield under Colonel Joseph Ellis,
February 4 to March 9,1778." In addition, Nieukirk was on the "rolls March
18th, 1778; in service at Swedesboro during (the) invasion of the enemy, April 4
1778" and that Nieukirk "commanded his company in service at Pittsgrove,
guarding effects of Tories, April 13 to 21, 1778."

Frank Stewart in his "Salem County in the Revolution" gives the complete
names of the officers and men of Nieukirk's company of foot militia, when they
were on duty in Pittsgrove from April 13th to the 21st. The company consisted
of the following:

Cornelius Nieukirk, Capt.
David Sithen, Lieut.
Robert Patterson, Sergeant
Aaron Brown, Sergeant

Joseph Fauver, Corporal

Privates

Obadiah Crothers	John Nealy
John Nieukirk	Cornelius DuBois
Gabriel Nelson	Thom. Eastburn
Patrick Conner	Daniel Russel
David Nelson	Jerediah DuBois
Elias Craig	Judah Foster
Joseph Brown	John Elwell
Benj. Dubois	John Mayhew
Joseph Vanmeter	Daniel Goalder
John Hutton	Wm. Aarons
David DuBois	Ananias Clark
Thomas Rose	Thomas Mayhew

In connection with Captain Nieukirk's presence at Swedesboro "during the invasion" of April 4th, 1778, it is clear that it was his company, plus others, that was there, when, according to the Rev. Nicholas Collin, "at daybreak on April 4, 300 refugees (Tories) and English troops arrived in three divisions to surround the militia which escaped with great difficulty" from Swedesboro. In addition, Collin tells us that "they burnt down the school house for the simple reason that their friends had been kept prisoners there." When and by whom, it is not known.

The Rev. Collin concluded by reporting that the American " . . . militia returned after a while, took up their position.on a wooded hill (close by) and began to fire (on British and Tories). A terrible alarm ensued. I and some others went out to look on, but both parties aimed badly, that the bullets flew in all directions, so that it was best to stay inside."

In addition to Captain Nieukirk's troops at Swedesboro, Colonel Bodo Otto and units of his First Regiment of "Old Gloucester County" Militia were present. A very cursory examination of Revolutionary War service records reveals that Lt. Ward Pierce's company participated at Swedesboro and that two brothers, Jacob and Leonard Fisler, were privates serving under Lt. Pierce. Interestingly, modern day Clayton, New Jersey, was earlier known as Fislerville.

Colonel Elijah Hand, commanding officer of the Cumberland County Militia, had two detachments of his troops at Swedesboro during March and April of 1778. In particular, Captain Jonathan Beesley commanded his company of 25 men from Cumberland County at Swedesboro. Lastly, Private Jacob Wright of Salem County served at Swedesboro and was probably a member of Captain John Till's company. Of course, Captain Robert Brown, a native of Swedesboro, commanded a company of troops against the British and he had the further responsibility of guarding the mouth of Raccoon Creek so that smaller British naval vessels could not use that water-way.

Writing from Haddonfield on March 28th, 1778, Colonel Israel Shreve of the Second New Jersey Regiment, Continental Line, informed General George Washington of the unhappy situation in "Old Gloucester County:"

> "The tories to the number of one hundred and fifty are in arms
> fortifying at Billingsport with the assistance of some marines; a great
> number of the disaffected inhabitants are trading with the enemy."

Colonel Shreve reported further that "yesterday (March 27th), sixty tories and marines commanded by one (Captain John) Cox went to Swedesboro, took Lt. (Bateman) Lloyd of the fourth Regiment, New Jersey, with two recruits, plundered the house of Capt, (Robert) Brown, stripped his wife and children, carried off or destroyed everything in the house. Several others houses shared the same fate. Every civil and military officer is forced to fly from home." In addition, many of the South Jersey Militia were taken prisoner by the Tories and sent to Philadelphia.

On March 25th, according to Colonel Shreve, "three days ago, three of the militia took a covered wagon and three horses with baggage and stores belonging to Daniel Cozens, a Tory Captain; yesterday (March 27th) Col. Ellis with a small party of horse took a certain David Chew, one of the tory gang; he acknowledges he has borne arms against the States . . . "

Captains Daniel Cozens and John Cox were residents of "Old Gloucester County" and both of them defected to the British early in 1778. Cozens, in fact, was made an officer by the British on January 1, 1778 and by March, he was in command of the Tory garrison at Billingsport, where he was later joined by Cox and Hugh Cowperthwaite from Pittsgrove in Salem County. Incidently, Cox and Cozens had been friends and neighbors in Woolwich Township prior to obtaining their military commissions from the British.

Due to their roots in "Old Gloucester County" and nearby Pittsgrove, the captains Cowperthwaite, Cox and Cozens were responsible for many raids and crimes against their former neoghbors. Of Cowperthwaite, it has been said that he led his own Tory troops on many reprisal missions and that several American Continental Officers fell into his hands, perhaps even Captain Bateman Lloyd at Swedesboro.

The force of British and Tory troops at Billingsport continued to be a serious menace to the Americans and an important post for the British until their evacuation from Philadelphia on June 18th. Billingsport was also important to the American cause, for sometime during the month of May 1778, the Rev. Nicholas Collin informs us that "a division of American troops was stationed in Swedesborough for some weeks. Although the weather was fine, they, nevertheless, took up their quarters in the church and filled it with filth and vermin, so that no Divine service could be held." Unfortunately, the identity of this American division has not been established as of this writing.

While the British post at Billingsport still remained strategically of value, it was to become less and less important for foraging. When the decision had been made to march most of the British and Hessian soldiers to New York City through New Jersey, the area from Gloucester City to Cooper's Ferry was to become vital to British evacuation plans.

B—Events Around Cooper's Ferry

While Billingsport was of critical geo-strategic value to the British in case of a possible naval evacuation of Philadelphia, the area of South Jersey opposite the city was of crucial importance should the British decide to ferry their troops over the Delaware River and march them through New Jersey to New York City. Cooper's and Gloucester ferries, both in "Old Gloucester County," would need to be secured for any land evacuation.

The British decision to evacuate Philadelphia was worked out in London by King George III and his ministers after it had been learned that France was about to enter into commercial and military alliances with the United States. By February 6th, 1778, Benjamin Franklin, Silas Deane and Athur Lee had reached an agreement with the French, whereby it was noted that " . . . the essential and direct end" of the treaty "was to maintain . . . the liberty, sovereignty, and independence, absolute and unlimited, of the United States."

News of the Franco-American Alliance did not reach the British in Philadelphia until April 13th, for in "The American Journal of Ambrose Serle," he wrote on that date: "Intelligence was also brought, but not confirmed, that the French Court has signed a Treaty with the Rebel Agents, & that in consequence a Declaration of War was looked upon as inevitable."

The most poignant reasons for the British withdrawal were the grim prospects of facing another winter in Philadelphia and the news of the French treaty and alliance with the Americans. In addition, there was the real possibility that the British fleet in the Delaware River could easily be blockaded by a French fleet. In any event, King George III personally ordered Sir Henry Clinton to evacuate Philadelphia when the Franco-American news became public. From the "Journal" of Ambrose Serle, it is noted in his May 8th, 1778 entry, that "France has been base enough to conclude a Treaty of Commerce with our profligate & abandoned Rebels about the Middle of March, & that in consequence a War with that Power, & therefore with Spain, was inevitable."

Almost two months to the day that Colonel Charles Mawhood returned to Philadelphia after his relatively unsuccessful foraging expedition to Salem County, the British officially notified Joseph Galloway, a prominent Tory and Superintendent of Philadelphia, of the decision to evacuate the city. As Serle tells us, this evacuation information "was soon circulated about the Town, & filled all of our Friends with melancholy of the Apprehension of being speedily deserted, now a Rope was it were) about their necks & and all their Property subject to Confiscation." Indeed, the pro-British Americans were advised "to make . . .Peace with the States, who . . . would not treat them harshly . . . "

From the "Diary of the American War" by the Hessian Captain Johann Ewald, it is learned:

> "All of the loyal inhabitants, who had taken our protection, put their heads together and lamented that they now had to give up all their property. They also told us to our faces that the army had come only to make them miserable . . . The heart of every honest man bled on hearing these people complain, who had an absolute right to do so."

While Philadelphia's Tories were frightened and saddened by the turn of events, the news of the French involvement on the side of the Americans produced great joy among the troops at Valley Forge. The Hessian Captain Friedrich von Muenchhausen noted in his "Diary" on May 10th: "The rebels have been deserting less since they have learned of the alliance with the French, which has induced General George Washington to light bon fires." Two days later, he wrote: "There hace been continuous celebrations in Washington's camp near Valley Forge because of their alliance with France." John Jackson tells us in his "With the British Army in Philadelphia," the British heard "thirteen cannon fired three times and from the direction of Valley Forge . . . "

As for George Washington himself, the treaty with France overjoyed him. As Marcus Cunliffe wrote in his "George Washington: Man and Monument," the commander-in-chief was heard to explain: "I believe no event was ever received with more heartfelt joy."

Evacuation Preparations

Even before the actual evacuation plans were put into effect, Cooper's Ferry and the area from it to Haddonfield were frequently the scene of British foraging parties. In addition, when General Anthony Wayne was bringing the cattle out of Salem and into "Old Gloucester County," the British attempted to cut him off. We learn from Wayne's letter of February 26th from Mount Holly to General Washington:

> " . . . at two o'clock this evening 1800 more (British) crossed at Cooper's Ferry who immediately marched to Haddonfield where they were joined with five hundred (at the dawn of day) from those who landed at Billingsport . . . "

Against such a British force, Wayne could boast of only "two little detachments which at this moment don't exceed 550 men."

Fortunately, General Wayne's modest "army" was supplemented by several hundred of Colonel Joseph Ellis' South Jersey Militia which were stationed at Haddonfield, the military capitol of South Jersey. Infact, from the "Diary" of Captain von Muenchhausen, it is learned that on April 4th:

> "At Haddonfield, in Jersey, six miles from Cooper's Ferry, opposite Philadelphia, on the other side of the Delaware, 300 rebels with two cannon have been stationed again the last few days."

Von Muenchhausen further reported that " . . . at Coopers Ferry there is also a picket of 50 men, with sentries along the bank of the Delaware." Of particular worry to the British was the fact that the American officers had been given "very large and good field glasses by Washington." This allowed the Americans said Muenchhausen to " . . . observe every move on our side, and since most of the Philadelphia. On June 19th, Captain John Montresor reported in his "Journal"

To rectify this situation and to inflict an element of surprise, 500 light infantry were ferried over to Billingsport, from whence they marched to Swedesboro on the morning of April 4th, 1778. Then according to von Muenchhausen, "they proceeded to Haddonfield, which the enemy had just left because they had received from their patrols news of our advance."

Unfortunately, the South Jersey Militia leaders, said von Muenchhausen " . . . forgot to advise their command at Coopers Ferry, most of whom fell into our hands, together with their field glasses . . . We captured the commanding major, two lieutenants, and 58 rank and file. One captain and some men were left on the field." Of this encounter, Frank Stewart has written, in his "Salem County in the Revolution," that "A horseman sent to warn the guard at Cooper's Ferry was killed, also a number of militiamen,"

The "commanding major" at Cooper's Ferry was Major William Ellis of the "Old Gloucester County" Militia. The two lieutenants captured were Abraham Stout and John Hutchins, both of Colonel Isreal Shreve's Second New Jersey Regiment, Continental Line. Incidentally, Colonel Shreve had dispatched Major Richard Howell of Fairton, Cumberland County, to attack Billingsport, but he was unable to do so because hoped-for South Jersey militia units did not appear. Howell was later to serve eight years as the Governor of New Jersey, 1792—1800.

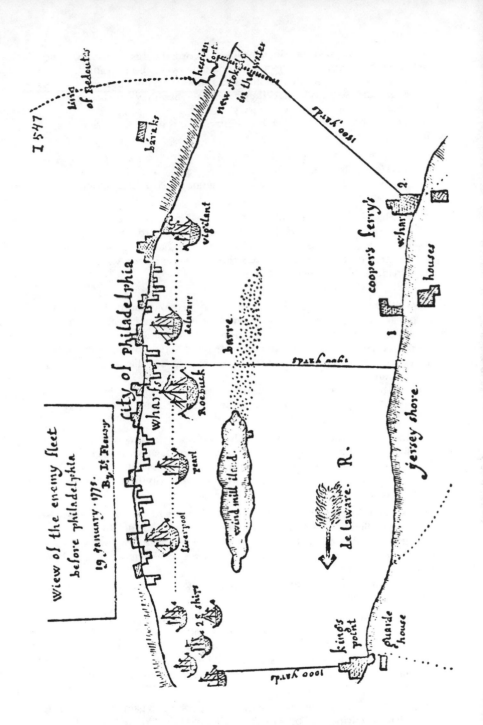

Lt. Fleury's Map of January 19th, 1778 showing part of the British Fleet at Philadelphia

On April 23rd, Captain von Muenchhausen recorded in his "Diary" that "the Rebel militia had gathered in Jersey and apparently were about to attack Billingsport, where our Jersey volunteers had about 80 men stationed in a redoubt. But after some rifle shots they retreated when they found our men determined to defend themselves bravely."

From the "Journal" of Captain John Montresor, it is noted in his April 28th entry:

> "At 7 this morning I embarked in flat boats with the 1st Battalion and Light Infantry and crossed the Delaware and landed in the Jersies at Cooper's Ferry . . . after fixing upon a Post for covering the wood cutters."

In the "Diary" of Archibald Robertson, he noted in his April 28th entry that he " . . . went with Sir William (Howe) to Cooper's Ferry in the Jersey's to reconnoiter a Proper Place for taking post to secure the cutting of fire wood." It is significant to note Sir William Howe's visit to Cooper's Ferry was the only one he ever made to "Old Gloucester County."

On April 29th, from the "Letters" of Major Carl Leopold Baurmeister, it is also learned that "General Erskine and Captain Montresor of the Engineers crossed the Delaware under cover of six British grenadier companies. Landing in Jersey at Cooper's Ferry, they searched for a suitable place behind the ferry that might be sufficiently fortified to serve as a camp for one brigade. They returned again toward evening."

The British were now beginning to suffer from a low supply of firewood, food and forage. Of the wood situation, Captain von Muenchhausen commented on May 3rd:

> "There is a dense woods a short mile from Coopers Ferry on the other side of the Delaware in Jersey. This morning at six o'clock the 55th and 63rd English regiments were ferried across with many wood-cutters. They immediately started to throw up three redoubts to cover the working party."

"It was" according to von Muenchhausen, "necessary to fill our magazines with firewood. Being short of it would excusable only if Philadelphia were occupied by a small force that could depend on nearby sources of wood." Obviously, for miles around Philadelphia, the source had been depleted by both the Amercans and the British.

Captain John Montresor actually participated in this mission and he wrote in his "Journal" on May 3rd:

> "At 6 this morning (Sunday) calm and fine weather. I proceeded to the Jersies with the 55th and 63rd Regts. and 12 Philadelphia Horse and began the Defenses on the Confluence of the Delaware and Cooper Creek by 4 Redoubts and flanked by the Cornwallis Galley. Our Horse pursued some Rebels; took one and cut anothers arm off."

From the "Letters" of Major Baurmeister, it is possible to gain further insights into the British activities at Cooper's Ferry. He noted that "on the 3rd (of May) two English infantry regiments, the 55th and 63rd crossed over to Jersey and encamped behind Cooper's Ferry. Since then a working party has been detached from here every day to fortify their camp." With them, Baurmeister continued, "is an officer and thirty dragoons for patroling the country. This is being done with the intent of acquiring fresh food and forage more easily from the country people and also of cutting firewood and bringing it to the local magazines. All the work is being accomplished without interference."

On May 5th, 1778 it is further learned that " . . . Brigadier General Erskine advanced with a dragoon patrol too far in the direction of "Hackenfield (Haddonfield) in Jersey. He was driven back with the loss of three dragoons and was almost captured himself."

By May 6th, Captain John Montresor reported laconically: "Finished our Works in the Jersies." In order to futher protect the British at Cooper's Ferry, Montresor noted on May 7th that "Allen's and Clifton's Regt. of Provincials (the later Roman Catholics) crossed over into the Jersies to join the 55th and 63rd Regts. posted opposite this city (Philadelphia) for the protection of the wood-cutters." There were 120 men in Lt. Colonel William Allen's Pennsylvania Loyalists and 174 troops in Lt. Colonel Alfred Clifton's Roman Catholic Volunteers. Add these to the 55th Westmoreland Regiment, 261 men, and the 63rd West Suffolk, 450 men, it is found that of May 7th 1778, there were slightly over 1000 British troops stationed at Cooper's Ferry (Camden) in "Old Gloucester County."

On May 8th, General, Sir Henry Clinton arrived at Billingsport "in the Greyhound Frigate from New York." Indeed, Billingsport remained an important post for the British, as outgoing and incoming ships had to pass the still narrow passage through the Chevaux de Frise.

Sir Henry Clinton arrived in Philadelphia on May 9th to relieve Lord William Howe as commanding officer of the British Army in and around Philadelphia, as well as those now at Billingsport and Cooper's Ferry. Regarding Clinton's arrival, it is foot-noted in the "Papers of William Livingston" that on the day after coming to Philadelphia, Clinton "received a letter from Lord George Germain enclosing orders from George III (both dated march 21st) ordering Clinton to evacuate Philadelphia." From the large movement of troops to Cooper's Ferry, it would appear that the evacuation had already begun.

Despite the movement of British troops to New Jersey, there were those in Philadelphia who thought the Americans could still be defeated. Ambrose Serle recorded an interesting comment in his "Journal" entry of May 14th:

"Had some Conversation with Mr. Andw. Allen. His most material Remark was, that from the Persuasion, that five Sixths of the Province (Pennsylvania) were against the Rebels, our Army had only to drive off Washington & put arms in the Hands of the well-affected, anf the Chain of Rebellion would be broken . . . "

Captain Van Munchhausen also evidensed dismay in his "Diary" entry of May 23rd:

"General von Knyphausen visited General Howe with all the Hessian staff officers to bid him farewell. It is maintained that our Army will leave Philadelphia. Nobody knows why, for counting heads, our army is twice as strong as the one of the rebels, and with respect to courage, a hundred times as strong. Many surmise that the reason is the fear of the French fleet, which could blockade the mouth of the Delaware."

A day earlier, Captain Johann Ewald recorded in his "Diary" that " . . . We began to work on three redoubts at Cooper's Ferry on the left bank of the

Delaware, where two English Regiments were ferried across for protection. They were to cover the army during the crossing of the Delaware."

General George Washington had been apprised by American intelligence that the British were preparing to evacuate Philadelphia by sea and land. In addition, the increased British activity at Cooper's Ferry was known to him, thus as early as May 25th, Brigadier General William Maxwell was ordered to Mount Holly to take command of the four New Jersey Regiments. Maxwell's troops were under orders from Washington to " . . . cover the country, and annoy the enemy, should they attempt to pass through the Jerseys."

Interestingly, Ambrose Serle's "Journal" entry of May 26th anticipated General Washington's orders to Maxwell:

" . . . Washington has sent off his heavy Baggage from his present camp (Valley Forge), from which he is ready to run; his People being almost ever under arms; that he has sent to the Jersies, apprehending that we mean to pass through them, to raise the (South Jersey) Militia to annoy us . . . "

By May 30th according to Captain John Montresor, " . . . the 7th and 26th crossed the Delaware to Cooper's Ferry in the Jersies to join the Corps posted there under the command of Brig. Genl. Leslie . . . Transports falling down (the Delaware River)." They were to pass through the Chevaux de Frize at Billingsport.

On June 2nd, Montresor recorded that additional ships were "Dropping down." That evening, "the 15th Regt, embarked for Billingsport to join the New Jersey Volunteers at that Post." With the evacuation now proceeding in earnest, the importance of the redoubts at Billingsport grew in importance in order to secure the safe passage of the transports, the vessels of war and those Hessian troops who went to New York City by water, lest they desert to the Americans. In addition, there were thousands of Loyalists who wished to leave for New York by sea. While estimates vary, between three and five thousand Loyalists boarded British transports and left Philadelphia forever.

On June 4th, Captain Johaan Ewald recorded in his "Diary" that "for several days all the pleasures and trade in the city have come to an end," Indeed, he said:

"All the loyalist families are engaged in packing up and fleeing before the wrath of Congress. The streets are full of wagons loaded with personal effects, which are being taken to the ships which have provided for these unfortunate people. It is said there are about fifteen hundred families which are leaving the city . . . "

Captain John Montresor has given us a very interesting account in June 8th:

"the market people on their return from this city stopped by some rebels & the whole branded W.H. William Howe . . . Waggons all this night crossing the Delaware from hence to the Jersies . . . "

By June 9th, two of the Hessian Anspach regiments sailed from Philadelphia and according to Montresor, they "go in the tide below the Chevaux dr Frises (near Billingsport)." In addition, during the night of June 9th, "the 46th Regiment embarked for Cooper's Ferry in New Jersey opposite this City to join the Troops at that Post."

The movement of the British and Hessian troops continued to Cooper's Ferry and on June 12th, Montresor commented that the " . . . waggons (were) crossing over to the Jersies from hence all night and the Park of Artillery. No waggons now left behind in Philadelphia.

The South Jersey Militia under Colonel Joseph Ellis attacked the British in and around Cooper's Ferry on June 13th, for Montresor's "Journal" informs us that:

> "This morning the Patrol of Provincial Calvary were attacked near the Post in the Jersies; we had 1 killed and 1 wounded. The rebels left 2 killed. All the Intrenching Tools to be carried with the Army were sent by me to Cooper's Ferry in New Jersey."

By the next day, many British horses had been sent over the Delaware River to Cooper's Ferry and on June 15th, "all officers horses ordered over to the Jersies." In addition, according to Montresor, on that date, A Brigade of Hessians embarked in flat boats and crossed the Delaware into the Jersies, as did the 33d in the night."

June 16th was a very active day for the British, as " . . . the 2 Regts. of Dragoons 16th and 17th crossed over from hence into the Jersies leaving 2 troops of each" in Philadelphia. On the same day, Montresor wrote that "Lt. Genl. Kniphuysen and the Hessians and the Hessian Grenadiers and Major Genl. Grant crossed into the Jersies. The Hessian Grenadiers by mistake, as they were to form part of the Rear Guard."

Archibald Robertson wrote in his "Diary" that from June 6th to the 7th, the British "were employ'd in Embarking Stores, Crossing the Calvary Provision trains, Waggons, etc, etc., to Cooper's Ferry. Likewise the 5th Brigade and all the Hessians, some of whom were advanced to Haddonfield the 16th in the morning. The 15th Regiment has likewise been for some time at Billingsport to reinforce Colonel Van Dyke's Corps." On the evening on June 17th, Robertson wrote that he had "joind General Knyphausen at Cooper's Ferry. About 8000 British remain'd as Rear Guard in Phila."

From the "Journal" of Lt. John Charles Philip von Kraft, a Hessian, it is learned that on June 15th " . . . at noon all the baggage had to be transported across the Delaware, also all officers, grooms and horses." By five in the afternoon, von Kraft recorded:

> "We marched almost to the end of the city...where we were at once shipped on board the boats awaiting us and taken across the Delaware. There we waited some time until the whole regiment was together. The place was called 'Coppers (Cooper's) Ferry.' We marched about 2½ English miles and the greater part of our regiment was directed to camp in a wood..."

By Tuesday morning, the 16th of June, the Hessians were given orders to erect huts, for as von Kraft noted: "...we were to remain here (Haddonfield) until all had over-taken us from Philadelphia," thus thousands of British and Hessian troops were in "Old Gloucester County" from Cooper's Ferry to Haddonfield, for more than a week until the start of the grand march towards New York City.

It was not until June 17th that von Kraft noted: "In the morning Genr'r'l von Knipphaussen as also all the Grenadiers and Yagers arrived in the camp from Philadelphia." Early in the morning of the 18th, von Kraft recorded: "...We all set out at 4 A.M. and proceeded 6½ English miles until we passed through the little town of "Hottenfeldt" (Haddonfield), where, at about 8 o'clock, we who were on the extreme right camped under huts on a fallow field."

On June 18th, 1778, the British Army was to withdraw all of its forces from

Philadelphia forever. Captain John Montresor stated in his "Journal" that:

> "This morning early the Kings Troops evacuated the city of
> Philadelphia and the several Redoubts and works that form its
> Defences and retired by land to Gloucester Point...and there
> embarked in Flat Bottomed Boats and crossed the river Delaware
> into New Jersey at Gloucester (City), after which the armed vessels
> and Flat Boats proceeded down the river to Billingsport..."

From the "Journal" of Major John Andre, it is noted in his June 18th entry that "...as soon as the Troops were passed (to South Jersey), General Knyphausen, with the Hessian Grenadiers and the 1st and 2d Brigades, marched to Haddonfield. Lord Cornwallis with the Light Infantry, British Grenadiers, Guards and the 3d and 4th Brigade followed soon after and halted for the night within two miles of Haddonfield."

For another view of the British evacuation of Philadelphia, Archibald Robertson wrote the following on June 18th:

> "We moved from Cooper's Ferry early in the Morning with all the
> Provision Train, Hessians, 5th Brigade, and Jagers, and Rangers.
> Arrived at Haddonfield at 8 o'clock. After halting two hours, I
> attended Brigadier General Leslie...We march'd about 7 miles
> through a very thick Country on the Road leading to Mount
> Holly...and encamped at Eve's Bridge on the fork of Moores Creek
> (Pennsauken Creek) that divides Gloster from Burlington County.
> We had a little skirmishing, but lost nobody..."

The "Journal" of Major John Andre provides an insight into the last day that the British and Hessians were in "Old Gloucester County." Andre wrote on June 20th, 1778:

> "General Leslie's Corps joined the rear of the Column. The Rebels,
> supposed to be about 900 in number, under General (William)
> Maxwell, had quitted Mount Holly the morning before. General
> Knyphausen...marched early the 20th to Moorestown, and on the
> 21st came to Mount Holly."

At long last, Andre commented that the British and Hessians were "now assembled in one body" and would shortly begin the march that would lead them to Monmouth County. They were to be harrassed all the way by the troops of General William Maxwell and the South Jersey Militia of Colonel Joseph Ellis. Indeed, Ellis and his troops played an important role in the Battle of Monmouth on June 28th, 1778.

The British, in order to insure their fleet's safety, had stationed a regiment of troops at Billingsport, which was to be picked up after the withdrawl from Philadelphia. On June 19th, Captain John Montesor reported in his "Journal" that the "15th Regt. posted at Billingsport and having sent 150 men to forage too far, they were intercepted by a considerable body of the Rebels with 2 field pieces and got to Red Bank and were taken off, horses & all by the Vigilant's Boats; she having fortunately got around near that place," thus it was that Billingsport and Red Bank were involved in the last British military activity in that part of "Old Gloucester County" which bordered on the Delaware River.

Gone were the British troops and the ravages of the American Revolution; however, citizens living in that part of "Old Gloucester County" which bordered on the Atlantic Ocean were to yet taste an invasion that produced death and destruction of a brutal, almost wanton, nature.

147

Chapter VIII
The Affair at Chesnut Neck

When the British evacuated Philadelphia on June 18th, 1778, the war was gone for most residents of "Old Gloucester County;" however, those who resided along the Atlantic coast in what is now Atlantic County were to experience additional devastation at the hands of the British Army and Navy in October, especially in the area of the Little Egg Harbor on Mullica River.

The genesis of the British invasion of Little Egg Harbor lay in the fact that the rivers and creeks of South Jersey lent themselves well to privateering, a very profitable business for those who brought in British merchantmen loaded with food, forage and military supplies for the troops of Sir Henry Clinton, now safe at New York City after his harrowing experiences at the Battle of Monmouth.

The situation became so bad that, according to Harold F. Wilson in his seminal work, "The Jersey Shore," by 1778 and 1779, no vessel bound for New York was safe from attack unless escorted by a warship on itself heavily armed. The Jersey seahawks proved no respector of persons." Over the years from 1776 to 1778, hundreds of British vessels were brought into Little Egg Harbor and their cargoes made available to the American Army and profiteering merchants.

In addition to the increased boldness of American profiteers, Henry Clinton was concerned about the iron-works at Batsto and other small production centers up the Little Egg Harbor River. If a British mission to stop these American Privateers were successful, it might also be possible to raze Batsto and stop the supply of cannon balls, cannon and other iron products needed by the American military.

Harold Wilson has written that "the strike at Chestnut Neck was long-planned" by the British in New York City. In any event, the Affair at Chestnut Neck, also known a the "Massacre of Little Egg Harbor," began on September 30th, when Captain Patrick Ferguson left New York City with a force of 300 British troops, plus 100 New Jersey Loyalists.

The 400 soldiers were carried by a British fleet of three sloops, four boats and two galleys, the flagship, "the Zebra" and some ten other smaller vessels. Due to high seas, the British expedition took four and one half days to sail down the Atlantic coast some seventy seven miles, thus it was not until October 5th that Major Ferguson's forces were ready to strike against the American ships and soldiers up the Little Egg Harbor River.

Due to the delays encountered by Patrick Ferguson, his mission became known by American intelligence and on October 6th Governor William Livingston wrote to Lord Stirling (General William Alexander) that he had received a letter from Colonel Coxe in Philadelphia, in which it was noted that Count Casimer Pulaski had been ordered by the American Congress to proceed to "Egg Harbour where the enemy have made their appearence with about 20 vessels of different sorts."

At daybreak on October 7th, Ferguson made his move against Chestnut Neck, then a small community protected by a small fortification, called Foxburrows. This fort had been constructed by Lt Colonial Elijah Clark and Major Richard Wescott of the "Old Gloucester County" Militia. In addition, Clark and Wescott had purchased defensive cannons at their own expense.

In short order, Fort Foxburrows at Chestnut Neck was over-run and destroyed by Ferguson's forces. In addition, they scuttled some thirty vessels belonging to the American privateers and then proceeded to burn the 12 houses in the tiny village as well as wharfs. wharehouses, barns, etc. At that point, Ferguson had accomplished his mission; however the Zebra went aground and much time had to be used to refloat it. Rather than have his men idle, they were ordered to conduct a series of wanton raids on homes and farms.

By October 8th,Ferguson's mission had been accomplished; however the weather would not cooperate and the fleet stood idle because of no wind to fill its sails. On this same day, Count Casimer Pulaski arrived to observe the havoc wrought by the British. In addition, Captain Thomas Proctor's Pennsylvania Artillery was enroute to Chestnut Neck. Unfortunately, at the time of Ferguson's attack there were no more than 50 inexperienced American militia in the Little Egg Harbor area.

There continued a military stale-mate at Little Egg Harbor for several days and finally early in the morning of October 14th, Ferguson's troops landed on Osborne's Island in the "Great Bay" at Little Egg Harbor, where Pulaski had stationed a detachment of approximately 50 men. The 250 British troops quickly overpowered the Americans, who lost forty of their men by the bayonet, with 5 taken as prisoners. Those who tried to escape were "cut to pieces," according to Major Ferguson.

Of this incident, it is learned in the "Diary" of Captain Johann Ewald of the Hessians:

> "Over sixty men were cut down, among whom were a French
> lieutenant colonel, two Polish captains, and four American officers.
> They took two hundred and fifty prisoners and captured four
> cannons and much baggage, including a cashbox of paper money.
> Luckily for Count Pulaski it had occurred to him the previous day
> to look for another post, as this one did not seem safe enough, and
> consequently he was not present."

While different sources give different estimates of American casualties at Chestnut Neck, it is certain that Ferguson's men were guilty of an unnecessary massacre, which aroused the citizens of Little Egg Harbor to a high pitch of patriotism. In addition, the arrival of Colonel Thomas Proctor, with three pieces of artillery, placed the Americans in a stronger position.

Aware that he had no artillery, Captain Patrick Ferguson loaded his troops on the waiting ships and sailed back to the safety of New York City. Captain Johann Ewald noted that "on the 24th (October) Major Ferguson returned from his expedition, which had sailed from New York on two galleys and four small vessels four weeks ago with a detachment. He had landed in Egg Harbor and destroyed and burned a number of ships. Afterward, he had burned several plantations on the Jersey coast and destroyed an enemy magazine and a salt works there."

Governor William Livingston of New Jersey had his own version of what transpired at Little Egg Harbor, for he wrote to Lord Stirling on October 11th that he forgot to give him the intelegence he had received about Ferguson's mission:

> "That they were about 2000 strong. That they had 5 ships, 1 Brigg, 4
> sloops, 2 row gallies, 5 quarter gallies, & 1 11 boats that carry 25
> men each."

Livingston further commented that the British "had burnt the buildings at Chestnut Neck, the saltworks at Osborns & Faulkenbridge Island; and that they give out they have Instructions to destroy all the salt works on that shore. That they have also burnt the buildings at the mouth of the Bass River . . . That in the evening of the 8th instant 5 sails of their vessels went into great Egg Harbor . . . "

Despite the brutality, the casualties and the destruction of public property by the Ferguson mission to the Little Egg Harbor River area, the patriotic citizens of "Old Gloucester County"continued their zeal for privateering and the war effort. Indeed, as Harold Wilson has commented: "Little Egg Harbor started to resume privateering activity, which 'was as bad as ever (for the British) in a few weeks' time.'"

APPENDIX ONE

Gloucester County In History
The Yorktown Bicentennial, 1781—1981
By Robert W. Harper

Memories of the 1976 Bicentennial of the American Declaration of Independence will be rekindled throughout the United States and in New Jersey as Americans honor the great victory at the Siege at Yorktown, Virginia.

The events which took place at Yorktown, during the period September 28th - October 19th, 1781, were not in any sense a military battle. Rather, there took place a classical "Siege at Yorktown,"where a combined American—French force, plus the French Navy, of 16,000 slowly drew the noose tighter around the entrapped Lord Cornwallis and his approximately 8,000 British and Hessian troops.

Lord Cornwallis, who led over 5,000 victorious Redcoats and Hessians up the King's Highway to Woodbury, during November of 1777, never envisioned that he would have to undergo a disastrous siege on land and a French naval blackade of the York River at his rear. To the end, he hoped that the British Navy would relieve him and take his troops back to the safety of British—held New York City.

Romantic historians have long led us to believe that Lord Cornwallis's surrender at Yorktown ended the American Revolution for all intents and purposes. A more realistic view was expressed by General George Washington who wrote that the capture of the British at Yorktown was "an interesting event that may be productive of much good if properly improved, but if it should be the means of relaxation and sink us into supine and (false) security, it had better not have happened"

The Winter of 1780/81

The American Army, mainly quartered at Morristown, New Jersey, and in the highlands along the lower Hudson River, was hungry, ill-paid and too often without warm clothing and wearable shoes. Indeed, the winter of 1780/81 saw the American morale at a new low ebb, perhaps worse than at Valley Forge, 1777/78.

Death, desertion and mutiny were prevalent and when six of General Anthony Wayne's Pennsylvania regiments mutinied against their officers and marched off for Philadelphia to complain to the Continental Congress, there were fears that the ragged army would further disintegrate. The march of the mutinous three New Jersey Regiments towards Trenton was quickly thwarted; however, a European observer of Washington's Army noted that "It is incredible that soldiers composed of men of every age, even of children of fifteen, of whites and blacks, almost naked, unpaid and rather poorly fed can march so well and stand fire so steadfastly."

During the disheartening spring of 1781, General Washington "never felt the embarrassment of his situation more keenly than in the early part of the year 1781. He could do little to assist the South, and saw no flattering prospects of achieving anything important in the North." Indeed, the British were in a strong position in the south and General Clinton held New York City firmly in his grip.

Enthusiasm for the Revolutionary War had reached a state of apathy among both civilians and soldiers. General Washington noted in his Military Journal: "Instead of having a magazine filled with provisions, we have a scanty pittance scattered here and there in the different States . . . . Instead of having the regiments completed to the new establishment, scarce any state in the Union has, at this hour, an eighth part of its quota in the field, and little prospect, that I can see, of even getting more than half. In a word, instead of having everything in readiness to take the field, we have nothing."

During May 1781 then, George Washington could never have envisioned that he would be at Yorktown the following October and that Lord Cornwallis would allow himself to be trapped and to surrender. Indeed, unless important French fiscal and military contributions were forthcoming, no offensive against the British in 1781 could occur.

It was Washington's hope that he might attack New York City; however, he had less than 3,500 troops at hand, plus the possibility of adding the New Jersey and New York regiments. In addition, the Count de Rochambeau had four thousand crack French troops at Newport, Rhode Island, It was hoped that a large French fleet, plus additional French soldiers, under Admiral de Grasse, might arrive in American waters by mid-summer of 1781

The Virginia Plan

While the New York Plan remained General Washington's choice, events in his native Virginia were such that Governor Thomas Jefferson feared that Lord Cornwallis was intent in re-establishing British rule over Virginia. If this came to pass, the 13 Colonies (States) would be cut in half and the British Army would be able to crush all resistance in the south and then move back to New York City, thus causing an American surrender. Such was the significance of Yorktown. Realizing this state of military affairs, the French insisted that Admiral de Grasse's fleet would be more effective if it gained control of Chesapeake Bay, thus preventing the British forces at Yorktown from evacuating.

By July 6, 1781, the four thousand French troops had marched from Rhode Island to the Hudson River, where Washington let it be known that New York City was to be attacked; however, this was a clever ruse, especially after it was learned that the French fleet, plus 3200 soldiers, would sail directly from the West Indies for Chesapeake Bay. De Grass had informed General Washington that his fleet could remain in American waters until the middle of the coming October. There was no choice but to march the Franco-American troops through New Jersey and down to the Elk River in Maryland.

Fortunately, General Clinton, the British Commander at New York City, learned too late that Washington and Rochambeau were off to Virginia, not however before the allied forces had given Clinton the impression that Staten Island was to be attacked from North Jersey.

On August 20, 1781, the French and Americans began to cross the Hudson River and by the 28th, they were still within striking distance of New York; however, they suddenly disappeared. Little did General Clinton realize that the allied troops were well on their way towards the Delaware River.

By September 18th, the French and Americans were safely aboard French frigates. Their destination was Williamsburg, Virginia, a short eleven miles from Yorktown, where Lord Cornwallis was leisurely completing fortification. On September 28th, General Washington ordered the march to Yorktown.

It was felt by many of the British officers that Cornwallis "might defend that position (Yorktown) for twenty-one days, open trenches, against 20,000 men and a proportionable artillary." By October 5th, General Clinton advised Lord Cornwallis that a British fleet of twenty-three ships and 5,000 soldiers were about to sail to Chesapeake Bay.

Day by day, the French and Americans inched closer and closer to Yorktown, aided in their efforts by British withdrawal from their outer defenses; however, the actual "Siege at Yorktown" began at night on October 6th, when as a result of the intense shelling of the town by French artillery and cannon from Admiral de Grasse's warships, the British were continually forced into a smaller defense area.

The Final Days at Yorktown

The first American troops to occupy forward trenches were those under the command of the Marquis de Lafayette, who had gained valuable military experience against the British and Hessians during the fighting from Haddonfield to Gloucester City during the last week of November 1777 when Lord Cornwallis was attempting to move his army back to Philadelphia. At Yorktown, Lafayette was now a general and in command of a Light Infantry Division and his Division Inspector was Major William Barber of New Jersey.

Lafayette's division was divided into two brigades and seven battalions. Lt. Colonel Francis Barber of New Jersey commanded the 3rd Battalion of the First Brigade and the Surgeon's Mate for Barber's Battalion was Jacob Harris of Salem County. Also present with Lafayette was a detail from Captain Alexander Mitchell's (Gloucester County) Company of the First Regiment of the New Jersey Line.

Lt. John Blair of Salem County commanded a detail from Captain Jonathan Dayton's Company, Privates Lawrence Carney, Salem County, and Joseph Fowler, Gloucester County, were in the detail from Captain Joseph J. Anderson's Company, First Regiment. In addition Private John Bryant of Gloucester County was in the detail from Captain John Holmes' Company First Regiment. All told, 148 New Jersey officers and men served at Yorktown in Lafayette's Light Infantry Division

Major General Benjamin Lincoln of Massachusetts commanded "Lincoln's Division" and in that group were Dayton's Brigade of 705 officers and men from New Jersey. Colonel Elias Dayton, senior New Jersey officer at Yorktown, had served in a very distinguished manner during the American Revolution and was a personal friend of General Washington. Under Dayton's command were his own Second New Jersey Regiment (276 officers and men).

The surgeon for the 2nd regiment was Dr. Ebenezer Elmer of Cumberland County, a man who served throughout the Revolution and who, as a general, was in command of Fort Billings (Paulsboro) during the War of 1812. Lt. Samuel Conn of Salem County served Colonel Dayton as a Recruiting Officer.

Sgt. Isaac Carty of Gloucester County was in Captain Nathaniel Bowman's Company and Captain Nathaniel Leonard of Gloucester County commanded his own Company at the "Siege at Yorktown."

Major John Noble Cummings of Salem County was second in command of Colonel Ogden's First New Jersey Regiment and after Captain Aaron Ogden was wounded at Yorktown, Ensign John Bishop of Cumberland County assumed command of Ogden's Company.

While the company of Captain Alexander Mitchell of Gloucester County was in Colonel Ogden's First Regiment, the company was actually commanded by Lt.

Nathan Wilkinson. Serving in this company were Privates John Coleman of Gloucester County and John Cunningham of Salem County.

Private John Berry of Gloucester County served in General George Washington's "Life Guards," a very elite group of 100 officers and men who were responsible for the safety of their commander-in-chief.

At the present level of research, it has not been possible to identify the military units with which Privates David Fisher and John Wilson served at Yorktown; however, the Revolutionary War pension records of these two Gloucester County patriots indicate that they were present.

The Cost of Yorktown

Despite the intense trench fighting and the heavy artillery exchanges between the Allied and British forces, plus the shelling of the British by the French Navy, the Siege at Yorktown resulted in a relatively small number af casualties, considering that close to 25,000 men were involved on both sides for approximately 19 days, September 28-October 17, 1781. Indeed, the cost of this great American victory was slight, as noted in the following statistics:

	Killed	Wounded	Total
American	23	65	88
British and Hessians	156	326	482
French	52	134	186

Again, when viewing the large number of Jersey troops at Yorktown, 853, the killed and wounded figures are minimal: Three officers, Lt. Colonel Francis Barner, Major William Barber and Captain Aaron Ogden were wounded; Privates Jahiel Hull, Benjamin Lewis, William Minthorn and John Whitaker were killed; Private Remington Ewing lost a leg at Yorktown; and Private Thomas Chummard died in Virginia on October 24, 1781, five days after the surrender of Lord Cornwallis. Sgt. David Lee, possibly of Gloucester County, died on November 4, 1781, thus making the final New Jersey casualties at Yorktown as follows: 3 officers wounded, plus Private Remington Ewing; four privates killed in battle; and two post-Yorktown deaths, no doubt from wounds incurred during the fighting.

The New Jersey troops, as well as the Allied and French forces, had contributed to a great - but not final - victory; thus when the British and Hessian troops began to lay down their arms at noon on October 19, 1781, the Siege at Yorktown was concluded and the defeated British Army had helped to contribute to a "World Turned Upside Down," a world in which the United States of America was to become finally free and independent by 1783.

From the:
Bulletin from the Gloucester County Historical Facility, December 1982.

APPENDIX TWO

Captain John Barry: Fox of the Capes

By Robert W. Harper

During the American Revolution, much of the success of both the Continental and Pennsylvania navies was due to the herculean sfforts of an Irish immigrant, John Barry.

Before the war became a reality, Barry had gained a high level of respect in Delaware Valley shipping circles as a shipmaster out of Philadelphia. When the Revolution became imminent, the 31 year-old Irishman's loyalty was never in question and his immense contributions to the defense of the waters from Egg Harbor to Cape May and around the coasts of Cumberland and Salem counties were more widely appreciated and better known two hundred years ago than they are in this post-Bicentennial period.

Fortunately, builders and namers of great bridges sometimes appear to have a keener appreciation of historical contributions than some historians themselves. A case in point is Captain John Barry. Even though the Commodore Barry Bridge over the Delaware River is a testimonial to Barry, few histories of the United States afford us much information about him. Consensus historians have created a naval image around the career of John Paul Jones, an immigrant Scot, whose Revolutionary War contributions equaled those of Barry but hardly exceeded them.

Who, then, was Barry and why wasn't the new bridge from Chester to South Jersey named John Paul Jones Bridge? Perhaps it was because Barry was the man who outfitted the first Continental fleet, for in his own words, he wrote:

"I was employed by the Congress to fit for Sea the first fleet that sailed from Phil . . ."

In addition, Barry commanded the last American warship, the "Alliance," to engage the British in a naval battle. The engagement against the British frigate, the "Sybil,"occurred on March 10, 1783, five weeks after Great Britain finally proclaimed "the end of hostilities on February 4, 1783." Above all, Barry knew the Delaware River and the New Jersey coastline more intricately than any other American Naval officer.

The concern here then will be with Barry's securing the New Jersey coast during the crucial spring and early summer months of 1776, for it was on March 25 that British men-of-war first appeared off Cape May and entered Delaware Bay. Immediately, Henry Fisher of Lewes, Delaware, who was responsible for notifying the Committee of Safety at Philadelphia of the approach of British was vessels, dispatched the following communique up the river:

"This serves to inform you that there is a Sloop of War now coming into o⌣. Road with a small tender. And as it is now night, I cannot inform you whether they are bound up the Bay or not; the Wind is at the South, therefore have Reason to believe that they will proceed up the Bay . . ."

With the coming of daylight, Henry Fisher was able to send more definitive information up the river to Philadelphia:

"This Comes Express to all Whom it may concern, giving notice that last

Evening came into Whore-kiln Road a Man of War, not less than forty Guns; this morning they took a sloop at the mouth of Lewes Creek and my Pilot Boat . . . all persons along the Bay are hereby Warn'd to be on their guard . . ."

It was obvious that the British were going th attempt to obstruct American shipping in and out of Delaware Bay, thus at Philadelphia it was ordered that "four of the Armed Boats, well filled & manned" be immediately sent "down the River, as far, if necessary, as Reedy Island, and to direct the commanding officer and other officers . . . to Act in concert with, and by the advice of Cap't Barry, of the Brig't, Lexington, (in the Continental Service), and exert themselves their utmost endeavors to take or destroy all such Vessels of the Enemy as they shall find in the River Delaware."

On April 1st, 1776, Henry Fisher at Lewes sent the following alarming report to Philadelphia:

". . . the man of War . . . took a Small Sloop . . . belonging to Egg Harbour; they also took two other small sloops from Philadelphia . . .Stripped and scuttled the adsd three Sloops and set them adrift; by these People we learned that it was Captain Hamond of the Kings Ship the 'Roebuck' of forty four guns . . ."

Three days earlier, the Pennsylvania Evening Post informed its readers of the severity of the British attacks upon New Jersey shipping and individual citizens:

"We hear a tender, with ten or twelve swivels . . . is cruzing between Sandy Hook and our capes; that she has taken two sloops and a brig of Egg Harbour; that they landed in Abscomb (Absecon) Beach, where they plundered a house, inhabited by one Steelman, whom they robbed and stripped of everything, even to the clothes on the children's back."

Fortunately, Barry had been warned by Henry Fisher that the larger British man-of-war was possessed of 44 guns, thus an attack upon the "Roebuck" was out of the question. Instead, Barry opted to elude the British vessels and make it safely out to sea. Fisher provides a good account of Barry's movements: " . . . the Brig (Lexington) Capt. Barry came down under Cape May and on Sunday morning went out . . .

The Ship and Tender put out to Sea also after the Brig but returned on Sunday into the Road," Captain Andrew Snape Hamond noted in the "Roebuck's" Journal that on March 31, 1776 at six on the morning the man-of-war "weighed and made Sail after a Brig (Barry's) under Cape May, but being obliged to go around the overfalls, at 8 lost sight of her . . ." Captain John Barry had outfoxed Captain Hamond and the "Lexington" was to play a vital roll in the capture of British supply vessels sailing off the New Jersey coast from Sandy-Hook to Cape May, and down to the Virginias.

Silas Deane, a delegate to the Continental Congress from Connecticut, who was enroute from Philadelphia to France to perform a secret American diplomatic mission to obtain "clothing and arms for twenty-five thousand men, with suitable quantity of ammunition, and one hundred field pieces," found it difficult to get out of Delaware Bay because of the weather and the British meri-of-war. It was Deane's hope, however, that "as Capt. (John) Barry has got out & will Cruzie from Sandy Hook to the Capes of Virginia, no small vessels of war will keep the Coast, and if you prevent their lying in the Eastern or Cape May Channel, your Navigation will be in great Measure Free."

On April 7,1776, Captain Barry notified the Continental Marine Committee of the Continental Congress that "at one P.M. this day I fell in with the sloop 'Edward' belonging to the 'Liverpool' frigate. She engaged us near two glasses.

They killed two of our men, wounded two more. We shattered her in a terrible manner . . ." Barry was safely to bring the prize, captured off the Virginia Capes, to Egg Harbor, New Jersey.

Captain Hamond of the "Roebuck" reported this incident to Lord Dunmore, the Royal Governor of Virginia, as follows:

"The 'Lexington' . . . took possession of her (the 'Edward') and carried her towards Egg Harbour, where he landed Mr. Boger & his People, who were marched from thence to Philadelphia. The vessel he (Barry) sent thro' Cape May Channel in the Night . . ."

Once again, John Barry was able to run the British blockade of the entrance to the Delaware Bay. Captain Hamond of the "Roebuck had been outfoxed and he admitted to Lord Dunmore that "all the North side of Delaware Bay is encompassed with shoals & water, having a chanel of about 13 or 14 foot water within them; and this passage Mr. (John) Barry is at present master of. I have chaced (sic) him several times, but can never draw him into the Sea."

Regarding the British prisoners from the "Edward," Captain Barry issued the following orders to Captain Timothy Shalor at Egg Harbor on April 15th, 1776:

"You are hereby desired to take with you to Philadelphia and there deliver the prisoners which I have taken out of the Sloop 'Edward,' and to supply them with sufficient meat Drink & Lodging during their journey . . ."

Despite the heroics of Captain John Barry and the crew of the "Lexington," the "Roebuck" and the "Liverpool," stationed in the lower reaches of Delaware Bay, were taking a heavy toll on American shipping.

Captain Hamond, who had long desired to move up the river against Philadelphia, weighed anchor on the morning of May 6 and the Committee of Safety at Philadelphia was notified "that the men of war were coming up the river, and between ten and eleven the alarm guns were fir'd; and at ten o'clock last night another express came from Reedy Island which said that . . . two Men of War with several tenders and prizes were in sight" of Reedy Island. On both side of the Delaware River, it became apparent that a naval battle was imminent

On May 8 and 9, the Philadelphia Navy, with the assistance of Captain Barry, engaged the British Squadron in the general area of today's Delaware Memorial Bridge. The "Roebuck" ran aground on the Jersey shore but was refloated during the early morning of May 9, at which time Captain Hamond turned back down the Delaware River to repair the extensive damages inflicted by the rather primitive Row Galleys of the Pennsylvania Navy.

As May drew to an end, Captain Barry had once more slipped by the British men-of-war and Henry Fisher at Lewes, Delaware, reported to Philadelphia that "Capt. Barry & Alexander were over in our Road . . . I went on board to give them the best information that I could in regard the 'Liverpool,' upon which they went over to Cape May . . . and now they are all over under our Cape in quest of the Pirate . . ."

Barry continued to harass British shipping and to protect American merchant vessels attempting to enter or leave Delaware Bay. Robert C. Alexander. in 1953, wrote interestingly of "The Battle of Turtle Gut Inlet," noting that the "Lexington" and other American men-of-war were stationed in the Cape May area so that they might protect 15 merchant-men attempting to get out to sea.

Unexpectedly, an American vessel, the "Nancy," inbound to Cape May with a mixed cargo of gunpowder, rum, textiles and sugar, was sighted by two British men-of-war, the "Kingfisher" and the "Orpheus,"which were attempting to blockade Cape May and the entrance to Delaware Bay.

Captain James Montgomery of the "Nancy" spotted the British vessel and realized that he would have to sail north into one of the numerous inlets above Cape May.

Montgomery chose Turkey Gut Inlet, located two hundred years ago in the Wildwood area, as a likely place to land the vitally needed cargo before the British could send in armed boats to prevent the landing.

Despite a brief respite from a typical South Jersey fog, the "Nancy" was soon approached by British sailors in armed boats. The ensuing "Battle of Turtle Gut Inlet" was to prove costly to the crew of the "Kingfisher." From the Pennsylvania Ledger of July 6, 1776, it is learned ". . . that a brig from St. Thomas's with 400 barrels of powder, arms, dry goods, &c, coming into our Capes on Saturday last (June 28th), was chased by the 'King-Fisher,' and run aground off Cape May. Captain Barre (John Barry) and Weekes (Lambert Wickes) sent their boats to assist in unloading her."

A contemporary letter from Philadelphia, dated July 6th, 1776, noted the crews of Barry and Wickes took out of the "Nancy" a substantial amount of the cargo: "62 firelocks, 260 barrels of powder, and some dry goods; but the fog clearing away, the (British) ships came within shot, and sent five barges full of men to attack her; the brigs people finding it impossible to keep her any longer started 30 or 40 barrels of powder in the cabin, and about 50 in the main-sail, in which they wrapped some fire, with an intent to communicate to the powder and quitted her . . . ."

At this moment, an unsung American hero, John Hancock, returned to the "Nancy" th retrieve the flag. The British viewed the lowering of the flag as an indication of surrender, thus they boarded the abandoned American vessel. The unknown letter writer from Philadelphia informs us that the British sailors were firing on the retreating Americans " . . . when the fire took effect on the powder, and sent 30 or 40 of them . . . into the air."

The blast of the "Nancy's" powder was heard all over South Jersey and the British casualties were severe: "They have taken up eleven bodies, two laced hats. and a leg with a white spatter dash . . . The water was covered with heads, legs, arms, entrails, &c."

The Americans suffered only two casualties, both from British gunfire. Third Lieutenant Richard Wickes of the "Reprisal"died from wounds through the body and Joshua Griffin, a young boy of the "Nancy's"crew, was seriously wounded from bullet wounds of the thigh.

Two days before the Declaration of Independence, the Marine Committee of the Continental Congress informed Barry that he would be leaving the water off New Jersey that he knew so well:

"As we find out coast is now lined with Men of War of too great force for you to cope With, We think it can be of little use for you to remain cooped up at Cape May . . . We think it a piece of justice due to your Merit to allow you to Make a cruize in the 'Lexington' for one or two months, in hopes that fortunate (sic) may favour your industry and reward it with some good prizes . . . "

The Marine Committee went on to suggest to Barry that "North Carolina is likely to remain unmolested by the Men of Warr, and, if so, your prizes may probably get safe in there—Cape May or Egg Harbour may also be safe places, however, you must use your own discretion in this respect."

Thus it was that Captain John Barry, the fox and master of the South Jersey capes, sailed southward to inflict further havac on British shipping.

Of all the Revolutionary War contributions of Captain John Barry that have relevance to South Jersey, perhaps none exceeds in importance than that mission to Salem County on February 19, 1778. It occurred during the tragic winter at Valley Forge when the starving remnants of George Washington's decimated army were on the brink of capitulation.

In a last ditch effort to obtain food, Washington dispatched General Anthony Wayne to South Jersey; however, the Delaware River was filled with ice and the availability of boats was not assured.

Fortunately, Captain Barry had been able to elude the British and was in hiding up one of the creeks near Wilmington, This intellegence was made known to General Wayne and it was decided that Barry's Row Galleys would transport the American troops over the river to Salem County.

The Barry—Wayne mission proved exciting and highly successful and was a major contribution to the ultimate American victory and independence. General Wayne was able to bring back to Valley Forge approximately 250 head of cattle and important quantities of goods obtained from British cargo vessels captured by Barry while the cattle were being rounded up.

In order to insure the safety of their mission, Barry and Wayne decided that all of the available hay in Salem and Gloucester counties would be purchased from farmers and burned at the appropriate time. Captain Barry and his crews ignited the hay, which ultimately filled the Delaware Valley air with flame and smoke. The confusion at Philadelphia caused by Barry's hay-burning expedition delayed the crossing of the British troops who had been alerted to Wayne's cattle drive. By the time the British had crossed the river and were rowing towards Salem, General Wayne and the cattle had reached Mount Holly and the success of the mission was assured.

Once again, Captain Barry had outfoxed the British and the beef that reached the starving American troops at Valley Forge made it possible for them to survive and ultimately turn the tide of battle. Small wonder, then, that today's Commodore Barry Bridge rests in the general area where Captain Barry transported General Wayne's troops and where the smoke-screen from the burning hay insured the safety of the cattle-drive.

Sunday Press, January 1977, Atlantic City, N.J.

BIBLIOGRAPHY

Andre, John. "Major Andre's Journal: Operation of the British Army under General Sir William Howe and Sir Henry Clinton, June 1777 to November 1778." Edited by William Abbatt. New York: 1930.

Archives of the State of New Jersey, 2nd ser. 5 vols. Trenton, 1901-17.

Baurmeister, Carl Leopold, "Letters of Major Baurmeister during the Philadelphia Campaign, 1777-1778." Edited by Bernhard A. Uhlendorg and Edna Vosper. Pennsylvania Magazine of History and Biography #59 (1935), #60 (1936).*

* The Pennsylvania Magazine of History and Biography will be referred to as PMHB.

Bean, Theodore W. "Washington at Valley Forge: One Hundred Years After." Norristown, Pennsylvania, 1876.

Bill, Alfred J. "New Jersey and the Revoluntionary War." New York: 1964.

Boucher, Jack E. "Of Batsto and Bog Iron." Batsto, New Jersey, 1964, 1973 & 1980.

Brown, Henry Armitt. "Oration at Valley Forge, June 19, 1878." Philadelphia, 1911.

Carrington, Henry B. "Battles of the American Revolution 1775-1781. New York: 1888.

Clark, William Bell and Morgan, W.J., eds. "Naval Documents of the American Revolution." 6 vols. Washington, D.C., 1961.

Cunliffe, Marcus. "George Washington: Man and Monument." New York, 1958.

David, Ebenezer. "A Rhode Island Chaplain in the Revolution: Letters of Ebenezer David to Nicholas Brown, 1775-1778." Edited by Jeanette Dr. Black and William Green Roelker. Providence, 1949.

Drinker, Elizabeth. "Extracts from the Journal of Mrs. Henry Drinker, from September 25, 1777 to July 8, 1778." PMBH, #13 (1889).

Ewald, Johann, Captain. "Diary of the American War: A Hessian Journal, 1777-1778." (Translated and Edited by Joseph P. Tustin). New Haven, 1979.

Ewing, George. "The Military Journal of George Ewing." New York, 1928.

Farish, Hunter D. (ed), "The Journal of Philip Vickers Fithian." Williamsburg, Virginia, 1943.

Flexner, James T., "Washington: The Indispensable Man." Boston, 1974.

Foner, Jack D. "Blacks and the Military in American History." New York, 1969.

Foner, Philip S. "Blacks in the American Revolution." New York, 1974.

Force, Peter

Ford, Worthington C., Ed. "Defences of Philadelphia in 1777." Brooklyn, 1897.

Frazer, Persifor. "Gen. Persifor Frazer: A Memoir." Philadelphia, 1907.

Gibson, James E., "Dr. Bodo Otto and the Medical Background of the American Revolution." Springfield, Illinois, 1937.

Glassboro State College, New Jersey. (Special Collections) The Stewart Collection.

Gerlach, Larry R. "New Jersey in the American Revolution, 1763-1783: A Documentary History." Trenton, 1975.

Gerlach, Larry R., "The Road to Revolution." Trenton, N.J., 1975.

Gifford, Edward S., Jr., "The American Revolution in the Delaware Valley." Philadelphia, 1976.

Gloucester County Historical Society, Woodbury, New Jersey (Stewart Papers)

Greenman, Jeremiah. "Diary of a Common Soldier in the American Revolution, 1775-1781." Edited by Robert C. Bray and Paul E. Bushnell. DeKalb, Illinois, 1978.

Griscom, Lloyd E. "Burlington County and the American Revolution." Burlington, New Jersey, 1976.

Historical Society of Pennsylvania (Manuscripts).

Jackson, John W. "The Pennsylvania Navy, 1775-1781: The Defense of the Delaware." New Brunswick, 1974.

Jackson, John W. "Fort Mercer: Guardian of the Delaware." Woodbury: Gloucester County Bicentennial Committee, 1977.

Jackson, John W. "With the British Army in Philadelphia, 1777-1778." San Rafael, California, 1979.

Johnson, Henry P., "The Yorktown Campaign and surrender of Cornwallis, 1781." New York, 1881.

*The Pennsylvania Magazine of History and Biography will be referred to as PMHB.

Laird, Robert F., Timmins, William D., and Harper, Robert W. "Quinton's Bridge '78." Salem: Salem County Cultural and Heritage Commission, 1978.

Lee, Francis B., "New Jersey as a Colony and as a State." Vol. II. New York, 1902.

Lender, Mark E., "The New Jersey Soldier." Trenton, N.J., 1975.

Lossing, Benson J. "Pictorial Field Book of the American Revolution." 2 vols. New York, 1860.

Kraft, John Charles Philip von. "Journal of Lieutenant John Charles Philip von Kraft, 1776-1784." Collections of the New York Historical Society for the Year 1882. New York, 1883.

McGeorge, Isabella C. "The Heroine of Red Bank." A Paper Read Before the Gloucester County Historical Society, January 11, 1904.

McGeorge, Wallace. "The Battle of Gloucester." A Paper Read Before the Gloucester County Historical Society, January 9, 1906.

Mickle, Isaac. "Reminiscences of Old Gloucester or Incidents in the History of the Counties of Gloucester, Atlantic and Camden, New Jersey." Philadelphia, 1845.

Miers, Earl S. "Crossroads of Freedom." New Brunswick, 1971.

Marshall, Christopher. "The Diary of Christopher Marshall." Albany, New York, 1877.

Martin, James M. and Mark E. Lender, "A Respectable Army: The Military Origins of the Republic, 1763-1789." Arlington Heights, Illinois, 1982.

Morton, Robert. "The Diary of Robert Morton, Kept in Philadelphia While that City Was Occupied by the British Army in 1777." PMBH #1 (1877).

Montresor, John. "The Montresor Journals." Edited and annotated by G.D. Scull. Collections of the New York Historical Society for the year 1881. New York, 1882.

Muenchhausen, Captain Friedrich von. "At General Howe's Side, 1776-1778." Translated by Ernst Kipping and annotated by Samuel S. Smith. Monmouth Beach, 1974.

Owen, Lewis F., "The Revolutionary Struggle in New Jersey, 1776-1783." Trenton, N.J., 1975.

"Papers of William Livington." Vol. 2. Edited by Carl E. Prince and Dennis P. Ryan. Trenton, 1980.

Peckham, Howard H. "The War for Independence." Chicago, 1958.

Pennsylvania Archives, 1st series. Vols. 5, 6, 7 and 9.

Pingeon, Frances D., "Blacks in the Revolutionary Era." Trenton, N.J., 1975.

Quarles, Benjamin. "The Negro in the American Revolution." Chapel Hill, North Carolina, 1961.

Quarles, Benjamin. "The Negro in the Making of America." New York, 1969.

Reed, John F. "Valley Forge: Crucible of Victory." Monmouth Beach, 1969.

Rutman, Darrett B. "The Morning of America, 1603-1789." Boston, 1971.

Salem County History Society (Manuscripts).

Salem County Court House (Archives).

Scheer, George E. (Editor) "Private Yankee Doodle: Being a Narrative ... of a Revolutionary Soldier by Joseph Plumb Martin." New York, 1962.

Scull, G.D. (Editor) "The Evelyns in America, 1608-1805." Oxford, England, 1881.

Sickler, Joseph. "The History of Salem County, New Jersey." Salem, 1937.

Smith, Samuel Stelle. "Fight for the Delaware." Monmouth Beach, 1970.

Stewart, Frank H. "Battle of Red Bank." Woodbury, New Jersey, 1927.

Stewart, Frank H. "Foraging for Valley Forge, etc." Woodbury, New Jersey, 1929.

Stewart, Frank H. "Salem County in the Revolution." Salem, 19

Stewart, Frank H. "Notes on Old Gloucester County." Vol. 3, Woodbury, 1937.

Timmerman, William and Ruth H. "The Great Cow Chase, 1776-1976." Woodstown, New Jersey, 1976. (Privately printed)

Waldo, Albigence. "Diary of Surgeon Albigence Waldo of the Connecticut Line." PMHB, #21 (1897).

Ward, Christopher. "The War of the Revolution." Edited by John R. Alden. 2 vols. New York, 1952.

Wildes, Harry E. "Valley Forge." New York, 1938.

Wilson, Harold F. "The Jersey Shore: A Social and Economic History of the Counties of Atlantic, Cape May, Monmouth and Ocean." New York, 1953.

INDEX

174